C, C++, JAVA & J2EE Interview Questions

(With Ready Answers)

PROF. (DR.) R.N. SATPATHY
Ph.D (Utkal), Ph.D (CU), Postdoc (NIT)
Grand Ph.D (WCU), D.Sc (FMU)
Professor of Computer Science & Engineering
Presently Principal of Hi-Tech Institute of Technology, Bhubaneswar

PROF. BIMAL KUMAR SAHOO
MCA, M.TECH, BPUT University, Bhubaneswar, Odisha

KHANNA BOOK PUBLISHING CO. (P) LTD.

Publisher of Science, Technology and Engineering Books

4C/4344, Ansari Road, Darya Ganj, New Delhi-110002
Phone: 011-23244447-48 **Mobile:** +91-99109 09320
E-mail: contact@khannabooks.com
Website: www.khannabooks.com

Price : ₹ 295/-

C, C++, JAVA & J2EE INTERVIEW QUESTIONS

Prof. (Dr.) R.N Satpathy
Prof. Bimal Kumar Sahoo

ISBN: 978-93-82609-71-7

Edition: 2016

Published by:

KHANNA BOOK PUBLISHING CO. (P) LTD.
4C/4344, Ansari Road, Darya Ganj, New Delhi-110 002
Phone: 011-23244447-48 **Mobile:** +91-9910909320
E-mail: contact@khannabooks.com

Laser Typeset by:
Book One Graphics, New Delhi

Printed in India by:
India Book Printers & Binders, Delhi

Dedicated to

The almighty
My Beloved Parents

Dedicated to

The almighty

My Beloved Parents

Preface

This book, Java Frequently Ask Questions is a book of C, C++, Java & J2EE interview related questions prepared especially for those people who have interview call letter(s) in their hands and harbor an intention of going through the books on Java. If you have very little time at your hands to prepare for the interview, you may find it difficult to go through several books on Java available – each with thousands of pages. Time may elapse just in selecting a book.

This book is intended for a quick review of what has been taught earlier in the institutions – a collective as well as selective information. It is selective because examiners generally prefer to ask tricky questions that you will not find in any book (all carry straight-forward questions). In this book it is easy to get the answers for the questions that are frequently asked during interviews. Every question is done so elaborately, so that students can easily guess the trick questions themselves.

Java satisfies today's need for early instruction in an object-oriented language, while avoiding the complexities of C++. At the same time, Java is similar enough to C++ to serve as a steppingstone to that language.

Here I cover all traditional C, C++ programming concepts and core java concepts such as data types, conditionals, and loops, abstraction, interfaces, array, multithreading, iostream, applet, AWT, event handling, exception handling, string handling, networking, collection framework; J2EE concepts and UML concepts are crucial to lay a foundation for future studies in Java.

Chapter 1 covers C programming concepts, control statements, arrays, functions, pointer, structure & union, dynamic memory allocation, file handling, preprocessor, etc.

Chapter 2 covers C++ object oriented programming concepts, constructors, inheritance, friend function, polymorphism etc.

Chapter 3 covers OOP concepts, operators, data types, classes, constructors & methods, overloading, overriding, inheritances, polymorphism, abstraction, interface, variables, JVM, modifiers, Byte Code, etc.

Chapter 4 covers sting handling like sting pool, string methods, StringBuffer class, and various operations on string operations.

Chapter 5 covers exceptions, exception types and assertions.

Chapter 6 covers multithreading, synchronization, deadlock can make your program more responsive and interactive, and enhance the performance.

Chapter 7 covers garbage collector, how garbage collection work in java etc.

Chapter 8 covers File class, iostream, serialization, transient, Externalizable etc.

Chapter 9 covers all components of AWT, different layout managers, clipping, canvas, different controls in AWT.

Chapter 10 covers types of event handling model, listeners, and adapter classes.

Chapter 11 covers swing components, Event-Driven-Thread, different containers.

Chapter 12 covers applet, security on applet, life cycle of applet, passing parameters to applet.

Chapter 13 covers Java Collections Framework which defines the Java API for handling common data structures tasks in Java. It defines classes and interfaces for storing and manipulating data in sets, lists, and maps.

Chapter 14 covers JDBC API, JDBC drivers, steps involving in writing JDBC programs, connection pooling, transaction, batch updates, resultset & rowset.

Chapter 15 covers networking related stubs, sockets, serversockets, factory methods, URL, caching of HTTP requests.

Chapter 16 covers steps involved in developing RMI object, RMI architecture.

Chapter 17 covers of description to different UML diagrams, relationship between classes.

Chapter 18 covers all J2EE stubs like J2EE servers, components, architecture, providers, EJB concepts, JMS concepts, and XML.

There is no doubt that in spite of our arduous efforts, error might remain in the text. Programmers are serious error-conscious people. We will be grateful if they could communicate to us any error they discover.

Introduction

Thanks for buying this book. This book is prepared for students/ professionals who intend to attend interview calls on Java platform. Generally, while preparing for an interview, you struggle to find out and browse only through some useful concepts, which you feel, might be asked in an interview. Such a frantic search consumes a lot of time and energy, as you have to go through huge volumes on Java.

The following are the topics based on which the questions were prepared:

1. C
2. C++
3. Basic Java
4. String Handling
5. Exception Handling
6. Multithreading
7. Garbage Collector
8. IO Stream
9. AWT
10. Event Handling
11. Java Swing
12. Java Applet
13. Collection Framework
14. JDBC
15. Java Networking
16. RMI
17. UML
18. J2EE & XML

Acknowledgement

We would like to laud the role played by The Almighty for encouraging us constantly whenever our spirits were squeezed. We would like to thank our parents for never leaving us throughout our career and during the writing of this book. They have been our constant inspiration and consistent motivation throughout. They are like the irreplaceable spinalcord, hence we dedicate this book to people who brought us onto this earth.

Acknowledgement

We would like to laud the role played by The Almighty for encouraging us constantly whenever our spirits were squeezed. We would like to thank our parents for spearheading us throughout our career and during the writing of this book. They have been our constant inspiration and consistent motivation throughout. They are like the irreplaceable spinalcord; hence we dedicate this book to people who brought us onto this earth.

During the course of penning down this book, we have received a lot of impetus, rejuvenation from our near & dear ones. The book would have not been possible without a strong team in the background. Without their uninterrupted & impeccable efforts this book would never have been possible.

In this regard we are thankful to all our friends, colleagues and students who really helped us in preparing the manuscript. We owe the titanic acknowledgement to Mr. Kumar Surjeet Chaudhury (Asst. Prof. HIT, BBSR), for his immense support and assistance.

A magnanimous proportion of credit is equally owed to our befitting colleagues of CSE dept; due to their latent, yet incredible co-operation.

We are thankful to our editor Mr. N.K. Singh for his minutely specific inputs and bringing this book out in a quick run. We bestow a huge thanks to Khanna Book Publishing Co. (P) Ltd. for providing excellent support and advice in the materialisation of the manuscript.

Authors

Acknowledgement

We would like to laud the role played by The Almighty for encouraging us constantly when our spirits were squeezed. We would like to thank our parents for [illegible] us throughout our career and during the writing of this book. They have been our constant inspiration and consistent motivation throughout. They are like the irreplaceable [illegible] hence we dedicate this book to people who brought us onto this earth.

During the course of penning down this book, we have received a lot of impetus from our [illegible] near & dear ones. The book would have not been possible without a strong team in the background. Without their uninterrupted & impeccable efforts this book would never have been possible.

In this regard we are thankful to all our friends, colleagues and students who really helped us in preparing the manuscript. We owe the innate acknowledgement to Mr. Kumar [illegible] (Asst. Prof. IIT, BBSR) for his immense support and assistance.

A magnanimous proportion of credit is equally owed to our befitting colleagues of CSE dept. due to their latent, yet incredible co-operation.

[illegible] Mr. N.K. Singh for his minutely specific inputs and bringing this book out in a quick run. We bestow a huge thanks to Khanna Book Publishing Co. (P) Ltd. for providing excellent support and advice in the materialisation of the manuscript.

Authors

Contents

1

C

1. What is C language?

Answer:

- C language is a structure/procedure oriented, middle level programming language developed at Bell Laboratories in 1972 by Dennis Ritchie.
- C language was invented for implementing UNIX operating system.
- In 1978, Dennis Ritchie and Brian Kernighan published the first edition "The C Programming Language".
- Also, C language is an ANSI/ISO standard and powerful programming language for developing real time applications

2. Who developed C language?

Answer: C programming language was developed at Bell Laboratories in 1972 by Dennis Ritchie.

3. Where is C programming language used or uses of C language?

Answer: C language is used to develop system applications that forms major portion of operating systems such as Windows, UNIX and Linux. Operating systems, C compiler and all UNIX application programs are written in C language. Below are some examples of uses of C language.

- Database systems
- Graphics packages
- Word processors
- Spread sheets
- Operating system development
- Compilers and Assemblers
- Network drivers
- Interpreters

4. **What is the difference between C and C++?**

Answer: Even though C and C++ programming languages are belonging to middle level languages, both are differed in below.

- C is structure/procedure oriented programming language whereas C++ is object oriented programming language.
- C language program design is top down approach whereas C++ is using bottom up approach.
- Polymorphism, virtual function, inheritance, Operator overloading, namespace concepts are not available in C programming language. Whereas C++ language supports all these concepts and features.
- C language gives importance to functions rather than data. Whereas C++ gives importance to data rather than functions.
- So, data and function mapping is difficult in C. But, data and function mapping is simple in C++ that can be done using objects.
- C language does not support user define data types. Whereas C++ supports user define data types.
- Exception handling is not present in C programming language. Whereas exception handling is present in C++ language.
- C language allows data to freely flow around the functions. But, data and functions are bound together in C++ which does not allow data to freely flow around the functions.

5. **What is the difference between top down approach and bottom up approach in programming languages?**

Answer: Top down approach and bottom up approach are involved in software development. These approaches are not involved in program execution.

- Structure/procedure oriented programming languages like C programming language follows top down approach. Whereas object oriented programming languages like C++ and Java programming language follows bottom up approach.
- Top down approach begins with high level design and ends with low level design or development. Whereas, bottom up approach begins with low level design or development and ends with high level design.
- In top down approach, main() function is written first and all sub functions are called from main function. Then, sub functions are written based on the requirement. Whereas, in bottom up approach, code is developed for modules and then these modules are integrated with main() function.
- Now-a-days, both approaches are combined together and followed in modern software design.

6. What is the difference between C and Java?

Answer:

- C is structure/procedure oriented programming language whereas Java is object oriented programming language.
- C language program design is top down approach whereas Java is using bottom up approach.
- C language is middle level language whereas Java is high level language.
- Exception handling is not present in C programming language. Whereas exception handling is present in Java.
- Polymorphism, virtual function, inheritance, Operator overloading, namespace concepts are not available in C programming language. Whereas Java supports all these concepts and features.

7. C language has been developed in which language?

Answer: C language has been developed using assembly level language.

8. Which year C language is developed?

Answer: C programming language was developed at Bell Laboratories in 1972 by Dennis Ritchie.

9. What is meant by programming language and give some examples?

Answer:

- Programming language is nothing but a language designed to communicate to machines through instructions and commands.
- Normally machines are computers. Programs are written using some programming languages to control the behaviour of machines/computers and to make them to perform required tasks.
- Programming language example: Assembly language, C language, C++ language, Java, C#, .NET, Python etc.

10. Describe about C standards.

Answer:

- C89/C90 standard – First standardized specification for C language was developed by American National Standards Institute in 1989. C89 and C90 standards refer to the same programming language.
- C99 standard – Next revision was published in 1999 that introduced new futures like advanced data types and other changes.
- C11 standard adds new features to C and library like type generic macros, anonymous structures, improved Unicode support, atomic operations, multi-threading, and bounds-checked functions. It also makes some portions of the existing C99 library optional, and improves compatibility with C++.

11. What are the key features or characteristics of C language?

Answer:

- Reliability
- Portability
- Flexibility
- Interactivity
- Modularity
- Efficiency and Effectiveness

12. What is embedded C?

Answer:

- Embedded C is the extension of C programming language.
- Embedded C is used to develop micro controller based applications.
- Embedded C includes features not available in normal C like fixed-point arithmetic, named address spaces, and basic I/O hardware addressing.
- Cell phones, MP3 players are some example for embedded systems in which embedded C is used to program and control these devices.

13. Which level is C language belonging to?

Answer:

- C language is belonging to middle level language. C language behaves as a bridge between machine level (low level) languages and high level languages.
- C language is more user friendly than machine level languages. And, C language does not support all the concepts that high level languages offer. So, C programming language is called as middle level language.

14. What do you mean by high level, middle level and low level languages and give an example for each?

Answer: High level languages –

- These level languages provide almost everything that the programmer might need to do as already build into the language.
- Example: Java, Python

Middle level languages –

- These languages don't provide all the built-in functions found in high level languages, but provide all building blocks that we need to produce the result we want.
- Example: C, C++

Low level languages –

- These languages provide nothing other than access to the machine's basic instruction set.

- Example: Assembly language

15. What is the difference between structured oriented, object oriented and non-structure oriented programming language?

Answer: Structured oriented programming language –

- In this type of language, large programs are divided into small programs called functions.
- Prime focus is on functions and procedures that operate on data
- Data moves freely around the systems from one function to another
- Program structure follows "Top Down Approach"
- Example: C, Pascal, ALGOL and Modula-2

Object oriented programming language –

- In this type of language, programs are divided into objects
- Prime focus is on the data that is being operated and not on the functions or procedures
- Data is hidden and cannot be accessed by external functions
- Program structure follows "Bottom UP Approach"
- Example: C++, JAVA and C# (C sharp)

Non-structure oriented programming language –

- There is no specific structure for programming this language.
- Example: BASIC, COBOL, FORTRAN

16. What is compiler?

Answer: Compiler is a program that converts human readable code into machine readable code. This process is called compilation.

17. What is the difference between assembler, compiler and interpreter?

Answer:

- Assembler is a program that converts assembly level language (low level language) into machine level language.
- Compiler compiles entire C source code into machine code. Whereas, interpreters converts source code into intermediate code and then this intermediate code is executed line by line.

18. What is printf()?

Answer:

- printf() is an inbuilt library function in C which is available in C library by default. This function is declared and related macros are defined in "stdio.h" header file.
- printf() function is used to print the "character, string, float, integer, octal and hexadecimal values" onto the output screen.

19. What is scanf()?

Answer:

- scanf() function is an inbuilt library function in C which is available in C library by default. This function is declared and related macros are defined in "stdio.h" header file.
- scanf() function is used to read character, string, numeric data from keyboard.

20. What is meant by protocol?

Answer: Protocol is nothing but a set of rules to be followed by a programmer.

21. Execution of a C program starts from which function?

Answer: Always, execution of a C program starts from main() function.

22. What are all the sections that a C program may/must have?

Answer: There are many sections in a C program structure. They are,

- Documentation section
- Link Section
- Definition Section
- Global declaration section
- Function prototype declaration section
- Main function
- User defined function section

main() function section is the important section in a C program as program execution starts from main() function only in C language. A C program may not have all other sections except main() function.

23. What is IDE?

Answer:

- IDE is nothing but Integrated Development Environment. IDE is a tool that provides user interface with compilers to create, compile and execute C programs.
- Example: Turbo C++, Borland C++ and DevC++. These provide Integrated Development Environment with compiler for both C and C++ programming language.

24. List out some of C compilers.

Answer: There are so many compilers available in market for Windows operating system and UNIX. We are listing some of them here for your reference.

- AMPC
- CCS C Compiler
- ch

- clang
- Cygwin
- Digital mars
- GCC compiler
- MikroC Compiler
- Portable C Compiler, Power C, QuickC, Ritchie C Compiler, Small-C

25. What is header file in C language?

Answer:

- Header file is a file that contains function declaration and macro definition for C in-built library functions.
- All C standard library functions are declared in many header files which are saved as file_name.h.
- We are including these header files in our C program using "#include <file_name.h>" command to make use of the functions those are declared in the header files.
- When we include header files in our C program using "#include <filename.h>" command, all C code of the header files are included in C program. Then, this C program is compiled by compiler and executed.

26. Is C language case sensitive?

Answer: Yes. C language instructions/commands/functions and everything used in C program are case sensitive.

27. What is data type in C?

Answer:

- Data types in C language are defined as the data storage format that a variable can store a data to perform a specific operation.
- Data types are used to define a variable before to use in a program.
- Size of variable, constant and array are determined by data types.

28. What is the difference between int, char, float & double data types?

Answer:

- Integer data type allows a variable to store numeric values. The storage size of int data type is 2 or 4 or 8 byte. It varies depend upon the processor in the CPU.
- Character data type allows a variable to store only one character. Storage size of character data type is 1.
- Float data type allows a variable to store decimal values. Storage size of float data type is 4. This also varies depend upon the processor in the CP.
- Double data type is also same as float data type which allows up-to 10 digits after decimal.

29. What is the use of sizeof() function in C?

Answer: sizeof() function is used to find the memory space allocated for each data type in C.

30. What is modifier in C?

Answer:

- The amount of memory space to be allocated for a variable is derived by modifiers.
- Modifiers are prefixed with basic data types to modify (either increase or decrease) the amount of storage space allocated to a variable.
- For example, storage space for int data type is 4 byte for 32 bit processor. We can increase the range by using long int which is 8 byte. We can decrease the range by using short int which is 2 byte.

31. What are different types of modifiers in C?

Answer: There are 5 modifiers available in C language. They are,

- short
- long
- signed
- unsigned
- long long

32. What is enum in C?

Answer:

- Enumeration is a data type that consists of named integer constants as a list.
- It start with 0 (zero) by default and value is incremented by 1 for the sequential identifiers in the list.

33. What is void in C?

Answer: Void is an empty data type that has no value.

- We use void data type in functions when we don't want to return any value to the calling function.

Example:

void sum (int a, int b); – This function won't return any value to the calling function.

int sum (int a, int b); – This function will return value to the calling function.

- We use void data type in pointer like "void *p". It means, pointer "p" is neither pointing to int data type nor char data type. It acts as generic pointer. We are using void pointer when we are not sure on the data type that this pointer will point to. We can use void pointer to refer either integer data or char data. But, this void pointer should not be dereferenced without explicit type casting.

- We use void in functions as "int function_name (void)". Here void means, this function does not pass any argument.

34. What is token in C?

Answer:

- C tokens are the basic buildings blocks in C language which are constructed together to write a C program.
- Each and every smallest individual unit in a C program are known as C tokens.

35. What are the types of C tokens?

Answer: C tokens are of six types. They are,

- Keywords (eg: int, while),
- Identifiers (eg: main, total),
- Constants (eg: 10, 20),
- Strings (eg: "total", "hello"),
- Special symbols (eg: (), {}),
- Operators (eg: +, /,-,*)

36. What is identifier in C?

Answer:

- Each program elements in a C program are given a name called identifiers.
- Names given to identify Variables, functions and arrays are examples for identifiers.
- Example: x is a name given to integer variable in above program

37. What is keyword in C?

Answer:

- Keywords are pre-defined words in a C compiler. Each keyword is meant to perform a specific function in a C program.
- Since keywords are referred names for compiler, they can't be used as variable name.

38. List out some keywords available in C language.

Answer:

- Below are some of keywords that C language offers.
- auto, double, int, struct, break, else, long, switch, case, enum, register, typedef, char, extern, return, union, const, float, short, unsigned, continue, for, signed, void, default, goto, sizeof, volatile, do, , if, static, while

39. What is constant in C?

Answer:

- Constants refer to fixed values. They are also called as literals.
- C Constants are also like normal variables. But, only difference is, constant values can't be modified by the program once they are defined. Constants may be belonging to any of the data type.

40. What are the types of constants in C?

Answer:

- Integer constants
- Real or Floating point constants
- Octal & Hexadecimal constants
- Character constants
- String constants
- Backslash character constants

41. What is variable in C?

Answer:

- C variable is a named location in a memory where a program can manipulate the data. This location is used to hold the value of the variable.
- The value of the C variable may get change in the program.
- C variable might be belonging to any of the data type like int, float, char etc.

42. What is the difference between constant and variable in C?

Answer: Constant values can't be modified by the program once it is declared. But, variable values can be modified by the program.

43. Can variable name start with numbers?

Answer: No. Variable names can't start with numbers as per the variable naming rule.

44. What is the difference between variable declaration and variable definition in C?

Answer:

- Variable declaration tells the compiler about data type and size of the variable. Whereas, variable definition allocates memory to the variable
- Variable can be declared many times in a program. But, definition can happen only one time for a variable in a program.
- Variable declaration is for assignment of properties and identification to a variable. Whereas, variable definition is for assignments of storage space to a variable

45. What are the different types of variable in C?

Answer:

- Local variable
- Global variable
- Environment variable

46. What is local variable in C?

Answer:

- The variables which are having scope/life only within the function are called local variables.
- These variables are declared within the function and can't be accessed outside the function.

47. What is global variable in C?

Answer:

- The variables which are having scope/life throughout the program are called global variables.
- Global variable is defined outside the main function. So, this variable is visible to main function and all other sub functions.

48. What is environment variable in C?

Answer:

- Environment variable is a variable that will be available for all C applications and C programs.
- Once environment variables are exported, we can access them from anywhere in a C program without declaring and initializing in an application or C program.

49. What is operator in C?

Answer:

- The symbols which are used to perform logical and mathematical operations in a C program are called C operators.
- These C operators join individual constants and variables to form expressions. Operators, functions, constants and variables are combined together to form expressions.

50. What are the different types of operators in C?

Answer: C language offers many types of operators. They are,

1. Arithmetic operators
2. Assignment operators
3. Relational operators

4. Logical operators
5. Bit wise operators
6. Conditional operators (ternary operators)
7. Increment/decrement operators
8. Special operators

51. What is the syntax for ternary operator in C?

Answer:

- Ternary operator is same as if else control statement in C.
- Syntax : (Condition? true_value: false_value);
- Example: (A > 100? 0: 1);

52. What is arithmetic operator in C?

Answer:

- C Arithmetic operators are used to perform mathematical calculations like addition, subtraction, multiplication, division and modulus in C programs.
- Arithmetic operators are +, -, *, /, %

53. What is assignment operator in C?

Answer:

- Assignment operators are used to assign the values to the variables.
- Assignment operators are =, +=, -=, /+, %= etc.

54. What is the relational operator in C?

Answer:

- Relational operators are used to find the relation between two variables. i.e. to compare the values of two variables in a C program.
- Relational operators are >, <, >=, <=, ==, !=

55. What is the logical operator in C?

Answer:

- Logical operators are used to perform logical operations on the given expressions.
- There are 3 logical operators in C language. They are,
  1. logical AND (&&)
  2. logical OR (||)
  3. logical NOT (!)

56. What is bitwise operator in C?

Answer:

- Bitwise operators are used to perform bit operations. Decimal values are converted into binary values which are the sequence of bits and bit wise operators work on these bits.
- Bit wise operators in C language are & (bitwise AND), | (bitwise OR), ~ (bitwise OR), ^ (XOR), << (left shift) and >> (right shift).

57. Differentiate between the expression "++a" and "a++"?

- With ++a, the increment happens first on variable a, and the resulting value is used. This is called as prefix increment.
- With a++, the current value of the variable will be used in an operation. This is called as postfix increment.

58. What are all decision control statements in C?

Answer: There are 3 types of decision making control statements in C language. They are,

1. if statements
2. if else statements
3. nested if statements

59. What are all loop control statements in C?

Answer:

- Loop control statements in C are used to perform looping operations until the given condition is true. Control comes out of the loop statements once condition becomes false.
- There are 3 types of loop control statements in C language. They are,
  1. for
  2. while
  3. do-while

60. What is the difference between while and do-while loops in C?

Answer:

- While loop is executed only when given condition is true.
- Whereas, do-while loop is executed for first time irrespective of the condition. After executing while loop for first time, then condition is checked.

61. What is the difference between single equal "=" and double equal "==" operators in C?

Answer:

- Single equal is an assignment operator used to assign the values to the variables.
- But, double equal is relational operator used to compare two variable values whether they are equal are not.

62. What is the difference between pre increment operator and post increment operator in C?

Answer:

- Pre increment operator is used to increment variable value by 1 before assigning the value to the variable.
- Post increment operator is used to increment variable value by 1 after assigning the value to the variable.

63. What is the difference between pre decrement operator and post decrement operator?

Answer:

- Pre decrement operator is used to decrement variable value by 1 before assigning the value to the variable.
- Post decrement operator is used to decrement variable value by 1 after assigning the value to the variable.

64. What is "&" and "*" operators in C?

Answer:

- "*" Operator is used as pointer to a variable. Example: * a where * is pointer to the variable a.
- & operator is used to get the address of the variable. Example: &a will give address of a.

65. What will happen if break statement is not used in switch case in C?

Answer:

- Switch case statements are used to execute only specific case statements based on the switch expression.
- If we do not use break statement at the end of each case, program will execute all consecutive case statements until it finds next break statement or till the end of switch case block.

66. Why is default statement used in switch case in C?

Answer: Switch case statements are used to execute only specific case statements based on the switch expression. If switch expression does not match with any case, default statements are executed by the program.

67. What is the use of "goto" statement?

Answer: goto statement is used to transfer the normal flow of a program to the specified labl in the program. Below is the syntax for goto statement in C.

```
{
…….
goto label;
…….
…….
LABEL:
statements;
}
```

68. What value will be assigned to the variable X if a = 10, b = 20, c = 30, d = 40 in below expression?

Answer: X = a/b+c*d-c;

- The above arithmetic operation is performed based on the precedence of the operators.
- In above mentioned expression, c*d will be performed first. Then, a/b, then (c*d)-c, then (a/b) + ((c*d)-c).
- Please check the operator precedence table to know the priority and associativity of the C operators.
- Output of the above expression is 1170.

Example program:

```
#include <stdio.h>
#include <stdlib.h>
int main()
{
    int a = 10, b = 20, c = 30, d = 40, X ;

    X = a/b+c*d-c;
    printf(" Value of X = %d\n", X);
    return 0;
}
```

Output : Value of X = 1170

69. What value is assigned to the below variables?

Answer: int X1 = 13/3;

int X2 = 13%3;

- The value of X1 is 4
- The value of X2 is 1

70. What is the difference between auto variable and register variable in C?

Answer: Storage class of all variables are auto by default unless we specify a variable is register or static or extern in C program.

- Both auto variable and register variable are local variables. Register variables are stored in register memory. Whereas, auto variables are stored in main CPU memory.
- Register variables will be accessed very faster than the normal/auto variables since they are stored in register memory rather than main memory.
- But, only limited variables can be used as register since register size is very low. (16 bits, 32 bits or 64 bits)

71. What is the difference between auto variable and static variable in C?

Answer:

- Both auto and static variables are local variables.
- Static variables can retain the value of the variable between different function calls.
- But, scope of auto variable is within the function only. It can't retain the value of the variable between different function calls.

72. Where should type cast function not be used in C?

Answer:

- Type cast function should not be used in const and volatile declaration.
- Because, constant value can't be modified by the program once they are defined.
- And, volatile variable values might keep on changing without any explicit assignment by the program as operating system will be modifying these values.

73. How will you print "Hello World" without semicolon?

Answer:

```
int main(void){
    if (printf("Hello World")) ;
}
```

74. Why is C language being considered a middle level language?

Answer: This is because C language is rich in features that make it behave like a high level language while at the same time can interact with hardware using low level methods. The use of a well structured approach to programming, coupled with English-like words used in functions, makes it act as a high level language. On the other hand, C can directly access memory structures similar to assembly language routines.

75. What are the different file extensions involved when programming in C?

Answer: Source codes in C are saved with .C file extension. Header files or library files have the .H file extension. Every time a program source code is successfully compiled, it creates an .OBJ object file, and an executable .EXE file.

76. What are reserved words?

Answer: Reserved words are words that are part of the standard C language library. This means that reserved words have special meaning and therefore cannot be used for purposes other than what it is originally intended for. Examples of reserved words are int, void, and return.

77. Why is c considered as a high level language and a low level language?

Answer: C is a high-level language because it abstracts away a large part of the underlying machine; instead of dealing with registers and op codes, you are dealing with objects and expressions. Streams are abstractions of communications channels, pointers are abstractions of memory addresses, etc. However, Cs abstractions are fairly basic; you still have to be aware of limitations on memory, you have to be aware of how types and operations may be mapped onto the underlying hardware, and you have to be aware that some aspects of the language are left to the individual implementation (compiler or interpreter) to define. C makes you *think* you are working at the hardware level, even though you aren't in most cases. Compare this with languages like Haskell or Lisp, where there is no hint of an underlying hardware platform; types are not limited by what an individual platform can represent (as opposed to C), there are no obvious constraints on memory (until performance begins to suffer, anyway).

78. What is the difference between getch() and getche()?

Answer: Both getch() and getche() are used to read single character there is very little difference

- Both functions accept a character input value from the user.
- When getch() is used, the key that was pressed will not appear on the screen. It is automatically captured and assigned to a variable.
- While when getche() is used, the key that was pressed by the user appears on the screen and is assigned to a variable.

79. How do you construct an increment statement or decrement statement in C?

Answer: There are actually two ways you can do this. One is to use the increment operator ++ and decrement operator –. For example, the statement "x++" means to increment the value of x by 1. Likewise, the statement "x –" means to decrement the value of x by 1. Another way of writing increment statements is to use the conventional + plus sign or – minus sign. In the case of "x++", another way to write it is "x = x +1".

80. Are comments included during the compilation stage and placed in the EXE file as well?

Answer: No, comments that were encountered by the compiler are disregarded. Comments are mostly for the guidance of the programmer only and do not have any other significant use in the program functionality.

81. What is a sequential access file?

Answer: When writing programs that will store and retrieve data in a file, it is possible to designate that file into different forms. A sequential access file is such that data are saved in sequential order: one data is placed into the file after another. To access a particular data within the sequential access file, data has to be read one data at a time, until the right one is reached.

82. What is variable initialization and why is it important?

Answer: This refers to the process wherein a variable is assigned an initial value before it is used in the program. Without initialization, a variable would have an unknown value, which can lead to unpredictable outputs when used in computations or other operations.

83. What is spaghetti programming?

Answer: Spaghetti programming refers to codes that tend to get tangled and overlapped throughout the program. This unstructured approach to coding is usually attributed to lack of experience on the part of the programmer. Spaghetti programing makes a program complex and analyzing the codes difficult, and so must be avoided as much as possible.

84. Differentiate Source Codes from Object Codes

Answer: Source codes are codes that were written by the programmer. It is made up of the commands and other English-like keywords that are supposed to instruct the computer what to do. However, computers would not be able to understand source codes. Therefore, source codes are compiled using a compiler. The resulting outputs are object codes, which are in a format that can be understood by the computer processor. In C programming, source codes are saved with the file extension .C, while object codes are saved with the file extension .OBJ

85. In C programming, how do you insert quote characters (' and ") into the output screen?

Answer: This is a common problem for beginners because quotes are normally part of a printf statement. To insert the quote character as part of the output, use the format specifiers \' (for single quote), and \" (for double quote).

86. What is the use of a '\0' character?

Answer: It is referred to as a terminating null character, and is used primarily to show the end of a string value.

87. What is the difference between the = symbol and == symbol?

Answer: The = symbol is often used in mathematical operations. It is used to assign a value to a given variable. On the other hand, the == symbol, also known as "equal to" or "equivalent to", is a relational operator that is used to compare two values.

88. What is the modulus operator?

Answer: The modulus operator outputs the remainder of a division. It makes use of the percentage (%) symbol. For example: 10 % 3 = 1, meaning when you divide 10 by 3, the remainder is 1.

89. What is a nested loop?

Answer: A nested loop is a loop that runs within another loop. Put it in another sense, you have an inner loop that is inside an outer loop. In this scenario, the inner loop is performed a number of times as specified by the outer loop. For each turn on the outer loop, the inner loop is first performed.

90. What is gets() function?

Answer: The gets() function allows a full line data entry from the user. When the user presses the enter key to end the input, the entire line of characters is stored to a string variable. Note that the enter key is not included in the variable, but instead a null terminator \0 is placed after the last character.

91. The % symbol has a special use in a printf statement. How would you place this character as part of the output on the screen?

Answer: You can do this by using %% in the printf statement. For example, you can write printf("10%%") to have the output appear as 10% on the screen.

92. Which of the following operators is incorrect and why? (>=, <=, <>, ==)

Answer: <> is incorrect. While this operator is correctly interpreted as "not equal to" in writing conditional statements, it is not the proper operator to be used in C programming. Instead, the operator != must be used to indicate "not equal to" condition.

93. Compare and contrast compilers from interpreters.

Answer: Compilers and interpreters often deal with how program codes are executed. Interpreters execute program codes one line at a time, while compilers take the program as a whole and convert it into object code, before executing it. The key difference here is that in the case of interpreters, a program may encounter syntax errors in the middle of execution, and will stop from there. On the other hand, compilers check the syntax of the entire program and will only proceed to execution when no syntax errors are found.

94. What are header files and what are its uses in C programming?

Answer: Header files are also known as library files. They contain two essential things: the definitions and prototypes of functions being used in a program. Simply put, commands that you use in C programming are actually functions that are defined from within each header files. Each header file contains a set of functions. For example: stdio.h is a header file that contains definition and prototypes of commands like printf and scanf.

95. What is the use of a semicolon (;) at the end of every program statement?

Answer: It has to do with the parsing process and compilation of the code. A semicolon acts as a delimiter, so that the compiler knows where each statement ends, and can proceed to divide the statement into smaller elements for syntax checking.

96. Finding a number which is a power of 2 in a single step

Answer:

```
int x=64;
if(x&&(x&(x-1))) printf(" x is not the power of 2");
else printf("x is power of 2");
```

97. What is syntax error?

Answer: Syntax errors are associated with mistakes in the use of a programming language. It maybe a command that was misspelled or a command that must was entered in lowercase mode but was instead entered with an upper case character. A misplaced symbol or lack of symbol, somewhere within a line of code can also lead to syntax error.

98. What is "Bus error"?

Answer: A bus error indicates an attempt to access memory in an illegal way,perhaps due to an unaligned pointer.

A 'bus error' is certain undefined behavior result type. The cause for such error on a system could not be specified by the C language. The memory accessibility which

CPU could not address physically, 'bus error' occurs. Also, any fault detected by a device by the computer system can also be a 'bus error'. These errors caused by programs that generate undefined behavior which C language no longer specifies what can happen.

99. What are variables and it what way is it different from constants?

Answer: Variables and constants may at first look similar in a sense that both are identifiers made up of one character or more characters (letters, numbers and a few allowable symbols). Both will also hold a particular value. Values held by a variable can be altered throughout the program, and can be used in most operations and computations. Constants are given values at one time only, placed at the beginning of a program. This value is not altered in the program. For example, you can assigned a constant named PI and give it a value 3.1415. You can then use it as PI in the program, instead of having to write 3.1415 each time you need it.

100. How do you access the values within an array?

Answer: Arrays contain a number of elements, depending on the size you gave it during variable declaration. Each element is assigned a number from 0 to number of elements-1. To assign or retrieve the value of a particular element, refer to the element number. For example: if you have a declaration that says "int scores[5];", then you have 5 accessible elements, namely: scores[0], scores[1], scores[2], scores[3] and scores[4].

101. Can I use "int" data type to store the value 32768? Why?

Answer: No. "int" data type is capable of storing values from -32768 to 32767. To store 32768, you can use "long int" instead. You can also use "unsigned int", assuming you don't intend to store negative values.

102. Can two or more operators such as \n and \t be combined in a single line of program code?

Answer: Yes, it's perfectly valid to combine operators, especially if the need arises. For example: you can have a code like " printf ("Hello\n\n\'World\'") " to output the text "Hello" on the first line and "World" enclosed in single quotes to appear on the next two lines.

103. Why is it that not all header files are declared in every C program?

Answer: The choice of declaring a header file at the top of each C program would depend on what commands/functions you will be using in that program. Since each header file contains different function definitions and prototype, you would be using only those header files that would contain the functions you will need. Declaring all header files in every program would only increase the overall file size and load of the program, and is not considered a good programming style.

104. When is the "void" keyword used in a function?

Answer: When declaring functions, you will decide whether that function would be returning a value or not. If that function will not return a value, such as when the purpose of a function is to display some outputs on the screen, then "void" is to be placed at the leftmost part of the function header. When a return value is expected after the function execution, the data type of the return value is placed instead of "void".

105. What are compound statements?

Answer: Compound statements are made up of two or more program statements that are executed together. This usually occurs while handling conditions wherein a series of statements are executed when a TRUE or FALSE is evaluated. Compound statements can also be executed within a loop. Curly brackets { } are placed before and after compound statements.

106. What is the significance of an algorithm to C programming?

Answer: Before a program can be written, an algorithm has to be created first. An algorithm provides a step by step procedure on how a solution can be derived. It also acts as a blueprint on how a program will start and end, including what process and computations are involved.

107. What is the advantage of an array over individual variables?

Answer: When storing multiple related data, it is a good idea to use arrays. This is because arrays are named using only 1 word followed by an element number. For example: to store the 10 test results of 1 student, one can use 10 different variable names (grade1, grade2, grade3... grade10). With arrays, only 1 name is used, the rest are accessible through the index name (grade[0], grade[1], grade[2]... grade[9]).

108. Can a variable be both const and volatile?

Answer: Yes. The const modifier means that this code cannot change the value of the variable, but that does not mean that the value cannot be changed by means outside this code. If a variable is both const and volatile, the two modifiers can appear in either order.

109. What is wrong in this statement? scanf("%d",whatnumber);

Answer: An ampersand & symbol must be placed before the variable name whatnumber. Placing & means whatever integer value is entered by the user is stored at the "address" of the variable name. This is a common mistake for programmers, often leading to logical errors.

110. How do you generate random numbers in C?

Answer: Random numbers are generated in C using the rand() command. For example: anyNum = rand() will generate any integer number beginning from 0, assuming that anyNum is a variable of type integer.

111. What could possibly be the problem if a valid function name such as tolower() is being reported by the C compiler as undefined?

Answer: The most probable reason behind this error is that the header file for that function was not indicated at the top of the program. Header files contain the definition and prototype for functions and commands used in a C program. In the case of "tolower()", the code "#include <ctype.h>" must be present at the beginning of the program.

112. What are comments and how do you insert it in a C program?

Answer: Comments are a great way to put some remarks or description in a program. It can serves as a reminder on what the program is all about, or a description on why a certain code or function was placed there in the first place. Comments begin with /* and ended by */ characters. Comments can be a single line, or can even span several lines. It can be placed anywhere in the program.

113. What is debugging?

Answer: Debugging is the process of identifying errors within a program. During program compilation, errors that are found will stop the program from executing completely. At this state, the programmer would look into the possible portions where the error occurred. Debugging ensures the removal of errors, and plays an important role in ensuring that the expected program output is met.

114. What does the && operator do in a program code?

Answer: The && is also referred to as AND operator. When using this operator, all conditions specified must be TRUE before the next action can be performed. If you have 10 conditions and all but 1 fails to evaluate as TRUE, the entire condition statement is already evaluated as FALSE.

115. What does the format %10.2 mean when included in a printf statement?

Answer: This format is used for two things: to set the number of spaces allotted for the output number and to set the number of decimal places. The number before the decimal point is for the allotted space; in this case it would allot 10 spaces for the output number. If the number of space occupied by the output number is less than 10, addition space characters will be inserted before the actual output number. The number after the decimal point sets the number of decimal places, in this case, its 2 decimal spaces.

116. What are logical errors and how does it differ from syntax errors?

Answer: Program that contains logical errors tend to pass the compilation process, but the resulting output may not be the expected one. This happens when a wrong formula was inserted into the code, or a wrong sequence of commands was performed. Syntax errors, on the other hand, deal with incorrect commands that are misspelled or not recognized by the compiler.

117. What are the different types of control structures in programming?

Answer: There are 3 main control structures in programming: Sequence, Selection and Repetition. Sequential control follows a top to bottom flow in executing a program, such that step 1 is first perform, followed by step 2, all the way until the last step is performed. Selection deals with conditional statements, which mean codes are executed depending on the evaluation of conditions as being TRUE or FALSE. This also means that not all codes may be executed, and there are alternative flows within. Repetitions are also known as loop structures, and will repeat one or two program statements set by a counter.

118. What is || operator and how does it function in a program?

Answer: The || is also known as the OR operator in C programming. When using || to evaluate logical conditions, any condition that evaluates to TRUE will render the entire condition statement as TRUE.

119. Not all reserved words are written in lowercase. TRUE or FALSE?

Answer: FALSE. All reserved words must be written in lowercase; otherwise the C compiler would interpret this as unidentified and invalid.

120. What is the difference between the expression "++a" and "a++"?

Answer: In the first expression, the increment would happen first on variable a, and the resulting value will be the one to be used. This is also known as a prefix increment. In the second expression, the current value of variable a would the one to be used in an operation, before the value of a itself is incremented. This is also known as postfix increment.

121. What would happen to X in this expression: X += 15; (assuming the value of X is 5)

Answer: X +=15 is a short method of writing X = X + 15, so if the initial value of X is 5, then 5 + 15 = 20.

122. In C language, the variables NAME, name, and Name are all the same. TRUE or FALSE?

Answer: FALSE. C language is a case sensitive language. Therefore, NAME, name and Name are three uniquely different variables.

123. What is an endless loop?

Answer: An endless loop can mean two things. One is that it was designed to loop continuously until the condition within the loop is met, after which a break function would cause the program to step out of the loop. Another idea of an endless loop is when an incorrect loop condition was written, causing the loop to run erroneously forever. Endless loops are oftentimes referred to as infinite loops.

124. Can the "if" function be used in comparing strings?

Answer: No. "if" command can only be used to compare numerical values and single character values. For comparing string values, there is another function called strcmp that deals specifically with strings.

125. What is a program flowchart and how does it help in writing a program?

Answer: A flowchart provides a visual representation of the step by step procedure towards solving a given problem. Flowcharts are made of symbols, with each symbol in the form of different shapes. Each shape may represent a particular entity within the entire program structure, such as a process, a condition, or even an input/output phase.

126. What is wrong with this program statement? void = 10;

Answer: The word void is a reserved word in C language. You cannot use reserved words as a user-defined variable.

127. Is this program statement valid? INT = 10.50;

Answer: Assuming that INT is a variable of type float, this statement is valid. One may think that INT is a reserved word and must not be used for other purposes. However, recall that reserved words are express in lowercase, so the C compiler will not interpret this as a reserved word.

128. What is a newline escape sequence?

Answer: A newline escape sequence is represented by the \n character. This is used to insert a new line when displaying data in the output screen. More spaces can be added by inserting more \n characters. For example, \n\n would insert two spaces. A newline escape sequence can be placed before the actual output expression or after.

129. Is it possible to initialize a variable at the time it was declared?

Answer: Yes, you don't have to write a separate assignment statement after the variable declaration, unless you plan to change it later on. For example: char planet[15] = "Earth"; does two things: it declares a string variable named planet, then initializes it with the value "Earth".

130. What is output redirection?

Answer: It is the process of transferring data to an alternative output source other than the display screen. Output redirection allows a program to have its output saved to a file. For example, if you have a program named COMPUTE, typing this on the command line as COMPUTE >DATA can accept input from the user, perform certain computations, then have the output redirected to a file named DATA, instead of showing it on the screen.

131. What are run-time errors?

Answer: These are errors that occur while the program is being executed. One common instance wherein run-time errors can happen is when you are trying to divide a number by zero. When run-time errors occur, program execution will pause, showing which program line caused the error.

132. What is the difference between functions abs() and fabs()?

Answer: These 2 functions basically perform the same action, which is to get the absolute value of the given value. Abs() is used for integer values, while fabs() is used for floating type numbers. Also, the prototype for abs() is under <stdlib.h>, while fabs() is under <math.h>.

133. What are control structures?

Answer: Control structures take charge at which instructions are to be performed in a program. This means that program flow may not necessarily move from one statement to the next one, but rather some alternative portions may need to be pass into or bypassed from, depending on the outcome of the conditional statements.

134. When is a "switch" statement preferable over an "if" statement?

Answer: The switch statement is best used when dealing with selections based on a single variable or expression. However, switch statements can only evaluate integer and character data types.

135. What are global variables and how do you declare them?

Answer: Global variables are variables that can be accessed and manipulated anywhere in the program. To make a variable global, place the variable declaration on the upper portion of the program, just after the preprocessor directives section.

136. What are enumerated types?

Answer: Enumerated types allow the programmer to use more meaningful words as values to a variable. Each item in the enumerated type variable is actually associated with a numeric code. For example, one can create an enumerated type variable named DAYS whose values are Monday, Tuesday... Sunday.

137. What does the function toupper() do?

Answer: It is used to convert any letter to its upper case mode. Toupper() function prototype is declared in <ctype.h>. Note that this function will only convert a single character, and not an entire string.

138. Is it possible to have a function as a parameter in another function?

Answer: Yes, that is allowed in C programming. You just need to include the entire function prototype into the parameter field of the other function where it is to be used.

139. What are multidimensional arrays?

Answer: Multidimensional arrays are capable of storing data in a two or more dimensional structure. For example, you can use a 2 dimensional array to store the current position of pieces in a chess game, or position of players in a tic-tac-toe program.

140. Which function in C can be used to append a string to another string?

Answer: The strcat function. It takes two parameters, the source string and the string value to be appended to the source string.

141. What is the difference between functions getch() and getche()?

Answer: Both functions will accept a character input value from the user. When using getch(), the key that was pressed will not appear on the screen, and is automatically captured and assigned to a variable. When using getche(), the key that was pressed by the user will appear on the screen, while at the same time being assigned to a variable.

142. Do these two program statements perform the same output? 1) scanf("%c", &letter); 2) letter=getchar()

Answer: Yes, they both do the exact same thing, which is to accept the next key pressed by the user and assign it to variable named letter.

143. What are structure types in C?

Answer: Structure types are primarily used to store records. A record is made up of related fields. This makes it easier to organize a group of related data.

144. Is it possible to create your own header files?

Answer: Yes, it is possible to create a customized header file. Just include in it the function prototypes that you want to use in your program, and use the #include directive followed by the name of your header file.

145. What is dynamic data structure?

Answer: Dynamic data structure provides a means for storing data more efficiently into memory. Using dynamic memory allocation, your program will access memory spaces as needed. This is in contrast to static data structure, wherein the programmer has to indicate a fix number of memory space to be used in the program.

146. What are the different data types in C?

Answer: The basic data types are int, char, and float. Int is used to declare variables that will be storing integer values. Float is used to store real numbers. Char can store individual character values.

147. What is the general form of a C program?

Answer: A C program begins with the preprocessor directives, in which the programmer would specify which header file and what constants (if any) to be used. This is followed by the main function heading. Within the main function lies the variable declaration and program statement.

148. What is the advantage of a random access file?

Answer: If the amount of data stored in a file is fairly large, the use of random access will allow you to search through it quicker. If it had been a sequential access file, you would have to go through one record at a time until you reach the target data. A random access file lets you jump directly to the target address where data is located.

149. In a switch statement, what will happen if a break statement is omitted?

Answer: If a break statement was not placed at the end of a particular case portion? It will move on to the next case portion, possibly causing incorrect output.

150. Describe how arrays can be passed to a user defined function

Answer: One thing to note is that you cannot pass the entire array to a function. Instead, you pass to it a pointer that will point to the array first element in memory. To do this, you indicate the name of the array without the brackets.

151. What are different storage class specifiers in C?

Answer: auto, register, static, extern

152. What is scope of a variable? How are variąbles scoped in C?

Answer: Scope of a variable is the part of the program where the variable may directly be accessible. In C, all identifiers are lexically (or statically) scoped.

153. When should we use pointers in a C program?

Answer:

1. To get address of a variable
2. For achieving pass by reference in C: Pointers allow different functions to share and modify their local variables.
3. To pass large structures so that complete copy of the structure can be avoided.C
4. To implement "linked" data structures like linked lists and binary trees.

154. What is NULL pointer?

Answer: NULL is used to indicate that the pointer doesn't point to a valid location. Ideally, we should initialize pointers as NULL if we don't know their value at the time of declaration. Also, we should make a pointer NULL when memory pointed by it is deallocated in the middle of a program.

155. What is Dangling pointer?

Answer: Dangling Pointer is a pointer that doesn't point to a valid memory location. Dangling pointers arise when an object is deleted or deallocated, without modifying the value of the pointer, so that the pointer still points to the memory location of the deallocated memory. Following are examples.

// EXAMPLE 1

```
int *ptr = (int *)malloc(sizeof(int));
.............
.............
free(ptr);
// ptr is a dangling pointer now and operations like following are
invalid
*ptr = 10;  // or printf("%d", *ptr);
```

// EXAMPLE 2

```
int *ptr = NULL
{
    int x  = 10;
    ptr = &x;
}
// x goes out of scope and memory allocated to x is free now.
// So ptr is a dangling pointer now.
```

156. What is memory leak? Why it should be avoided

Answer: Memory leak occurs when programmers create a memory in heap and forget to delete it. Memory leaks are particularly serious issues for programs like daemons and servers which by definition never terminate.

```
/* Function with memory leak */
#include <stdlib.h>
void f(){
    int *ptr = (int *) malloc(sizeof(int));
    /* Do some work */
    return; /* Return without freeing ptr*/
}
```

157. What are pointers?

Answer: Pointers point to specific areas in the memory. Pointers contain the address of a variable, which in turn may contain a value or even an address to another memory.

158. What is an lvalue?

Answer: An lvalue is an expression to which a value can be assigned. The lvalue expression is located on theleft side of an assignment statement, whereas an rvalue is located on the right side of an assignment statement. Each assignment statement must have an lvalue and an rvalue. The lvalue expression must reference a storable variable in memory. It cannot be a constant.

159. What is a pointer value and address?

Answer: A pointer value is a data object that refers to a memory location. Each memory location is numbered in the memory. The number attached to a memory location is called the address of the location.

160. What is wild pointer?

Answer: Wild pointers are also known as dangling pointers. Pointers that do not point to a valid object of the appropriate type, or to a distinguished null pointers value in language which support this.

161. What are the drawback of Pointer?

Answer: Since the pointers point to a memory location issues of dangling pointers and wild pointers can occur.

Dangling pointers are those pointers when the data at which they are pointed may have been modified or deleted.

But still the pointer points to that location.

The pointers that are not initialized lead to wild pointers because they will be pointing to some arbitrary memory.

Also memory leaks occur, if a memory is not released.

162. What is pointer in C?

Answer: Pointer is a variable that stores/points the address of another variable. Normal variable stores the value of the variable whereas pointer variable stores the address of the variable.

```
syntax: data_type *var_name;
```

Where, * is used to denote that "p" is pointer variable and not a normal variable.

163. What is null pointer in C?

Answer: Null pointer is a pointer which is pointing to nothing. Null pointer points to empty location in memory. Value of null pointer is 0. We can make a pointer to point to null as below.

```
int *p = NULL;
char *p = NULL;
```

164. What is NULL in C?

*Answer:*NULLisamacrowhichisdefinedinCheaderfiles.ThevalueofNULLmacrois0. It is defined in C header files as below.

```
#define NULL (void *) 0;
```

NULL is used for pointers only as it is defined as (void *) 0. It should not be used other than pointers. If NULL is assigned to a pointer, then pointer is pointing to nothing.

165. What is void pointer in C?

Answer:

- Void pointer is a generic pointer that can be used to point another variable of any data type.
- Void pointer can store the address of variable belonging to any of the data type. So, void pointer is also called as general purpose pointer.

Note: *i*nt pointer can be used to point a variable of int data type and char pointer can be used to point a variable of char data type.

166. What is dangling pointer in C?

Answer: When a pointer is pointing to non-existing memory location is called dangling pointer.

167. What is wild pointer in C?

Answer: Uninitialized pointers are called as wild pointers in C which points to arbitrary (random) memory location. This wild pointer may lead a program to behave wrongly or to crash.

168. What is file pointer in C?

Answer:

- File pointer is a pointer which is used to handle and keep track on the files being accessed. A new data type called "FILE" is used to declare file pointer. This data type is defined in stdio.h file. File pointer is declared as FILE *fp. Where, 'fp' is a file pointer.
- fopen() function is used to open a file that returns a FILE pointer. Once file is opened, file pointer can be used to perform I/O operations on the file. fclose() function is used to close the file.

169. When can void pointer and null pointer be used in C?

Answer: Void pointer is a generic pointer that can be used to point another variable of any data type. Null pointer is a pointer which is pointing to nothing.

170. What is const pointer in C?

Answer: Const pointer is a pointer that can't change the address of the variable that is pointing to.Once const pointer is made to point one variable, we can't change this pointer to point to any other variable. This pointer is called const pointer.

171. Is pointer arithmetic a valid one? Which arithmetic operation is not valid in pointer? Why?

Answer: Pointer arithmetic is not valid one. Pointer addition, multiplication and division are not allowed as these are not making any sense in pointer arithmetic.

But, two pointers can be subtracted to know how many elements are available between these two pointers.

172. Is void pointer arithmetic a valid one? Why?

Answer: Arithmetic operation on void pointer is not valid one. Void pointer is a generic pointer. It is not referring int, char or any other data type specifically. So, we need to cast void pointer to specific type before applying arithmetic operations.

Note:

- Pointer arithmetic itself is not valid one. Pointer addition, multiplication and division are not allowed as these are not making any sense in pointer arithmetic.
- But, two pointers can be subtracted to know how many elements are available between these two pointers.

173. What is the difference between null and zero?

Answer: NULLisamacrowhichisdefinedinCheaderfiles.ThevalueofNULLmacrois0. It is defined in C header files as below.

```
#define NULL (void *) 0;
```

- NULL is used for pointers only as it is defined as (void *) 0. It should not be used other than pointers. If NULL is assigned to a pointer, then pointer is pointing to nothing.
- 0 (zero) is a value.

174. What is the difference between null pointer and uninitialized pointer in C?

Answer: Null pointer is a pointer which is pointing to nothing. Null pointer points to empty location in memory. Value of null pointer is 0. We can make a pointer to point to null as below.

```
int *p =  NULL;
char *p = NULL;
```

Uninitialized pointers are called as wild pointers in C which points to arbitrary (random) memory location. This wild pointer may lead a program to behave wrongly or to crash.

175. Can array size be declared at run time?

Answer: Array size can't be declared at run time. Size of array must be known during compilation time. So, array size should be declared before compilation.

- Correct example: char array [10];
- Wrong example: char array[i];
- Always, Array subscript should be positive and it should not be either negative or any variable name.
- If we really don't know the size of an array, we can use dynamic memory allocation concepts in C which uses malloc(), calloc() functions to allocate memory during execution time.

176. What are local static variables? What is their use?

Answer: A local static variable is a variable whose lifetime doesn't end with a function call where it is declared. It extends for the lifetime of complete program. All calls to the function share the same copy of local static variables. Static variables can be used to count the number of times a function is called. Also, static variables get the default value as 0. For example, the following program prints "0 1"

```
#include <stdio.h>
void fun(){
   // static variables get the default value as 0.
```

```
    static int x;
    printf("%d ", x);
    x = x + 1;
}
int main(){
    fun();
    fun();
    return 0;
}
```

// Output: 0 1

177. What are static functions? What is their use?

Answer: In C, functions are global by default. The "static" keyword before a function name makes it static. Unlike global functions in C, access to static functions is restricted to the file where they are declared. Therefore, when we want to restrict access to functions, we make them static. Another reason for making functions static can be reuse of the same function name in other files.

178. Reallocating memory

Answer: When reallocating memory if any other pointers point into same piece of memory do you have to readjust these pointers or do they get readjusted automatically?

179. What is the difference between Call by Value and Call by Reference?

Answer: When using Call by Value, you are sending the value of a variable as parameter to a function, whereas Call by Reference sends the address of the variable. Also, under Call by Value, the value in the parameter is not affected by whatever operation that takes place, while in the case of Call by Reference, values can be affected by the process within the function.

180. What are actual arguments?

Answer: When you create and use functions that need to perform an action on some given values, you need to pass these given values to that function. The values that are being passed into the called function are referred to as actual arguments.

181. What are formal parameters?

Answer: In using functions in a C program, formal parameters contain the values that were passed by the calling function. The values are substituted in these formal parameters and used in whatever operations as indicated within the main body of the called function.

182. Can you pass an entire structure to functions?

Answer: Yes, it is possible to pass an entire structure to a function in a call by method style. However, some programmers prefer declaring the structure globally, and then pass a variable of that structure type to a function. This method helps maintain consistency and uniformity in terms of argument type.

183. Is there a built-in function in C that can be used for sorting data?

Answer: Yes, use the qsort() function. It is also possible to create user defined functions for sorting, such as those based on the balloon sort and bubble sort algorithm.

184. How do you convert strings to numbers in C?

Answer: You can write you own functions to do string to number conversions, or instead use C's built in functions. You can use atof to convert to a floating point value, atoi to convert to an integer value, and atol to convert to a long integer value.

185. How many arguments can be passed to a function in C?

Answer:

- Any number of arguments can be passed to a function. There is no limit on this. Function arguments are stored in stack memory rather than heap memory. Stack memory allocation is depending on the operating system.
- So, any number of arguments can be passed to a function as much as stack has enough memory. Program may crash when stack overflows.

186. What is static function in C?

Answer: All functions are global by default in a C program/file. But, static keyword makes a function as a local function which can be accessed only by the program/ file where it is declared and defined. Other programs/files can't access these static functions.

187. What is the difference between memcpy() & strcpy() functions in C?

Answer:

- memcpy() function is used to copy a specified number of bytes from one memory to another. Whereas, strcpy() function is used to copy the contents of one string into another string.
- memcpy() function acts on memory rather than value. Whereas, strcpy() function acts on value rather than memory.

188. What is the difference between memcpy() & memmove() functions in C?

Answer:

- memcpy() function is is used to copy a specified number of bytes from one memory to another.

- memmove() function is used to copy a specified number of bytes from one memory to another or to overlap on same memory.
- Difference between memmove() and memcpy() is, overlap can happen on memmove(). Whereas, memory overlap won't happen in memcpy() and it should be done in non-destructive way.

189. Is there any inbuilt library function in C to remove leading and trailing spaces from a string? How will you remove them in C?

Answer:

- There is no inbuilt function to remove leading and trailing spaces from a string in C. We need to write our own function to remove them.
- We need to check first non-space character in given string. Then, we can copy that string from where non space character is found. Then, we can check whether any spaces are available in copied string from the end of the string. If space is found, we can copy '\0' in that space until any character is found. Because, '\0'indicates the end of the string. Now, we have removed leading and trailing spaces in a given string.

190. What is the difference between strcpy() & strncpy() functions in C?

Answer:

- strcpy( ) function copies whole content of one string into another string. Whereas, strncpy( ) function copies portion of contents of one string into another string.
- If destination string length is less than source string, entire/specified source string value won't be copied into destination string in both cases.

191. If you want to execute C program even after main function is terminated, which function can be used?

Answer:

- "atexit()" function can be used if we want to execute any function after program is terminated normally.
- Syntax: int atexit (void (*func)(void));
- The function "func" will be called automatically without any arguments once program is terminated normally.

192. What is exit() function in C?

Answer:

- exit() function terminates the program/process normally and returns the status code to the parent program/process.
- Syntax: void exit(int status)

193. Is it possible to call atexit() function more than once in a C program?

Answer: Yes. We can call atexit() function more than once. But, they will be executed in reverse order as a stack.

Example program:

```
#include <stdio.h>
#include <stdlib.h>

void Exit1 (void){
    printf (“Exit1 function is called\n”);
}
void Exit2 (void){
    printf (“Exit2 function is called \n”);
}

int main (void){
    atexit (Exit1);
    atexit (Exit2);
    printf (“This is the end of this program.\n”);
    return 0;
}
```

Output:

This is the end of this program.

```
Exit2 function is called
Exit1 function is called
```

194. What is the difference between exit() and return() in C?

Answer:

- exit() is a system call which terminates current process. exit() is not an instruction of C language.
- Whereas, return() is a C language instruction/statement and it returns from the current function (i.e. provides exit status to calling function and provides control back to the calling function).

195. What is the use of “#define” in C?

Answer: #define is a pre-processor directive which is used to define constant value. This constant can be any of the basic data types.

196. What is the syntax for comments in C?

Answer: Below is the syntax for comments in C. The characters or words or anything which are given between "/*" and "*/", won't be considered by C compiler for compilation process. These will be ignored by C compiler during compilation.

```
Syntax: /* your comments here */
```

197. What is a stack?

Answer: A stack is one form of a data structure. Data is stored in stacks using the FILO (First In Last Out) approach. At any particular instance, only the top of the stack is accessible, which means that in order to retrieve data that is stored inside the stack, those on the upper part should be extracted first. Storing data in a stack is also referred to as a PUSH, while data retrieval is referred to as a POP.

198. What are linked list?

Answer: A linked list is composed of nodes that are connected with another. In C programming, linked lists are created using pointers. Using linked lists is one efficient way of utilizing memory for storage.

199. What is FIFO?

Answer: In C programming, there is a data structure known as queue. In this structure, data is stored and accessed using FIFO format, or First-In-First-Out. A queue represents a line wherein the first data that was stored will be the first one that is accessible as well.

200. What are binary trees?

Answer: Binary trees are actually an extension of the concept of linked lists. A binary tree has two pointers, a left one and a right one. Each side can further branch to form additional nodes, which each node having two pointers as well.

201. What are the advantages and disadvantages of a heap?

Answer: Storing data on the heap is slower than it would take when using the stack. However, the main advantage of using the heap is its flexibility. That's because memory in this structure can be allocated and remove in any particular order. Slowness in the heap can be compensated if an algorithm was well designed and implemented.

202. What is static memory allocation and dynamic memory allocation?

Answer:

- **Static memory allocation:** The compiler allocates the required memory space for a declared variable. By using the address of operator, the reserved address is obtained and this address may be assigned to a pointer variable. Since most of the declared variable has static memory, this way of assigning pointer value to a pointer variable is known as static memory allocation. Memory is assigned during compilation time.

- **Dynamic memory allocation:** It uses functions such as malloc( ) or calloc( ) to get memory dynamically. If these functions are used to get memory dynamically and the values returned by these functions are assigned to pointer variables, such assignments are known as dynamic memory allocation. Memory is assigned during run time.

203. What is the difference between "calloc" and "malloc"?

Answer: calloc and malloc are used for dynamic memory allocation. Calloc initializes the memory locations to zero by default but malloc memory contains garbage values.

204. Where is the function declared as static stored in memory?

Answer: The usage of static with a function or variable restricts their scope. Is this behavior memory related?

Yes static keyword would not affect where the function gets stored, even if it is static a function will always be stored in stack! But it hides the function from being used in other files other than in which it is declared.

205. What is pointer linking with operating system?

Answer: When we declare a null pointer it addresses the 0 address which is the address of operating system so we cannot use that address this is what the pointer is linked to OS.

206. Difference between program memory, data memory, stack memory and heap memory?

Answer: When the program is compiled and linked different parts of the program is organized in separate segments. That is our code will be in one segment code means the instructions to be executed this is called as code segment or program memory this is usually read-only. Then there are data which on which the code operates, these data get stored in a segment called data segment. Stack memory is a part of programs memory which will be used as stack in case of function calls to store the IP and parameters variables of the current function. The three types of memory specified above are owned by the corresponding process or program the linker will give info about where to store which data to the loader, based on these infos loader will load the corresponding image i.e. executable in the memory. Heap memory is the memory which is not owned by the process. OS has set of pages of memory which can be allocated to the process when a process requests for extra memory, these requests are done by the malloc and calloc function calls. This memory is allocated when the program is running and according to the current condition of the process i.e. allocated dynamically that's why this is called as dynamic allocation.

I have used words program and process invariably. Because a program needs physical primary memory when it gets executed and a program under execution is a process, Hope this explanation is clear.

207. C is a structural or high-level or middle level language which one is correct answer

Answer: C is a middle level language.
Because this language contains both the features of both high level language and low level languages. Also can be called as structured programming language.

208. What does the characters "r" and "w" mean when writing programs that will make use of files?

Answer: "r" means "read" and will open a file as input wherein data is to be retrieved. "w" means "write", and will open a file for output. Previous data that was stored on that file will be erased.

209. What is the difference between text files and binary files?

Answer: Text files contain data that can easily be understood by humans. It includes letters, numbers and other characters. On the other hand, binary files contain 1s and 0s that only computers can interpret.

210. How do you search data in a data file using random access method?

Answer: Use the fseek() function to perform random access input/ouput on a file. After the file was opened by the fopen() function, the fseek would require three parameters to work: a file pointer to the file, the number of bytes to search, and the point of origin in the file.

211. Difference between "printf" and "sprintf".

Answer: printf will write to the console. sprintf will write to the buffer

212. Difference between printf and cprintf

Answer: printf outputs to the standard output stream (stdout)
fprintf goes to a file handle (FILE*)
sprintf goes to a buffer you allocated. (char*)

213. Garbage Value

Answer: In C if a variable is not assigned a value then why does it take garbage value?

214. What are preprocessor directives?

Answer: Preprocessor directives are placed at the beginning of every C program. This is where library files are specified, which would depend on what functions are to be used in the program. Another use of preprocessor directives is the declaration of constants. Preprocessor directives begin with the # symbol.

215. What is Macro? Why do we use macro?

Answer:

- Macro is a name which is given to a value or to a piece of code/block in a program. Instead of using the value, we can use macro which will replace the value in a program.
- The reason for using macro is, consider below example.
- You are using a person's age as 50 in many places in your program. If you use direct value in all the places in your program, it is very difficult to change the age value in future if you want to change it to 60. If you use macro in your program, it is very simple to replace the value and we can change in only one place which will change the value in all places in your program.

Syntax: #define <MACRO_NAME> VALUE

Example: Original declaration – #define AGE 50

Modified declaration – #define AGE 60

216. What is "##" operator in C?

Answer: ## is a pre-processor macro in C. It is used to concatenate 2 tokens into one token.

Example program:

```
#include<stdio.h>
#define concatination(a,b) a ## b
int main (){
   int ab = 1000;
   printf("The concatenated value is:%d \n",concatination(a,b));
   return 0;
}
```

Output: The concatenated value is: 1000

217. How will you override an existing macro in C?

Answer: To override an existing macro, we need to undefine existing macro using "#undef". Then, we need to define same macro again with new value.

218. What is pragma in C? Or how will you execute functions before and after main function in C program?

Answer: #pragma is a pre-processor macro in C. It is used to call a function before and after main function in a C program.

Example program:

```
#include <stdio.h>
void function1( );
void function2( );
#pragma startup function1
#pragma exit function2
int main( ){
    printf ( "\n Now we are in main function" ) ;
    return 0;
}
void function1( ){
    printf("\nFunction1 is called before main function call");
}
void function2( ){
    printf ( "\nFunction2 is called just before end of " \
            «main function" ) ;"
}
```

Output:

```
Function1 is called before main function call
Now we are in main function
Function2 is called just before end of main function
```

219. How to check whether macro is defined or not in a C program?

Answer: "#ifdef" pre-processor directive checks whether particular macro is defined or not in a C program.

220. What is the difference between typedef & Macros?

Answer: Typedef is used to create a new name to an already existing data type. Redefine the name creates conflict with the previous declaration.

```
eg: typedef unsigned int UINT32
```

Macros [#define] is a direct substitution of the text before compling the whole code. In the given example, its just a textual substitution. Where there is a posibility of redifining the macro

```
eg: #define chPointer  char *
undef chPointer
#define chPointer int *
```

221. What are pre-processor directives?

- Pre-processor directives are placed at the beginning of a C program. They begin with # symbol.

- This is the place, where library files are specified depending on the functions to be used in the program.
- Pre-processor directives are also used for declaration of constants.

222. What is the difference between structure & union?

Answer: Differences are:

1. union allocates the memory equal to the maximum memory required by the member of the union but structure allocates the memory equal to the total memory required by the members.
2. In union, one block is used by all the member of the union but in case of structure, each member has their own memory space.
3. union is best in the environment where memory is less as it shares the memory allocated. But structure cannot implement in shared memory.
4. As memory is shared, ambiguity is more in union, but less in structure.
5. Self referential union cannot be implemented in any data structure, but self referential structure can be implemented.

223. What is wrong with this statement? myName = "Robin";

Answer: You cannot use the = sign to assign values to a string variable. Instead, use the strcpy function. The correct statement would be: strcpy(myName, "Robin");

224. How do you determine the length of a string value that was stored in a variable?

Answer: To get the length of a string value, use the function strlen(). For example, if you have a variable named FullName, you can get the length of the stored string value by using this statement: I = strlen(FullName); the variable I will now have the character length of the string value.

225. How do you declare a variable that will hold string values?

Answer: The char keyword can only hold 1 character value at a time. By creating an array of characters, you can store string values in it. Example: "char MyName[50]; " declares a string variable named MyName that can hold a maximum of 50 characters.

226. Can array subscripts have negative value in C?

Answer: No. Array subscripts should not have negative value. Always, it should be positive.

227. What is the difference between array and string in C?

Answer:

- Array can hold any of the data types. But, string can hold only char data type.
- Array size must be a constant value. So, array size can't be changed once declared. But, string size can be modified using char pointer.

- Array is not ended with null character by default. But, string is ended with null ('\0') character by default.

228. What is meant by core dump in C?

Answer:

- Core dump or core is a file, generated when a program is crashed or terminated abnormally because of segmentation fault or some other reason. Information of the memory used by a process is dumped in a file called core. This file is used for debugging purpose. Core dump has file name like "core.<process_id>"
- Core dump file is created in current working directory when a process terminates abnormally. Core dump is a typical error occurs because of illegal memory access.
- Core dump is also called as memory dump, storage dump or dump.

229. What is the purpose of "register" keyword?

Answer: It is used to make the computation faster.

The register keyword tells the compiler to store the variable onto the CPU register if space on the register is available. However, this is a very old technique. Todays processors are smart enough to assign the registers themselves and hence using the register keyword can actually slowdown the operations if the usage is incorrect.

230. What is the purpose of "register" keyword?

Answer: The keyword 'register' instructs the compiler to persist the variable that is being declared, in a CPU register.

Ex: register int number;

The persistence of register variables in CPU register is to optimize the access. Even the optimization is turned off; the register variables are forced to store in CPU register.

231. Explain the use of "auto" keyword.

Answer: When a certain variable is declared with the keyword 'auto' and initialized to a certain value, then within the scope of the variable, it is reinitialized upon being called repeatedly.

232. Explain the use of "auto" keyword.

Answer: The keyword 'auto' is used extremely rare. A variable is set by default to auto. The declarations:

auto int number; and int number;

has the same meaning. The variables of type static, extern and register need to be explicitly declared, as their need is very specific. The variables other than the above three are implied to be of 'auto' variables. For better readability auto keyword can be used.

2

C++

1. **What is C++?**

Answer: Released in 1985, C++ is an object-oriented programming language created by Bjarne Stroustrup. C++ maintains almost all aspects of the C language, while simplifying memory management and adding several features - including a new data type known as a class (you will learn more about these later) - to allow object-oriented programming. C++ maintains the features of C which allowed for low-level memory access but also gives the programmer new tools to simplify memory management.

2. **What is Object Oriented Programming?**

Answer: Object Oriented Programming (OOP) is a programming paradigm where the complete software operates as a bunch of objects talking to each other. An object is a collection of data and methods that operate on its data.

3. **Why OOP?**

Answer: The main advantage of OOP is better manageable code that covers following.

1. The overall understanding of the software is increased as the distance between the language spoken by developers and that spoken by users.
2. Object orientation eases maintenance by the use of encapsulation. One can easily change the underlying representation by keeping the methods same.

OOP paradigm is mainly useful for relatively big software. See this for a complete example that shows advantages of OOP over procedural programming.

4. **What are main features of OOP?**

Answer:

- Encapsulation

- Polymorphism
- Inheritance

5. What is encapsulation?

Answer: Encapsulation is referred to one of the following two notions.

1. Data hiding: A language feature to restrict access to members of an object. For example, private and protected members in C++.
2. Bundling of data and methods together: Data and methods that operate on that data are bundled together.

6. What is Polymorphism? How is it supported by C++?

Answer: Polymorphism means that some code or operations or objects behave differently in different contexts. In C++, following features support polymorphism.

- ***Compile Time Polymorphism:*** Compile time polymorphism means compiler knows which function should be called when a polymorphic call is made. C++ supports compiler time polymorphism by supporting features like templates, function overloading and default arguments.
- ***Run Time Polymorphism:*** Run time polymorphism is supported by virtual functions. The idea is virtual functions are called according to the type of object pointed or referred, not according to the type of pointer or reference. In other words, virtual functions are resolved late, at runtime.

7. What is Abstraction?

Answer: The first thing with which one is confronted when writing programs is the problem. Typically we are confronted with "real-life" problems and we want to make life easier by providing a program for the problem. However, real-life problems are nebulous and the first thing we have to do is to try to understand the problem to separate necessary from unnecessary details: We try to obtain our own abstract view, or model, of the problem. This process of modeling is called abstraction

8. What is the difference between realloc() and free()?

Answer: The free subroutine frees a block of memory previously allocated by the malloc subroutine. Undefined results occur if the Pointer parameter is not a valid pointer. If the Pointer parameter is a null value, no action will occur. The realloc subroutine changes the size of the block of memory pointed to by the Pointer parameter to the number of bytes specified by the Size parameter and returns a new pointer to the block. The pointer specified by the Pointer parameter must have been created with the malloc, calloc, or realloc subroutines and not been deallocated with the free or realloc subroutines. Undefined results occur if the Pointer parameter is not a valid pointer.

9. What is function overloading and operator overloading?

Answer: **Function overloading:** C++ enables several functions of the same name to be defined, as long as these functions have different sets of parameters (at least as far as their types are concerned). This capability is called function overloading. When an overloaded function is called, the C++ compiler selects the proper function by examining the number, types and order of the arguments in the call. Function overloading is commonly used to create several functions of the same name that perform similar tasks but on different data types.

Operator overloading allows existing C++ operators to be redefined so that they work on objects of user-defined classes. Overloaded operators are syntactic sugar for equivalent function calls. They form a pleasant facade that doesn't add anything fundamental to the language (but they can improve understandability and reduce maintenance costs).

10. What is the difference between declaration and definition?

Answer: The declaration tells the compiler that at some later point we plan to present the definition of this declaration.

```
E.g.: void stars () //function declaration
The definition contains the actual implementation.
E.g.: void stars () // declaratory
{
for(int j=10; j > =0; j--) //function body
cout << *;
cout << endl; }
```

11. What are the differences between references and pointers?

Answer: Both references and pointers can be used to change local variables of one function inside another function. Both of them can also be used to save copying of big objects when passed as arguments to functions or returned from functions, to get efficiency gain. Despite above similarities, there are following differences between references and pointers.

References are less powerful than pointers

1. Once a reference is created, it cannot be later made to reference another object; it cannot be reseated. This is often done with pointers.
2. References cannot be NULL. Pointers are often made NULL to indicate that they are not pointing to any valid thing.
3. A reference must be initialized when declared. There is no such restriction with pointers

Due to the above limitations, references in C++ cannot be used for implementing data structures like Linked List, Tree, etc. In Java, references don't have above restrictions, and can be used to implement all data structures. References being more powerful in Java are the main reason Java doesn't need pointers.

References are safer and easier to use:

1. Safer: Since references must be initialized, wild references like wild pointers are unlikely to exist. It is still possible to have references that don't refer to a valid location.
2. Easier to use: References don't need dereferencing operator to access the value. They can be used like normal variables. '&' operator is needed only at the time of declaration. Also, members of an object reference can be accessed with dot operator ('.'), unlike pointers where arrow operator (->) is needed to access members.

12. Explain Copy Constructor.

Answer: It is a constructor which initializes it's object member variable with another object of the same class. If you don't implement a copy constructor in your class, the compiler automatically does it.

13. When do you call copy constructors?

Answer: Copy constructors are called in these situations:

i. when compiler generates a temporary object
ii. when a function returns an object of that class by value
iii. when the object of that class is passed by value as an argument to a function
iv. when you construct an object based on another object of the same class

14. Differentiate between late binding and early binding. What are the advantages of early binding?

Answer:

a. Late binding refers to function calls that are not resolved until run time while early binding refers to the events that occur at compile time.
b. Late binding occurs through virtual functions while early binding takes place when all the information needed to call a function is known at the time of compiling. Early binding increases the efficiency. Some of the examples of early binding are normal function calls, overloaded function calls, and overloaded operators etc.

15. What are the advantages of inheritance?

Answer: It permits code reusability. Reusability saves time in program development. It encourages the reuse of proven and debugged high-quality software, thus reducing problem after a system becomes functional.

16. **What do you mean by inline function?**

Answer: The idea behind inline functions is to insert the code of a called function at the point where the function is called. If done carefully, this can improve the application's performance in exchange for increased compile time and possibly (but not always) an increase in the size of the generated binary executables.

17. **What is public, protected, private?**

Answer: Public, protected and private are three access specifier in C++. Public data members and member functions are accessible outside the class. Protected data members and member functions are only available to derived classes. Private data members and member functions can't be accessed outside the class. However there is an exception can be using friend classes.

Write a function that swaps the values of two integers, using int* as the argument type.

```
void swap(int* a, int*b) {
int t;
t = *a;
*a = *b;
*b = t;
}
```

18. **What is virtual constructors/destructors?**

Answer: Answer 1

Virtual destructors:

If an object (with a non-virtual destructor) is destroyed explicitly by applying the delete operator to a base-class pointer to the object, the base-class destructor function (matching the pointer type) is called on the object.

There is a simple solution to this problem declare a virtual base-class destructor. This makes all derived-class destructors virtual even though they don't have the same name as the base-class destructor. Now, if the object in the hierarchy is destroyed explicitly by applying the delete operator to a base-class pointer to a derived-class object, the destructor for the appropriate class is called. Virtual constructor: Constructors cannot be virtual. Declaring a constructor as a virtual function is a syntax error.

Answer 2

Virtual destructors: If an object (with a non-virtual destructor) is destroyed explicitly by applying the delete operator to a base-class pointer to the object, the base-class destructor function (matching the pointer type) is called on the object.

There is a simple solution to this problem – declare a virtual base-class destructor.

This makes all derived-class destructors virtual even though they don't have the same name as the base-class destructor. Now, if the object in the hierarchy is destroyed explicitly by applying the delete operator to a base-class pointer to a derived-class object, the destructor for the appropriate class is called.

19. Explain storage qualifiers in C++.

Answer:

i. Const - This variable means that if the memory is initialized once, it should not be altered by a program.

ii. Volatile - This variable means that the value in the memory location can be altered even though nothing in the program code modifies the contents.

iii. Mutable - This variable means that a particular member of a structure or class can be altered even if a particular structure variable, class, or class member function is constant.

20. What is the type of "this" pointer? When does it get created?

Answer: It is a constant pointer type. It gets created when a non-static member function of a class is called.

21. How would you differentiate between a pre and post increment operators while overloading?

Answer: Mentioning the keyword int as the second parameter in the post increment form of the operator++() helps distinguish between the two forms.

22. What are the advantages of inheritance?

Answer:

- It permits code reusability.
- Reusability saves time in program development.
- It encourages the reuse of proven and debugged high-quality software, thus reducing problem after a system becomes functional.

23. What is a template?

Answer: Templates allow to create generic functions that admit any data type as parameters and return value without having to overload the function with all the possible data types. Until certain point they fulfill the functionality of a macro. Its prototype is any of the two following ones:

```
template <class indetifier> function_declaration;
template <typename indetifier> function_declaration;
```

The only difference between both prototypes is the use of keyword class or typename, its use is indistinct since both expressions have exactly the same meaning and behave exactly the same way.

24. Define a constructor - What it is and how it might be called (2 methods).

Answer: *Answer 1*

Constructor is a member function of the class, with the name of the function being the same as the class name. It also specifies how the object should be initialized.

Ways of calling constructor:

1. Implicitly: automatically by complier when an object is created.
2. Calling the constructors explicitly is possible, but it makes the code unverifiable.

Answer 2

```
class Point2D{
int x; int y;
public Point2D() : x(0) , y(0) {} //default (no argument) constructor
};
main(){
Point2D MyPoint; // Implicit Constructor call. In order to allocate
memory on stack, the default constructor is implicitly called.
Point2D * pPoint = new Point2D(); // Explicit Constructor call. In
order to allocate memory on HEAP we call the default constructor.
We have two pairs: new() and delete() and another pair : alloc() and
free().
```

25. Explain differences between eg. new() and malloc()

Answer: Answer 1:

1. "new and delete" are preprocessors while "malloc() and free()" are functions. [we dont use brackets will calling new or delete].
2. no need of allocate the memory while using "new" but in "malloc()" we have to use "sizeof()".
3. "new" will initlize the new memory to 0 but "malloc()" gives random value in the new alloted memory location [better to use calloc()]

Answer 2:

new() allocates continous space for the object instace malloc() allocates distributed space.

new() is castless, meaning that allocates memory for this specific type, malloc(), calloc() allocate space for void * that is cated to the specific class type pointer.

26. What is the difference between class and structure?

Answer: Structure: Initially (in C) a structure was used to bundle different type of data types together to perform a particular functionality. But C++ extended the structure to contain functions also. The major difference is that all declarations inside a structure are by default public. Class: Class is a successor of Structure. By default all the members inside the class are private.

27. What is RTTI?

Answer: Runtime type identification (RTTI) lets you find the dynamic type of an object when you have only a pointer or a reference to the base type. RTTI is the official way in standard C++ to discover the type of an object and to convert the type of a pointer or reference (that is, dynamic typing). The need came from practical experience with C++. RTTI replaces many Interview Questions - Homegrown versions with a solid, consistent approach.

28. What is encapsulation?

Answer: Packaging an object's variables within its methods is called encapsulation.

29. What is an object?

Answer: Object is a software bundle of variables and related methods. Objects have state and behavior.

30. What do you mean by inheritance?

Answer: Inheritance is the process of creating new classes, called derived classes, from existing classes or base classes. The derived class inherits all the capabilities of the base class, but can add embellishments and refinements of its own.

31. What is namespace?

Answer: Namespaces allow us to group a set of global classes, objects and/or functions under a name. To say it somehow, they serve to split the global scope in sub-scopes known as namespaces.

The form to use namespaces is:

```
namespace identifier { namespace-body }
```

Where identifier is any valid identifier and namespace-body is the set of classes, objects and functions that are included within the namespace. For example:

namespace general { int a, b; } In this case, a and b are normal variables integrated within the general namespace. In order to access to these variables from outside the namespace we have to use the scope operator ::. For example, to access the previous variables we would have to put:

```
general::a general::b
```

The functionality of namespaces is especially useful in case that there is a possibility that a global object or function can have the same name than another one, causing a redefinition error.

32. What is virtual class and friend class?

Answer: Friend classes are used when two or more classes are designed to work together and need access to each other's implementation in ways that the rest of the world shouldn't be allowed to have. In other words, they help keep private things private. For instance, it may be desirable for class DatabaseCursor to have more privilege to the internals of class Database than main() has.

33. What is the difference between an object and a class?

Answer: Classes and objects are separate but related concepts. Every object belongs to a class and every class contains one or more related objects.

- A Class is static. All of the attributes of a class are fixed before, during, and after the execution of a program. The attributes of a class don't change.
- The class to which an object belongs is also (usually) static. If a particular object belongs to a certain class at the time that it is created then it almost certainly will still belong to that class right up until the time that it is destroyed.
- An Object on the other hand has a limited lifespan. Objects are created and eventually destroyed. Also during that lifetime, the attributes of the object may undergo significant change.

34. What is a class?

Answer: Class is a user-defined data type in C++. It can be created to solve a particular kind of problem. After creation the user need not know the specifics of the working of a class.

35. What is friend function?

Answer: As the name suggests, the function acts as a friend to a class. As a friend of a class, it can access its private and protected members. A friend function is not a member of the class. But it must be listed in the class definition.

36. Which recursive sorting technique always makes recursive calls to sort subarrays that are about half size of the original array?

Answer: Mergesort always makes recursive calls to sort subarrays that are about half size of the original array, resulting in O(n log n) time.

37. What is abstraction?

Answer: Abstraction is of the process of hiding unwanted details from the user.

38. What are virtual functions?

Answer: A virtual function allows derived classes to replace the implementation provided by the base class. The compiler makes sure the replacement is always called whenever the object in question is actually of the derived class, even if the object is accessed by a base pointer rather than a derived pointer. This allows algorithms in the base class to be replaced in the derived class, even if users don't know about the derived class.

39. What is a scope resolution operator?

Answer: A scope resolution operator (::), can be used to define the member functions of a class outside the class.

40. What do you mean by pure virtual functions?

Answer: Pure virtual function in object oriented programming is called as virtual method that acts as a function allowing its behavior to be overridden by the class that is inheriting the pure virtual function with the same signature. This is used in case of polymorphism. It is used when a base class is being driven by the derived class and an object of the derived class referred as base or derived class type. When a derived class overrides the base class method then the output or the behavior will be called as ambiguous. To use the virtual function a virtual keyword is used. This allows the function to be defined in every derived class and use the functionality of it.

40. What is polymorphism? Explain with an example?

Answer: "Poly" means "many" and "morph" means "form". Polymorphism is the ability of an object (or reference) to assume (be replaced by) or become many different forms of object. Example: function overloading, function overriding, virtual functions. Another example can be a plus '+' sign, used for adding two integers or for using it to concatenate two strings.

41. What is a conversion constructor?

Answer: A constructor that accepts one argument of a different type.

42. What is the difference between a copy constructor and an overloaded assignment operator?

Answer: A copy constructor constructs a new object by using the content of the argument object. An overloaded assignment operator assigns the contents of an existing object to another existing object of the same class.

43. Explain the ISA and HASA class relationships. How would you implement each in a class design?

Answer: A specialized class "is" a specialization of another class and, therefore, has the ISA relationship with the other class. An Employee ISA Person. This relationship is best implemented with inheritance. Employee is derived from Person. A class may have an instance of another class. For example, an employee "has" a salary, therefore the Employee class has the HASA relationship with the Salary class. This relationship is best implemented by embedding an object of the Salary class in the Employee class.

44. What is the Standard Template Library (STL)?

Answer: A library of container templates approved by the ANSI committee for inclusion in the standard C++ specification.

A programmer who then launches into a discussion of the generic programming model, iterators, allocators, algorithms, and such, has a higher than average understanding of the new technology that STL brings to C++ programming.

45. In C++, what is the difference between method overloading and method overriding?

Answer: Overloading a method (or function) in C++ is the ability for functions of the same name to be defined as long as these methods have different signatures (different set of parameters). Method overriding is the ability of the inherited class rewriting the virtual method of the base class.

46. What is a modifier?

Answer: A modifier, also called a modifying function is a member function that changes the value of at least one data member. In other words, an operation that modifies the state of an object. Modifiers are also known as 'mutators'.

47. What is an accessor?

Answer: An accessor is a class operation that does not modify the state of an object. The accessor functions need to be declared as const operations

48. Differentiate between a template class and class template.

Answer: Template class: A generic definition or a parameterized class not instantiated until the client provides the needed information. It's jargon for plain templates. Class template: A class template specifies how individual classes can be constructed much like the way a class specifies how individual objects can be constructed. It's jargon for plain classes.

49. Explain Stack & Heap Objects

Answer: The memory a program uses is divided into four areas:

a. The code area - this is where the compiled program sits in memory.

b. The global area - the place where global variables are stored.

c. The heap - the place where dynamically allocated variables are allocated from.

d. The stack -the place where parameters and local variables are allocated from.

50. Explain deep copy and a shallow copy

Answer:

a. Deep copy - It involves using the contents of one object to create another instance of the same class. Here, the two objects may contain the same information but the target object will have its own buffers and resources. The destruction of either object will not affect the remaining object.

b. Shallow copy -It involves copying the contents of one object into another instance of the same class. This creates a mirror image. The two objects share the same externally contained contents of the other object to be unpredictable. This happens because of the straight copying of references and pointers.

51. Explain virtual class and friend class

Answer:

a. **Virtual Base Class:**

It is used in context of multiple inheritances in C++.

If you want to derive two classes from a class, and further derive one class from the two classes in the second level, you need to declare the uppermost base class as 'virtual' in the inherited classes. This prevents multiple copies of the uppermost base class data members when an object of the class at the third level of hierarchy is created.

b. **Friend class:**

When a class declares another class as its friend, it is giving complete access to all its data and methods including private and protected data and methods to the friend class member methods.

Friendship is not necessarily bi-directional. If A declares B as its friend it does not imply that A can access private data of B. It only means that B can access all data of A.

Explain the of scope resolution operator

A scope resolution operator (::) is used to define the member functions of a class outside the class.

Mostly, a scope resolution operator is required when a data member is redefined by a derived class or an overridden method of the derived class wants to call the base class version of the same method.

52. **What are virtual functions?**

Answer: Virtual functions are used with inheritance, they are called according to the type of object pointed or referred, not according to the type of pointer or reference. In other words, virtual functions are resolved late, at runtime. Virtual keyword is used to make a function virtual.

Following things are necessary to write a C++ program with runtime polymorphism (use of virtual functions)

1. A base class and a derived class.
2. A function with same name in base class and derived class.
3. A pointer or reference of base class type pointing or referring to an object of derived class.

53. **What are the features that are provided to make a program modular?**

Answer: To create a program requires self sufficient resources, the way to make a piece of code modular so that it can be handled properly. This shows the relationship between different objects or in between the same objects. Different functions have to be used to keep the code different from the data provided. Object oriented programming allows creating a modular approach to make it more abstract and create the interactions between them. The features that are being provided in object oriented programming are:

- **Encapsulation:** it deals with the grouping of data and functions together at one place or it can be said in an object that defines the interface of their interaction and the relationship between them.
- **Inheritance:** it deals with the relationship that exists between the parent and child classes. A child can inherit the properties of the parent and it remains helpful in creating a hierarchy in the system to keep things more modular.
- **Polymorphism:** is a feature that deals with different values that can be used by only one function. It doesn't have to re-create the same function again and again for different values but, it uses the same function to call different data types.

3

Basic JAVA

1. **What is OOPs?**

   Answer: Object oriented programming organizes a program around its data, i.e. objects and a set of well defined interfaces to that data. An object-oriented program can be characterized as data controlling access to code.

2. **What is the difference between Procedural and OOPs?**

   Answer:

   a) In procedural program, programming logic follows certain procedures and the instructions are executed one after another.

   In OOPs program, unit of program is object, which is nothing but combination of data and code.

   b) In procedural program, data is exposed to the whole program whereas in OOPs program, it is accessible within the object and which in turn assures the security of the code.

3. **What is an Object?**

   Answer: An object is an entity with certain attributes or qualities and behaviors, for a simple example, a 'Laptop' is an object which has certain attributes like weight, color, screen size, manufacturer etc. It has various behaviors or activities to do or act upon, as play games, browse Internet, write/check emails, watch movies, listen music etc.

4. **What is a Class?**

   Answer: A class is a collection of attributes and behaviors of objects with certain similarities and an instance of a class is represented by an object. A simple example of class is a 'Car' which represents variety of Car objects with different attribute values and behaviors. The different objects of 'Car' class can be, for example: A Mercedes Car, a Toyota Car, two different objects from same class but different attributes and different behaviors too.

5. **What is OOAD?**

Answer: **Object Oriented Analysis and Design (OOAD)** is a methodology to analyze, design and develop application using objects and their relations and message based communication to each other. Everything in OOAD is visualized in terms of objects and classes. OOAD introduced a paradigm shift from thinking and programming procedurally to objects oriented programming. This approach helps in designing complex real time systems with ease. The features like Data Abstraction and Encapsulation, Inheritance and Polymorphism form fundamentals of object oriented programming.

Advantages:

- Enhanced Reusability
- Modular approach towards problem solving which will be
- Better Maintainability Better Performance if system is designed cautiously using OOAD concepts

6. **What is Data Abstraction?**

Answer: Data Abstraction is extraction of essential information for a particular purpose and ignoring the remainder of the information, e.g. a car is consisted of an engine, air filters, a carburetor, a gear box, a steering, a fuel tank, tyres etc. A driver of a car need not to be bothered about several finer points of the car, he/she should know what it requires to drive a car. Take another user, a car mechanic; he will require different set of information in order to repair the car.

7. **What is Data Encapsulation?**

Answer: Data Encapsulation is wrapping information's (attributes and behaviors) within an object. A suitable example is a class as it wraps methods and data within itself. The attributes of a class corresponds to its data members while behavior corresponds to member methods of the class.

8. **What is the difference between Data Abstraction and Information Hiding?**

Answer: Data Abstraction is often confused with information hiding while they altogether are two different technical concepts.

9. **What are Encapsulation, Inheritance and Polymorphism?**

Answer: Encapsulation is the mechanism that binds together code and data it manipulates and keeps both safe from outside interference and misuse.

Inheritance is the process by which one object acquires the properties of another object.

Polymorphism is the feature that allows one interface to be used for general class actions.

10. What is the difference between Assignment and Initialization?

Answer: Assignment can be done as many times as desired whereas initialization can be done only once.

11. What are Class, Constructor and Primitive data types?

Answer: Class is a template for multiple objects with similar features and it is a blue print for objects. It defines a type of object according to the data the object can hold and the operations the object can perform.

Constructor is a special kind of method that determines how an object is initialized when created.

Primitive data types are 8 types and they are:

byte, short, int, long
float, double
boolean
char

12. What is an Object and how do you allocate memory to it?

Answer: Object is an instance of a class and it is a software unit that combines a structured set of data with a set of operations for inspecting and manipulating that data. When an object is created using new operator, memory is allocated to it.

13. What are the supported platforms by Java Programming Language?

Answer: Java runs on a variety of platforms, such as Windows, Mac OS, and the various versions of UNIX/Linux like HP-Unix, Sun Solaris, Redhat Linux, Ubuntu, CentOS, etc.

14. What is the difference between constructor and method?

Answer: Constructor will be automatically invoked when an object is created whereas method has to be called explicitly.

15. What is difference between object oriented programming language and object based programming language?

Answer: Object based programming languages follow all the features of OOPs except Inheritance. Examples of object based programming languages are JavaScript, VBScript etc.

16. What are methods and how are they defined?

Answer: Methods are functions that operate on instances of classes in which they are defined. Objects can communicate with each other using methods and can call methods in other classes.

Method definition has four parts. They are name of the method; type of object or primitive type the method returns, a list of parameters and the body of the method. A method's signature is a combination of the first three parts mentioned above.

17. What is the use of bin and lib in JDK?

Answer: Bin contains all tools such as javac, appletviewer, awt tool, etc., whereas lib contains API and all packages.

18. What is casting?

Answer: Casting is used to convert the value of one type to another.

19. How many ways can an argument be passed to a subroutine and explain them?

Answer: An argument can be passed in two ways. They are passing by value and passing by reference. Passing by value: This method copies the value of an argument into the formal parameter of the subroutine.

Passing by reference: In this method, a reference to an argument (not the value of the argument) is passed to the parameter.

20. What is the difference between an argument and a parameter?

Answer: While defining method, variables passed in the method are called parameters. While using those methods, values passed to those variables are called arguments.

21. What is UNICODE?

Answer: Unicode is used for internal representation of characters and strings and it uses 16 bits to represent each other.

22. What is method overloading and method overriding?

Answer: **Method overloading:** When a method in a class having the same method name with different arguments is said to be method overloading.

Method overriding: When a method in a class having the same method name with same arguments is said to be method overriding.

23. What is difference between overloading and overriding?

Answer:

a) In overloading, there is a relationship between methods available in the same class whereas in overriding, there is relationship between a superclass method and subclass method.

b) Overloading does not block inheritance from the superclass whereas overriding blocks inheritance from the superclass.

c) In overloading, separate methods share the same name whereas in overriding, subclass method replaces the superclass.

d) Overloading must have different method signatures whereas overriding must have same signature.

24. What is Inheritance and what are different types of it?

Answer: Inheritance is a mechanism by which a specific object acquires attributes and behaviors of more general objects. In OOP terminology ,Inheritance is the mechanism which allows a Class 'A' to inherit properties of Class 'B' and we say 'A inherits from B' or in other words B is a 'Superclass'/'Parent class' while A is a 'Subclass'/'Child class'. A typical example of inheritance is a family tree which consists of son, father, grandfather, great grandfather and so on. The different types of Inheritance are:

1. Single Inheritance
2. Multiple Inheritances
3. Multilevel Inheritance
4. Hierarchical Inheritance
5. Hybrid Inheritance

25. Why Java uses singly rooted hierarchy?

Answer: All objects in Java are inherited from same base class called 'Object'. In Java all objects have common interface to implement and it makes implementation of Garbage collector lot easier in Java. The necessary implementation is provided in base class, and the garbage collector can then send the necessary messages to every object in the system. Without singly rooted hierarchy, it would have been difficult to implement garbage collection feature. It enables lot of ease to programmers not to be bothered about memory management while development. It greatly simplifies argument passing amongst object too on the heap. As Java started from scratch and has no backward compatibility issues with any existing language, it was a logical choice to use the singly-rooted hierarchy in common with most other object-oriented programming languages.

26. Why does Java not support Multiple Inheritances?

Answer: Java does not support multiple inheritances at least not the way it does in case of C++.In designer's view Multiple Inheritance poses many problems and confusions than it solves. E.g. famous Diamond problem. The diamond problem is an ambiguity that can occur when a class multiply inherits from two classes that both descend from a common super class. In such scenarios assuming if Java implements multiple inheritance then it would be difficult to know which method is to be called by an inheriting class object of two of the super classes. In Java, interfaces solve all these ambiguities caused by the diamond problem. Through interfaces, Java allows multiple inheritances of interface but not of implementation. Implementation, which includes instance variables and method implementations, is always singly inherited. As a result, confusion will never arise in Java over which inherited instance variable or method implementation to use.

27. Why is Java not 100% pure OOP language?

Answer: Java takes inspirations from C and C++.The native data types like 'char', 'int', 'float', 'double' are straight pick from C, which is not an Object Oriented Language. Reasonably enough, Java is not a 100% pure Object Oriented Language.

28. What is Early Binding?

Answer: The assignment of types to variables and expressions at compilation time is known as 'Early Binding', it is also called 'static binding' and 'static typing'.

29. What is Polymorphism/Late Binding?

Answer: When an object is sent a message then it does not know itself what type it is, the runtime environment will decide about function calling over an object. This feature of connecting an object with its associated message at runtime is known as Polymorphism or Late binding or Dynamic binding.

30. What is meant by Inheritance and what are its advantages?

Answer: Inheritance is the process of inheriting all the features from a class. The advantages of inheritance are reusability of code and accessibility of variables and methods of the super class by subclasses.

31. What is the difference between this() and super()?

Answer: this() can be used to invoke a constructor of the same class whereas super() can be used to invoke a super class constructor.

32. What is the difference between superclass and subclass?

Answer: A super class is a class that is inherited whereas sub class is a class that does the inheriting.

33. What modifiers may be used with top-level class?

Answer: public, abstract and final can be used for top-level class.

34. What is interface and its use?

Answer: Interface is similar to a class which may contain method's signature only but not bodies and it is a formal set of method and constant declarations that must be defined by the class that implements it.

Interfaces are useful for:

a) Declaring methods that one or more classes are expected to implement

b) Capturing similarities between unrelated classes without forcing a class relationship.

c) Determining an object's programming interface without revealing the actual body of the class.

35. What is an abstract class?

Answer: An abstract class is a class designed with implementation gaps for subclasses to fill in and is deliberately incomplete.

36. Difference between Abstraction and Encapsulation.

Answer: Abstraction is removing some distinctions between objects, so as to show their commonalities.

Encapsulation is hiding the details of the implementation of an object so that there are no external dependencies on the particular implementation.

37. Why are there no global variables in Java?

Answer: Global variables are considered bad form for a variety of reasons:

- Adding state variables breaks referential transparency (you no longer can understand a statement or expression on its own: you need to understand it in the context of the settings of the global variables).
- State variables lessen the cohesion of a program: you need to know more to understand how something works. A major point of Object-Oriented programming is to break up global state into more easily understood collections of local state.
- When you add one variable, you limit the use of your program to one instance. What you thought was global, someone else might think of as local: they may want to run two copies of your program at once.
- For these reasons, Java decided to ban global variables.

38. What does it mean that a class or member is final?

Answer: A final class can no longer be subclassed. Mostly this is done for security reasons with basic classes like String and Integer. It also allows the compiler to make some optimizations, and makes thread safety a little easier to achieve.

Methods may be declared final as well. This means they may not be overridden in a subclass.

Fields can be declared final, too. However, this has a completely different meaning. A final field cannot be changed after it's initialized, and it must include an initializer statement where it's declared. For example,

```
public final double c = 2.998;
```

It's also possible to make a static field final to get the effect of C++'s const statement or some uses of C's #define, e.g.

```
public static final double c = 2.998;
```

39. What does it mean that a method or class is abstract?

Answer: An abstract class cannot be instantiated. Only its subclasses can be instantiated. You indicate that a class is abstract with the abstract keyword like this:

```
public abstract class Container extends Component {
```

Abstract classes may contain abstract methods. A method declared abstract is not actually implemented in the current class. It exists only to be overridden in subclasses. It has no body. For example,

```
public abstract float price();
```

Abstract methods may only be included in abstract classes. However, an abstract class is not required to have any abstract methods, though most of them do.

Each subclass of an abstract class must override the abstract methods of its superclasses or itself be declared abstract.

40. What is the difference between Integer and int?

Answer:

a) Integer is a class defined in the java.lang package, whereas int is a primitive data type defined in the Java language itself. Java does not automatically convert from one to the other.

b) Integer can be used as an argument for a method that requires an object, whereas int can be used for calculations.

41. What is a cloneable interface and how many methods does it contain?

Answer: It is not having any method because it is a TAGGED or MARKER interface.

42. What is the difference between abstract class and interface?

Answer:

a) All the methods declared inside an interface are abstract whereas abstract class must have at least one abstract method and others may be concrete or abstract.

b) In abstract class, key word abstract must be used for the methods whereas interface we need not use that keyword for the methods.

c) Abstract class must have subclasses whereas interface can't have subclasses.

43. Can you have an inner class inside a method and what variables can you access?

Answer: Yes, we can have an inner class inside a method and final variables can be accessed.

44. What are wrapper classes?

Answer: Wrapper classes are classes that allow primitive types to be accessed as objects.

45. What is the difference between C++ & Java?

Answer: Both are Object Oriented. But Java does not support multiple inheritances; this is achieved in Java Through interfaces. In C++ there is no memory management; developer has to allocate and free the Memory resources deliberately which is error prone and cumbersome.

46. What is an Interface?

Answer: An **Interface** is a reference type, similar to a **class** that can contain only constants, method signatures, and nested types. There are no method bodies (abstract methods) means an **Interface** is a specification of **method prototype**.

→ An **Interface** may or may not have any methods.

→ An **Interface** can contain variables which are public, static, and final by default.

→ **Interfaces** cannot be instantiated—they can only be implemented by classes or extended by other **Interfaces**.

→ We can use **Interface** reference variable to refer **Implementation Class objects.**

→ An **Interface** can't implement another **Interface**.

→ An **Interface** can extend already existing **Interface.**

→ A single **Class** can implement multiple **Interfaces.**

47. How can we achieve Multiple Inheritances in Java?

Answer: Directly we can't achieve **Multiple Inheritance** in **Java**. Indirectly there are two ways, those are :

1. We can achieve **Multiple Inheritance** by implementing more than one **Interfaces**, because we can have chance to implement more than one **Interfaces** in Java.
2. Another indirect way to achieve **Multiple Inheritance** is, doing by repeated use of **Single Inheritance.**

Example:

```
Class z extends A, B --- Inavallid (bcz direct way)
Class B extends A
} ---- those are vallid (bcz indirect way)
Class Z extends B
```

So, here Class z can have all the features of Class B and Class A, but here we are doing indirect way with the help of **Single Inheritance**.

48. What is the difference between an abstract class and an interface?

Answer: An abstract class allows its subclasses to override the methods defined in it. It is never instantiated and a class can inherit from a single class, as Java doesn't support for Multiple Inheritance. It may contain both abstract and non-abstract methods.

An interface has public, abstract methods and may have public, static and final variables (read only). It introduces multiple inheritances by a class implementing several interfaces.

49. What modifiers may be used with an interface declaration?

Answer: An interface may be declared as public or abstract.

50. What is the use of interface?

Answer: An interface is a collection of public abstract methods and read only i.e. public, static and final variables. The concept of interfaces in Java makes Multiple Inheritance a reality. Two or more non-related classes can implement the same interface. A class can implement multiple interfaces. Whenever there has to be an ancestry associated with classes along with some concrete behaviors then it is good idea to come up with abstract classes in such scenario but when implementation is more generic in nature and not dependent upon class relations or type hierarchy then such behaviors should be packaged inside an interface. The methods defined inside an interface can be implemented by non related classes.

51. What is serializable interface?

Answer: In java.io package there is an interface called *java.io.Serializable,* which is a syntactic way of serializing objects. This interface does not define any method. The purpose of serialization is persistence, communication over sockets or RMI. In Object serialization an object can be converted into byte stream and vice versa.

52. Does a class inherit constructors from its superclass?

Answer: No. Constructors cannot be inherited. Constructors are used to initialize a valid sate of an object. Whenever a subclass instance is created then it calls no argument default constructor of super class. The following code will explain implicit call to default constructor of base class:-

```
class Base {
      Base() {
            System.out.println("I am constructing Base");
      }
}
class Child extends Base {
```

```
        Child() {
                System.out.println("I am constructing Child");
        }
    }
    public class A {
        public static void main(String[] args) {
                Child child = new Child();
        }
    }
```

Once executed this code will print:

I am constructing Base

I am constructing Child

It means when a child class object is created it inherently calls no arg default constructor of base class.

53. How many methods do u implement if implement the Serializable Interface?

Answer: The Serializable interface is just a "marker" interface, with no methods of its own to implement. Other 'marker' interfaces are

```
java.rmi.Remote , java.util.EventListener
```

54. What's the difference between constructors and other methods?

Answer: Constructors must have the same name as the class and cannot return a value. They are only called once while regular methods could be called many times.

55. What is constructor chaining and how is it achieved in Java?

Answer: A child object constructor always first needs to construct its parent (which in turn calls its parent constructor.). In Java it is done via an implicit call to the no-args constructor as the first statement.

56. If the method to be overridden has access type 'protected', can subclass have the access type as 'private'?

Answer: No, it must have access type as protected or public, since an overriding method must restrict access of the method it overrides.

57. If you use super() or this() in a constructor where should it appear in the constructor?

Answer: It should always be the first statement in the constructor.

58. What modifiers may be used with an inner class that is a member of an outer class?

Answer: A (non-local) inner class may be declared as public, protected, private, static, final, or abstract.

59. Can an inner class be defined inside a method?

Answer: Yes it can be defined inside a method and it can access data of the enclosing methods or a formal parameter if it is final.

60. What is an anonymous class?

Answer: It is a type of inner class with no name. Once defined an object can be created of that type as a parameter all in one line. It cannot have explicitly declared constructor. The compiler automatically provides an anonymous constructor for such class.

An anonymous class is never abstract. An anonymous class is always an inner class; it is never static. An anonymous class is always implicitly final.

61. Why Java does not support Multiple Inheritances?

Answer: **Java** design team strove to make **Java** as:

→ Simple, object oriented, and familiar

→ Robust and secure

→ Architecture neutral and portable

→ High performance

→ Interpreted, threaded, and dynamic

→ The reasons for omitting **Multiple Inheritance** from the **Java Language** mostly stem from the "simple, object oriented and familiar" goal.

→ **Multiple Inheritance** causes more problems and confusion than it solves. So the designers' of **Java Language** cut **Multiple Inheritance** from the language (just as they cut Operator overloading).

→ **Multiple Inheritance** leads to confusion for programmers. This is against to the design principle of the **Java** to be a Simple Programming Language.

62. How many types of Inheritances does Java support?

Answer: Yes, Ok but, basically there are two types of Inheritances are there, they are

1. Single Inheritance
2. Multiple Inheritances

And some other Inheritances are there those are

→ Multi Level

→ Hierarchical

→ Hybrid

→ But these come under again Basic Inheritances Single and Multiple only. So we can leave these types, and we can say only two types that is Single and Multiple Inheritances.

→ And Java support only Single Inheritance only.

63. What is JVM Heap Size? How does it affect the performance of the Application

Answer: The heap is the runtime data area from which memory for all class instances and arrays is allocated. The heap may be of a fixed size or may be expanded. The heap is created on virtual machine start-up. If you have complicated algorithms or big caching which might create lot of objects in memory you may need bigger heap size.

64. Is null a keyword?

Answer: The null value is not a keyword.

65. What is the difference between the >> and >>> operators?

Answer: The >> operator carries the sign bit when shifting right. The >>> zero-fills bits that have been shifted out.

66. How many bits are used to represent Unicode, ASCII, UTF-16, and UTF-8 characters?

Answer: Unicode requires 16 bits and ASCII require 7 bits. Although the ASCII character set uses only 7 bits, it is usually represented as 8 bits. UTF-8 represents characters using 8, 16, and 18 bit patterns. UTF-16 uses 16-bit and larger bit patterns.

67. Is sizeof a keyword?

Answer: The sizeof operator is not a keyword.

68. What are wrapped classes?

Answer: Wrapped classes are classes that allow primitive types to be accessed as objects.

69. What is the difference between the Boolean & operator and the && operator?

Answer: If an expression involving the Boolean & operator is evaluated, both operands are evaluated. Then the & operator is applied to the operand. When an expression involving the && operator is evaluated, the first operand is evaluated. If the first operand returns a value of true then the second operand is evaluated. The && operator is then applied to the first and second operands.

If the first operand evaluates to false, the evaluation of the second operand is skipped.

70. What is the difference between a break statement and a continue statement?

Answer: A break statement results in the termination of the statement to which it applies (switch, for, do, or while). A continue statement is used to end the current loop iteration and return control to the loop statement.

71. What must a class do to implement an interface?

Answer: It must provide all of the methods in the interface and identify the interface in its implements clause.

72. What is an abstract method?

Answer: An abstract method is a method whose implementation is deferred to a subclass.

73. What is the difference between a static and a non-static inner class?

Answer: A non-static inner class may have object instances that are associated with instances of the class's outer class. A static inner class does not have any object instances.

74. What is meant by Inheritance and what are its advantages?

Answer: Inheritance is the process of inheriting all the features from a class. The advantages of inheritance are reusability of code and accessibility of variables and methods of the super class by subclasses.

75. What is the difference between abstract class and interface?

Answer:

a) All the methods declared inside an interface are abstract whereas abstract class must have at least one abstract method and others may be concrete or abstract.

b) In abstract class, key word abstract must be used for the methods whereas interface we need not use that keyword for the methods.

c) Abstract class must have subclasses whereas interface can't have subclasses.

76. Can you have an inner class inside a method and what variables can you access?

Answer: Yes, we can have an inner class inside a method and final variables can be accessed.

77. Does Java provide any construct to find out the size of an object?

Answer: No there is not sizeof operator in Java. So there is not direct way to determine the size of an object directly in Java.

78. What t is the use of main method?

Answer: main method is used to start the execution of the program.

79. What is overloading?

Answer: Overloading is nothing but having the same name with different parameters. (or) The same function having different functionalities.

80. What restrictions are placed on method overriding?

Answer: Overridden methods must have the same name, argument list, and return type. The overriding method may not limit the access of the method it overrides. The overriding method may not throw any exceptions that may not be thrown by the overridden method.

81. What is overriding?

Answer: Overriding is nothing but having same name and method signature. It is between parent class and child class. Child class will always override parent class.

82. What is method overriding?

Answer: The method with same signature but with changed implementation lead to method overriding and that can occur in a parent child relation of classes. A method defined in parent class can be overridden in its child class with different implementation from its base class.

1. Pointers are supported in C++ while not in Java. The memory management is done automatically with help of part of JVM called Garbage Collector.
2. Multiple inheritances is not supported in Java but supported in C++.
3. There are no structures and unions in Java.
4. There is no scope resolution operator in Java (::).
5. There are no destructors in Java like C++.
6. There is no virtual keyword in Java because all non-static method use dynamic binding.

83. What are the access modifiers?

Answer: Public, Private, Protected and Default.

84. What is Method Signature?

Answer: Method signature is nothing but (return type of function + function name + no.of arguments).

85. What are the rules we have to follow in overloading?

Answer:

i) The no.of arguments must be different.

ii) the type of arguments must be different

iii) It will not depend on return type.

86. What are the Secondary Access Modifiers?

Answer: Static, abstract, final, transient and volatile.

87. What is Shadowing?

Answer: Declaring the same variables of parent class in the subclass is known as Shadowing.

Eg : e.super.x;

88. What are the types of data types in Java?

Answer: byte, short, int, float, long, double, char and Boolean

89. Can we call the non static variables into static methods?

Answer: No, vice versa is also not possible.

90. What is numeric promotion?

Answer: Numeric promotion is the conversion of a smaller numeric type to a larger numeric type, so that integer and floating-point operations may take place. In numerical promotion, byte, char, and short values are converted to int values. The int values are also converted to long values, if necessary. The long and float values are converted to double values, as required.

91. What is the difference between a public and a non-public class?

Answer: A public class may be accessed outside of its package. A non-public class may not be accessed outside of its package.

92. To what value is a variable of the boolean type automatically initialized?

Answer: The default value of the boolean type is false.

93. Is delete,next,main,exit or null keyword in java?

Answer: No.

94. What is the basic difference between the overloading and overriding?

Answer: It is necessary to check the method signature in overloading, whereas it is not necessary in overriding. Method overloading between the same class methods and method overriding is between parent class method and child class method.

95. What is java bytecode?

Answer: Bytecode is a highly optimized set of instructions designed to be executed by the java run time system, which is called the Java Virtual Machine (JVM)

96. What is java virtual machine?

Answer: Java VM is interpreter for the bytecode.

97. What is Encapsulation?

Answer: Encapsulation is the mechanism that binds together code and the data it manipulates, and keeps the safe from outside interference and misuse.

98. What is Data Abstraction?

Answer: Abstraction is nothing but keeping the data and methods in a single object.

99. What is inheritance?

Answer: Inheritance is the process by which one object acquires the properties of another object.

100. What are the types of inheritance?

Answer:

a) Single inheritance.
b) Multiple inheritance
c) Multi level inheritance
d) Hybrid inheritance.

101. Dose Java supports multiple inheritances?

Answer: No. nterfaces are used for this purpose.

102. What is polymorphism?

Answer: Polymorphism is a feature that allows one interface to be used for a general class of actions.

103. What is Type Costing?

Answer: The conversion of one data type to another data type is known as Type Costing. It is possible in higher data type to lower.

104. What is the range and width of long?

Answer: Range is -9,223,372,036,854,775,808 to 9,223,372,036,854,775,807 and the width is 64.

105. What is the range and width of int?

Answer: Range is -2,147,483,648 to 2,147,483,647 and width is 32.

106. What is the range and width of short?

Answer: Range is -32,768 to 32,767 and width is 16.

107. What is the range and width of byte?

Answer: Range is -128 to 127 and width is 8.

108. What is the declaration of an Array?

Answer: int Array[] = new int [5];

109. What is a class?

Answer: A class is a template for an object.

110. What is an Object?

Answer: Object is instance of a class.

111. What are called instance variables?

Answer: The data or variables defined within a class are called instance variables.

112. What is a Constructor?

Answer: Constructor is used to initialize the object. Constructors have no return type, not even void.

113. What are the types of Constructors?

Answer: Constructors are divided into two types: I) Implicit and 2) Explicit.

114. What are the types of explicit constructors?

Answer: Argument constructors and Default constructors.

115. Where we use the key word 'this'?

Answer: 'this' is always a reference to the object on which the method was invoked.

116. Can we get the output using Constructors?

Answer: No, These are used only for assigning values.

117. What is call by value and call by reference?

Answer: When a simple type is passed to a method, it is done by use of call by-by-value. Objects are passed call by reference.

118. What is Recursion?

Answer: It is a process of defining something in terms of itself.

119. What is recursive?

Answer: A method that calls itself is said to be recursive.

120. What is Static?

Answer: Static is the key word, which is used to create a member that can be used by itself, without reference to a specific instance. It is a class level variable. It is illegal to refer to any instance variables inside of a static method.

121. Can we refer instance variables inside of a static method?

Answer: No. We can't.

122. What is final?

Answer: The final prevents its contents from being modified.

123. What is Dynamic Method Dispatch?

Answer: Dynamic method dispatch is the mechanism by which a call to an overridden function is resolved at run time, rather than at compile time.

124. What is an abstract class?

Answer: Restriction of data is called Abstract. We can't create the instance. These are virtual classes. It is same as interface but we can implement the methods.

125. What does the "abstract" keyword mean in front of a method? A class?

Answer: Abstract keyword declares either a method or a class. If a method has a abstract keyword in front of it, it is called abstract method. Abstract method has no body. It has only arguments and return type. Abstract methods act as placeholder methods that are implemented in the subclasses.

Abstract classes can't be instantiated. If a class is declared as abstract, no objects of that class can be created. If a class contains any abstract method it must be declared as abstract

126. Which key word is used to prevent Overriding?

Answer: Final

127. What is an interface?

Answer: It is a task for specific contract. It does not actually define any implementations. It is not at all a class. It won't allow constructors.

128. What is public?

Answer: If we declare it as a public, classes, subclasses within the package and outside the package, can access it.

129. What is private?

Answer: It can't be accessed anywhere other than the same class.

130. What is protected?

Answer: It can be accessed in the same class, sub class of the same package but not other side of that package.

131. What are pass by reference and pass by value?

Answer: Pass by Reference means the passing the address itself rather than passing the value. Pass by Value means passing a copy of the value to be passed.

132. What is passed by ref and what by value?

Answer: All Java method arguments are passed by value. However, Java does manipulate objects by reference, and all object variables themselves are references

133. What is an abstract class?

Answer: Abstract class must be extended /subclassed (to be useful). It serves as a template. A class that is abstract may not be instantiated (i.e., you may not call its constructor), abstract class may contain static data. Any class with an abstract method is automatically abstract itself, and must be declared as such. A class may be declared abstract even if it has no abstract methods. This prevents it from being instantiated.

134. Can an abstract class be final?

Answer: An abstract class may not be declared as final

135. What is static in java?

Answer: Static means one per class, not one for each object no matter how many instance of a class might exist. This means that you can use them without creating an instance of a class. Static methods are implicitly final, because overriding is done based on the type of the object, and static methods are attached to a class, not an object. A static method in a superclass can be shadowed by another static method in a subclass, as long as the original method was not declared final. However, you can't override a static method with a non static method. In other words, you can't change a static method into an instance method in a subclass.

136. What is difference between static (class) method and instance method?

Answer:

static or class method	instance method
1. A method i.e. declared as static is known as static method.	A method i.e. not declared as static is known as instance method.
2. Object is not required to call static method.	Object is required to call instance methods.
3. Non-static (instance) members cannot be accessed in static context (static method, static block and static nested class) directly.	static and non-static variables both can be accessed in instance methods.
4. For example: public static int cube(int n){ return n*n*n;}	For example: public void msg(){...}.

137. Difference between method Overloading and Overriding.

Answer:

Method Overloading	Method Overriding
1. Method overloading increases the readability of the program.	Method overriding provides the specific implementation of the method that is already provided by its super class.
2. Method overloading is occurs within the class.	Method overriding occurs in two classes that have IS-A relationship.
3. In this case, parameter must be different.	In this case, parameter must be same.

138. Why we cannot override static method?

Answer: It is because the static method is the part of class and it is bound with class whereas instance method is bound with object and static gets memory in class area and instance gets memory in heap.

139. What is final?

Answer: A final class can't be extended i.e. final class may not be subclassed. A final method can't be overridden when its class is inherited. You can't change value of a final variable (is a constant).

140. What does the "final" keyword mean in front of a variable? A method? A class?

Answer: FINAL for a variable: value is constant

FINAL for a method: cannot be overridden

FINAL for a class: cannot be derived

141. What is the difference between instanceof and isInstance?

Answer: **instanceof** is used to check to see if an object can be cast into a specified type without throwing a cast class exception.

isInstance()

Determines if the specified Object is assignment-compatible with the object represented by this Class. This method is the dynamic equivalent of the Java language instanceof operator. The method returns true if the specified Object argument is non-null and can be cast to the reference type represented by this Class object without raising a ClassCastException. It returns false otherwise.

142. What is the output from System.out.println("Hello"+null);

Answer: Hellonull

143. Can you have virtual functions in Java?

Answer: Yes, all functions in Java are virtual by default.

144. What if the main method is declared as private?

Answer: The program compiles properly but at runtime it will give "Main method not public." message.

145. What if the static modifier is removed from the signature of the main method?

Answer: Program compiles. But at runtime throws an error "NoSuchMethodError".

146. What if I write static public void instead of public static void?

Answer: Program compiles and runs properly.

147. What if I do not provide the String array as the argument to the method?

Answer: Program compiles but throws a runtime error "NoSuchMethodError".

148. How many different ways to create a objects?

Answer: There are 4 ways of creating object in java

- By using new keyword, this common and mostly used to create object
```
MyClass object=new MyClass();
```
- If you know class name and it has public default constructor, you can create object by
```
Class.forName() MyClass object= (MyClass) Class.forName("MyClass").
newInstance();
```
- Using clone(),it can be used to create a copy of an existing object.
```
MyClass object=new MyClass();
MyClass anotherObject=object.clone();
```

- Using object deserialization

```
ObjectInputStream oi = new ObjectInputSteram(InputStream);
MyClass object = (MyClass) oi.readObject();
```

149. What is the first argument of the String array in main method?

Answer: The String array is empty. It does not have any element. This is unlike C/C++ where the first element by default is the program name.

150. Question: Why can't I say just abs() or sin() instead of Math.abs() and Math.sin()?

Answer: The import statement does not bring methods into your local name space. It lets you abbreviate class names, but not get rid of them altogether. That›s just the way it works, you›ll get used to it. It›s really a lot safer this way.
 However, there is actually a little trick you can use in some cases that gets you what you want. If your top-level class doesn›t need to inherit from anything else, make it inherit from java.lang.Math. That *does* bring all the methods into your local name space. But you can›t use this trick in an applet, because you have to inherit from java.awt.Applet. And actually, you can›t use it on java.lang.Math at all, because Math is a «final» class which means it can›t be extended.

151. Question: Is "abc" a primitive value?

Answer: The String literal «abc» is not a primitive value. It is a String object.

152. Can an application have multiple classes having main method?

Answer: Yes it is possible. While starting the application we mention the class name to be run. The JVM will look for the Main method only in the class whose name you have mentioned. Hence there is not conflict amongst the multiple classes having main method.

153. Question: What are the Object and Class classes used for?

Answer: The Object class is the highest-level class in the Java class hierarchy. The Class class is used to represent the classes and interfaces that are loaded by a Java program.

154. What is overriding?

Answer: When a class defines a method using the same name, return type, and arguments as a method in its superclass, the method in the class overrides the method in the superclass. When the method is invoked for an object of the class, it is the new definition of the method that is called, and not the method definition from superclass. Methods may be overridden to be more public, not more private.

155. What are different types of inner classes?

Answer: Nested top-level classes, Member classes, Local classes, Anonymous classes

Nested top-level classes- If you declare a class within a class and specify the static modifier, the compiler treats the class just like any other top-level class. Any class outside the declaring class accesses the nested class with the declaring class name acting similarly to a package. E.g, outer.inner. Top-level inner classes implicitly have access only to static variables. There can also be inner interfaces. All of these are of the nested top-level variety.

Member classes - Member inner classes are just like other member methods and member variables and access to the member class is restricted, just like methods and variables. This means public member class acts similarly to a nested top-level class. The primary difference between member classes and nested top-level classes is that member classes have access to the specific instance of the enclosing class.

Local classes - Local classes are like local variables, specific to a block of code. Their visibility is only within the block of their declaration. In order for the class to be useful beyond the declaration block, it would need to implement a more publicly available interface. Because local classes are not members; the modifiers public, protected, private, and static are not usable.

Anonymous classes - Anonymous inner classes extend local inner classes one level further. As anonymous classes have no name, you cannot provide a constructor.

156. Are the imports checked for validity at compile time? E.g. will the code containing an import such as java.lang.ABCD compile?

Answer: Yes the imports are checked for the semantic validity at compile time. The code containing above line of import will not compile. It will throw an error saying, cannot resolve symbol: class ABCD location: package io import java.io.ABCD;

157. What does it mean that a method or field is "static"?

Answer: Static variables and methods are instantiated only once per class. In other words they are class variables, not instance variables. If you change the value of a static variable in a particular object, the value of that variable changes for all instances of that class.

Static methods can be referenced with the name of the class rather than the name of a particular object of the class (though that works too). That's how library methods like System.out.println() work out is a static field in the java.lang.System class.

158. What is the difference between declaring a variable and defining a variable?

Answer: In declaration we just mention the type of the variable and its name. We do not initialize it. But defining means declaration + initialization. e.g. String s; is just a declaration while String s = new String ("abcd"); Or String s = "abcd"; are both definitions.

159. What is the default value of an object reference declared as an instance variable?

Answer: null unless we define it explicitly.

160. Can a top level class be private or protected?

Answer: No. A top level class cannot be private or protected. It can have either "public" or no modifier. If it does not have a modifier it is supposed to have a default access. If a top level class is declared as private the compiler will complain that the "modifier private is not allowed here". This means that a top level class cannot be private. Same is the case with protected.

161. What type of parameter passing does Java support?

Answer: In Java the arguments are always passed by value.

162. Primitive data types are passed by reference or pass by value?

Answer: Primitive data types are passed by value.

163. Objects are passed by value or by reference?

Answer: Java only supports pass by value. With objects, the object reference itself is passed by value and so both the original reference and parameter copy both refer to the same object.

164. How does Java handle integer overflows and underflows?

Answer: It uses those low order bytes of the result that can fit into the size of the type allowed by the operation.

165. What is the difference between a while statement and a do statement?

Answer: A while statement checks at the beginning of a loop to see whether the next loop iteration should occur. A do statement checks at the end of a loop to see whether the next iteration of a loop should occur. The do statement will always execute the body of a loop at least once.

166. Question: What is the difference between the prefix and postfix forms of the ++ operator?

Answer: The prefix form performs the increment operation and returns the value of the increment operation. The postfix form returns the current value all of the expression and then performs the increment operation on that value.

167. Question: What is the purpose of a statement block?

Answer: A statement block is used to organize a sequence of statements as a single statement group.

168. How many ways can one write an infinite loop?

Answer: Personally I would recommend following ways to implement infinite loop in Java but there can be other ways like calling a method recursively, though I never tested that.

```
- while (true)
- for (;;) { }
```

169. When do you use 'continue' and 'break' statements?

Answer: When one wants to complete the iteration of a loop prematurely then 'continue' statement is used.

While the 'break' statement is used to exit the entire loop whenever encountered.

170. What is the difference between 'while' and 'do while' loop?

Answer: In case of 'do-while' loop, body is always executed at least once, since test is performed at the end of the body. It should usually be ignored while coding.

171. What restrictions are placed on the values of each case of a switch statement?

Answer: During compilation, the values of each case of a switch statement must evaluate to a value that can be promoted to an int value.

172. What is the difference between an if statement and a switch statement?

Answer: If statement is used to select among two alternatives. It uses a boolean expression to decide which alternative should be executed. The switch statement is used to select among multiple alternatives. It uses an int expression to determine which alternative should be executed.

173. Can a for statement loop indefinitely?

Answer: Yes, a for statement can loop indefinitely. For example, consider the following: for(;;) ;

174. What is the range of the short type?

Answer: The range of the short type is - (2^15) to 2^15 - 1.

175. To what value is a variable of the String type automatically initialized?

Answer: The default value of an String type is null.

176. What is the difference between inner class and nested class?

Answer: When a class is defined within a scope od another class, then it becomes inner class.

If the access modifier of the inner class is static, then it becomes nested class.

177. What is the difference between static and non-static variables?

Answer: A static variable is associated with the class as a whole rather than with specific instances of a class. Non-static variables take on unique values with each object instance.

178. How are this() and super() used with constructors?

Answer: this() is used to invoke a constructor of the same class. super() is used to invoke a superclass constructor.

179. Can an unreachable object become reachable again?

Answer: An unreachable object may become reachable again. This can happen when the object's finalize() method is invoked and the object performs an operation which causes it to become accessible to reachable objects.

180. What modifiers are allowed for methods in an Interface?

Answer: Only public and abstract modifiers are allowed for methods in interfaces.

181. What are some alternatives to inheritance?

Answer: Delegation is an alternative to inheritance. Delegation means that you include an instance of another class as an instance variable, and forward messages to the instance. It is often safer than inheritance because it forces you to think about each message you forward, because the instance is of a known class, rather than a new class, and because it doesn't force you to accept all the methods of the super class: you can provide only the methods that really make sense. On the other hand, it makes you write more code, and it is harder to re-use (because it is not a subclass).

182. Which characters may be used as the second character of an identifier, but not as the first character of an identifier?

Answer: The digits 0 through 9 may not be used as the first character of an identifier but they may be used after the first character of an identifier.

183. How does Java handle integer overflows and underflows?

Answer: It uses those low order bytes of the result that can fit into the size of the type allowed by the operation.

184. What is Downcasting?

Answer: Downcasting is the casting from a general to a more specific type, i.e. casting down the hierarchy

185. Can a method be overloaded based on different return type but same argument type?

Answer: No, because the methods can be called without using their return type in which case there is ambiquity for the compiler

186. What happens to a static var that is defined within a method of a class ?

Answer: Can't do it. You'll get a compilation error

187. How many static init can you have?

Answer: As many as you want, but the static initializers and class variable initializers are executed in textual order and may not refer to class variables declared in the class whose declarations appear textually after the use, even though these class variables are in scope.

188. What modifiers may be used with an inner class that is a member of an outer class?

Answer: A (non-local) inner class may be declared as public, protected, private, static, final, or abstract.

189. What restrictions are placed on the location of a package statement within a source code file?

Answer: A package statement must appear as the first line in a source code file (excluding blank lines and comments).

190. A variable can be declared to be final, as in the declaration "static final int ballCount = 25;" What does it mean to declare the variable to be "final"? Why would you want to use such a variable in a program? (For extra credit: Why do you suppose that "final" variables are generally declared to be "static" as well?)

Answer: When a variable is declared to be "final," its value can never be changed from the value that is initially assigned to it. The variable is said to be a named constant. The two main reasons for using final variables are:

Using a meaningful name such as "ballCount" to represent a quantity, rather than an actual value such as 25, makes the program easier to read and understand.

Supose you want to modify your program to use a different value for the constant (for example, ballCount = 50 instead of ballCount = 25). It is easy to change the value of a final variable in the single line where it is declared. In general, it would be much harder to find and change an actual value every place it occurs in the program.

Extra credit: If a variable is non-static, then every object that belongs to the class gets its own copy of the variable. In the case of a final variable, all these copies would have the same value. It makes more sense to have a single copy, associated with the class. So final variables are usually declared to be static.

191. Explain what is meant by polymorphism, and give an example.

Answer: Polymorphism refers to the fact that a method call, such as shape.draw(), can call different methods, depending on the actual type of the object. If the variable, shape, is declared to be of type Shape, then it can refer to an object belonging to the class Shape or to any subclass of that class. Each of these subclasses might have its own version of the draw() method. The method that is actually called by the command shape.draw() depends on which class the shape object actually belongs to.

192. What is HotJava?

Answer: HotJava is a Browser provided by Sun. It is a modular, applet-aware, extensible WorldWide Web browser written entirely in Java. The security in HotJava provides a safe environment for the execution of imported code. The security is based on interlocking layers of security that range from the design of the Java language at the base to the file and network access protections at the top.

193. What is the sequence of interpretation, compilation of a java applet?

Answer: A java program is first compiled to byte code which is stored in a '.class file'. This file is downloaded as an applet to a browser which then interprets it by converting it into machine code appropriate to the hardware platform on which it is running.

194. How JAVA achieves platform independence?

Answer: Java is platform independent because of the consistent data sizes at all the platforms on which Java code is run. The output of a Java compiler is not an executable code it is bytecode. bytecode is highly optimized set of instructions designed to be executed by a virtual machine that the Java run-time system emulates. As Java programs are interpreted, rather than compiled it is much easier to run them in a variety of run-time environments.

195. Does Java support virtual functions?

Answer: No, Java does not support virtual functions directly as supported by C++. Virtual functions can be implemented in Java using abstract classes and interfaces. Abstract class is a class with declaration of methods, but without their implementation. The implementation of the methods takes place in the subclasses. Another example of virtual functions is interfaces. The only difference between an abstract class and an interface is that abstract classes can be used only when they are superclasses and the subclass implements their methods. Whereas in an interface the methods can be implemented even by classes, which are not inherited.

196. What software is needed to learn Java?

Answer: A Java compiler/development environment such as VJ++ is needed to learn Java.

197. What are the different int data types provided by Java?

Answer: The different data types supported by Java are-- int, short, long and byte. The byte wise representations are as follows:

- byte-8 byte
- short-16 byte
- int-32 byte
- long-64 byte.

198. What are different data types in Java?

Answer: Java supports following 8 primitive data types:
(click this picture to enlarge)

Data Type	Size	Default Value (for fields)	Range of Values(Min-Max)
byte	8 bits	0	-128(-2^7) to 127(2^7-1)
short	16 bits	0	-32,768(-2^15) to 32,767(2^15-1)
int	32 bits	0	-2,147,483,648(-2^31) to 2,147,483,647(2^31-1)
long	64 bits	0L	-9,223,372,036,854,775,808(-2^63) to 9,223,372,036,854,775,807(2^63-1)
float	32 bits	0.0f	N/A
double	64 bits	0.0d	N/A
char	16 bits	'\u0000'	'\u0000' (or 0) to '\uffff (or 65,535 -->(2^16-1) inclusive)
boolean	1 bit	false	true or false

199. What are expressions, statements and blocks in Java?

Answer: An expression is a construct made up of variables, operators, and method invocations, which are built-up according to the syntax of the language that evaluates to a single value.

Some examples of expression:

```
int val = 0;
iArr[0] = 20;
int var = 4 + 2; // var is now 6
```

A statement is complete unit of execution. Any expression which is:

- An assignment expression
- ++ or --
- Method invocation
- Object creation

200. What is the difference between Java and HTML?

Answer: Java is a full-fledged object oriented programming language. It is derived from C++ and shares the same basic syntax with that language. HTML (HyperText Markup Language) is not a programming language. It is simply used as a scripting tool to develop web pages. It is not an editor - it is a simple scripting language that defines how the text and images will appear on the web page. Java is used to create small applications (called applets) that run in the browser. It can also be used to develop full-fledged applications.

201. Which would be faster - an application developed in Java or an application developed in C++?

Answer: An application developed in C++ would be about 30 times faster than Java.

202. What is the difference between the >> and >>> operators?

Answer: The >> operator carries the sign bit when shifting right. The >>> zero-fills bits that have been shifted out.

203. How are memory leaks possible in Java

Answer: If any object variable is still pointing to some object which is of no use, then JVM will not garbage collect that object and object will remain in memory creating memory leak.

204. What would happen if you say this = null

Answer: this will give a compilation error as follows cannot assign value to final variable this.

205. How would you pass a java integer by reference to another function?

Answer: Passing by reference is impossible in JAVA but Java supports the object reference so. Object is the only way to pass the integer by reference.

206. Do multiple inheritances in Java?

Answer: It's not possible directly. That means this feature is not provided by Java, but it can be achieved with the help of Interface. By implementing more than one interface.

207. What is data encapsulation? What does it buy you?

Answer: The most common example I can think of is a java bean. Encapsulation may be used by creating 'get' and 'set' methods in a class which are used to access the fields of the object. Typically the fields are made private while the get and set methods are public.

dEncapsulation can be used to validate the data that is to be stored, to do calculations on data that is stored in a field or fields, or for use in introspection (often the case when using java beans in Struts, for instance).

208. What are the primitive types in Java?

Answer: According to Java in a Nutshell, 5th ed: boolean, byte, char, short, long float, double, int

209. What is heap in Java?

Answer: JAVA is fully Object oriented language. It has two phases first one is Compilation phase and second one is interpretation phase. The Compilation phase convert the java file to class file (byte code is only readable format of JVM) than Interpretation phase interoperate the class file line by line and give the proper result.

210. In Java, how are objects / values passed around?

Answer: In Java Object are passed by reference and Primitive data is always pass by value

211. Do primitive types have a class representation?

Answer: Primitive data type has a wrapper class to present.

Like for int - Integer , for byte Byte, for long Long etc ...

212. How all can you free memory?

Answer: With the help of finalize() method.

If a programmer really wants to explicitly request a garbage collection at some point, System.gc() or Runtime.gc() can be invoked, which will fire off a garbage collection at that time.

213. Does java do reference counting?

Answer: It is more likely that the JVMs you encounter in the real world will use a tracing algorithm in their garbage-collected heaps.

214. What does a static inner class mean? How is it different from any other static member?

Answer: A static inner class behaves like any ``outer" class. It may contain methods and fields.

It is not necessarily the case that an instance of the outer class exists even when we have created an instance of the inner class. Similarly, instantiating the outer class does not create any instances of the inner class.

The methods of a static inner class may access all the members (fields or methods) of the inner class but they can access only static members (fields or methods) of the outer class. Thus, f can access the field x, but it cannot access the field y.

215. What is the restriction imposed on a static method or a static block of code?

Answer: A static method should not refer to instance variables without creating an instance and cannot use "this" operator to refer the instance.

216. How do you declare constant values in java?

Answer: Using Final keyword we can declare the constant values. How all can you instantiate final member's Final member can be instantiate only at the time of declaration. Null.

217. What is the difference between the '&' operator and the '&&' operator?

Answer: '&&' is a Logical operator while '&' is a Bitwise operator.

e.g.

int x=12; binary represenation of 12---------> 1100

int y=10; 1010 binary represenation of 10---------> 1010

int z=x & y; binary represenation of (x & y)--------> 1000

Here value of z will be 8.

In case of logical operatior '&&':

condition1 && condition2

ifcondition1isfalsethen(condition1&&condition2)willalwaysbe false, that is the reason why this logical operator is also known as short circuit operator. if condition1 is true then condition2 is to be evaluated, if it is true then overall result will be true else it will be false.

218. Why main method of Java has public static void?

Answer: It is the main entry point of a java file. Every java file has just single copy of main method from where main thread is invoked and that's why main method is static. This method can be overloaded but JVM will distinguish public static void main from rest of the overloaded main methods.

219. What are the command line arguments?

Answer: Whenever a java file is executed it is done by java command given as below:

```
java Usage: java [-options] class [args...]
```

(to execute a class)

```
or java -jar [-options] jarfile [args...]
```

(to execute a jar file)

when some arguments are also passed with execution command then these arguments are called command line arguments as they are taken as an array of String as a parameter in main method.

220. Does Java support multi dimensional arrays?

Answer: The Java programming language does not really support multi-dimensional arrays. It does, however, support arrays of arrays. In Java, a two-dimensional array 'arr' is really an array of one-dimensional arrays:

```
int[][] arr = new int[4][6];
```

The expression arr[i] selects the one-dimensional array; the expression arr[i][j] selects the element from that array.

The built-in multi-dimensional arrays suffer the same indignities that simple one-dimensional arrays do: Array indices in each dimension range from zero to, where length is the array length in the given dimension. There is no array assignment operator. The number of dimensions and the size of each dimension is fixed once the array has been allocated.

221. What are the restrictions for static method?

Answer: Whenever you say something is static that means data or method is not associated with an object instance of that class. They are allocated when a class is loaded, during compile time. Only a single copy of that will be created for that class. So even if you have never created an object of a class you can always access static data and method of that class. If you have class by name 'Vehicle' and you have a static method 'drive()' then it can simply be invoked by ' Vehicle.drive()', no need of object creation in this scenario. A static method cannot access non static data and can invoke other static methods. All static methods are automatically final. It is redundant to make them final.

222. Why an abstract method cannot be static?

Answer: An abstract method is usually defined in an abstract class or an interface, for which implementation is provided in a subclass or a class implementing the interface. As static methods just have single copy per class and are interpreted at code compile time, not at runtime, so it is impossible to have polymorphic behavior out of them. In other words, they cannot be overridden.

An abstract class is one which cannot be instantiated but a static method defined in abstract class can be invoked without creating an instance. So there is no mechanism to ensure call of an abstract static method.

Moreover this is a design decision by language designers. :-)

223. Why Java does not support pointers?

Answer: As per the design decision Java does not support pointers explicitly. This greatly reduces the burden of dynamic memory management while coding from programmers. Though programmers dynamically allocate memory while coding but they need not worry about de-allocating this memory. The automatic garbage collection feature of Java collects dangling references of objects though it has a trade off on performance as programmer managed memory management will be efficient as compared to JVM driven automatic garbage collection.

224. Is 'sizeof' a keyword?

Answer: No, 'sizeof' is an operator used in C and C++ to determine the bytes of a data item, but it is not used in Java as all data types are standard sized in all machines as per specifications of the language.

A JVM is free to store data any way it pleases internally, big or little endian, with any amount of padding or overhead, though primitives must behave as if they had the official sizes. In JDK 1.5+ you can use java.lang.instrument. Instrumentation. getObjectSize() to get the object size.

On Java World, I have found an interesting article on Objects' size determination, read.

225. What is the precedence of operators in Java?

Answer: The precedence of operators suggests the sequence in which operators will be work upon in case of compounded statements containing several operators.

For example, in the expression

```
x = a + b * c;
```

the first "+" operator still first determines its left operand ("a" in this case) and then its right operand. But in this case the right operand consists of the expression "b*c". The multiplication operator "*" has a higher precedence than the additive "+".

Precedence can be overridden with parentheses, e.g.

```
x = (a + b) * c;
```

will force the addition of b to a, and then this sum is multiplied by c.

The table shown in image below is organized from higher precedence to low, when you traverse from top to the bottom of the table.

<table>
<tr><th>Operator Types</th><th>Operator</th></tr>
<tr><td>Unary</td><td>++x, --x, +x, -x, ~, !</td></tr>
<tr><td>Arithmetic (and shift)</td><td>*, /, %, +, - << >></td></tr>
<tr><td>Relational</td><td>>, <, >=, <=, ==, !=</td></tr>
<tr><td>Logical (and bitwise)</td><td>&&, ||, &, |, ^</td></tr>
<tr><td>Conditional (ternary)</td><td>A > B ? X : Y</td></tr>
<tr><td>Assignment</td><td>=, *=, /=, %=, +=, -=, <<=, >>=, >>>=, &=, ^=, |=</td></tr>
</table>

226. How is an argument passed in Java methods?

Answer: In Java no matter if the variable is primitive data type or an object when passed as an argument to a method; they are always passed by value.

This is a most common error that most of newcomers to language and even veterans do in understanding this concept.

Please go through to following link on java.sun.com website for a detailed discussion and understanding of this concept.

227. What is the difference between class variable, member variable and automatic (local) variable?

Answer: The *class variable* is a static variable and it does not belong to any instance of class but shared across all the instances.

The *member variable* belongs to a particular instance of class and can be called from any method of the class.

The automatic or local variable is created on a method entry and valid within method scope and they have to be initialized explicitly.

228. When are static and non static variables of a class initialized?

Answer: The static variables are initialized at class load time during compilation and non static variables are initialized just before the constructor is called.

229. Can shift operators be applied to float types?

Answer: No, shift operators are applicable only on integer or long types.

230. What are different Java declarations and their associated rules?

Answer: All variables in Java are introduced/declared with some basic data types with some basic values, e.g. every decimal value by default is a double. The names of variables must avoid reserved Java keywords. The local variables are explicitly initialized.

231. What are Java Modifiers?

Answer: Java classes, interfaces, and their members can be declared with one or more *modifiers*. They can be categorized as:

Class Modifiers

ClassModifier: one of public private (for inner classes) protected (for inner classes) abstract static final strictfp

Any top level class can either be public or package private (no explicit modifier)

Field Modifiers

FieldModifier: one of public protected private static final transient volatile

Method Modifiers

MethodModifier: one of public protected private abstract static final synchronized native strictfp

Constructor Modifiers

ConstructorModifier: one of public protected private

The following matrix of the all modifiers in Java shows which modifier maps to which element:-

Modifiers-Elements Matrix in Java

element / modifier	Data field	Method	Constructor	Class: top level (outer)	Class: nested (inner)	Interface: top level (outer)	Interface: nested (inner)
abstract	no	yes	no	yes	yes	yes	yes
final	yes	yes	no	yes	yes	no	no
native	no	yes	no	no	no	no	no
private	yes	yes	yes	no	yes	no	yes
protected	yes	yes	yes	no	yes	no	yes
public	yes	yes	yes	yes	yes	yes	yes
static	yes	yes	no	no	yes	no	yes
synchronized	no	yes	no	no	no	no	no
transient	yes	no	no	no	no	no	no
volatile	yes	no	no	no	no	no	no
strictfp	no	yes	no	yes	yes	yes	yes

232. Explain final modifier.

Answer: 'final' modifier can be applied to classes, methods and variables and the features cannot be changed. final class cannot be subclassed, methods cannot be overridden.

233. Can you change the reference of the final object?

Answer: No the reference cannot be changed, but the data in that object can be changed.

234. Can abstract class be instantiated?

Answer: No, an abstract class cannot be instantiated i.e. you cannot create a new object of this class. When does the compiler insist that the class must be abstract?

In following conditions, compiler insists 'abstract' keyword with a class:

- If one or more methods of the class are abstract.
- If class inherits one or more abstract methods from the parent abstract class and no implementation is provided for that method
- If class implements an interface and provides no implementation for those methods

235. Where can static modifiers be used?

Answer: They can be applied to variables, methods and even a block of code, static methods and variables are not associated with any instance of class. They are loaded at the class compile time.

236. Why is not recommended to have instance variables in Interface

Answer: By Default, All data members and methods in an Interface are public. Having public variables in a class that will be implementing it will be violation of the Encapsulation principal.

237. Can there be an abstract class with no abstract methods in it?

Answer: Yes

238. Can an Interface be final?

Answer: No

239. Can an Interface have an inner class?

Answer: Yes.

```
public interface abc {
static int i=0;
void dd();
class a1 {
a1() {
int j;
System.out.println("in interfia");
};
      public static void main(String a1[]) {
System.out.println("in interfia");
}
```

```
    }
}
```

240. What is Nested Interface?

Answer: An interface which is declared within another interface or class is known as nested interface. The nested interfaces are used to group related interfaces so that they can be easy to maintain. The nested interface must be referred by the outer interface or class. It can't be accessed directly.

Points to remember for nested interfaces

There are given some points that should be remembered by the java programmer.

- Nested interface must be public if it is declared inside the interface but it can have any access modifier if declared within the class.
- Nested interfaces are declared static implicitly.

Syntax of nested interface which is declared within the interface

```
interface interface_name{
 ...
        interface nested_interface_name{
                ...
        }
}

Syntax of nested interface which is declared within the class
class class_name{
        ...
        interface nested_interface_name{
                ...
        }
}
```

Example of nested interface which is declared within the interface

In this example, we are going to learn how to declare the nested interface and how we can access it.

```
interface Showable{
        void show();
        interface Message{
                void msg();
        }
}
```

```
class Test implements Showable.Message{
        public void msg(){System.out.println("Hello nested interface");}
        public static void main(String args[]){
                Showable.Message message=new Test();//upcasting here
                message.msg();
        }
}
```

Output: hello nested interface

As you can see in the above example, we are accessing the Message interface by its outer interface Showable because it cannot be accessed directly. It is just like almirah inside the room, we cannot access the almirah directly because we must enter the room first. In collection frameword, sun microsystem has provided a nested interface Entry. Entry is the sub interface of Map i.e. accessed by Map.Entry.

Internal code generated by the java compiler for nested interface Message

The java compiler internally creates public and static interface as displayed below:.

```
public static interface Showable$Message
{
        public abstract void msg();
}
```

Example of nested interface which is declared within the class

Let's see how can we define an interface inside the class and how can we access it.

```
class A{
        interface Message{
                void msg();
        }
}
 class Test implements A.Message{
        public void msg(){System.out.println("Hello nested interface");}
        public static void main(String args[]){
                A.Message message=new Test();//upcasting here
                message.msg();
        }
}
```

Output: hello nested interface

241. Can we define private and protected modifiers for variables in interfaces?

Answer: No

242. What are some alternatives to inheritance?

Answer: Delegation is an alternative to inheritance. Delegation means that you include an instance of another class as an instance variable, and forward messages to the instance. It is often safer than inheritance because it forces you to think about each message you forward, because the instance is of a known class, rather than a new class, and because it doesn't force you to accept all the methods of the super class: you can provide only the methods that really make sense. On the other hand, it makes you write more code, and it is harder to re-use (because it is not a subclass).

243. Why isn't there operator overloading?

Answer: Because C++ has proven by example that operator overloading makes code almost impossible to maintain. In fact there very nearly wasn't even method overloading in Java, but it was thought that this was too useful for some very basic methods like print(). Note that some of the classes like DataOutputStream have unoverloaded methods like writeInt() and writeByte().

244. Question: What does it mean that a method or field is "static"?

Answer: Static variables and methods are instantiated only once per class. In other words they are class variables, not instance variables. If you change the value of a static variable in a particular object, the value of that variable changes for all instances of that class.

Static methods can be referenced with the name of the class rather than the name of a particular object of the class (though that works too). That's how library methods like System.out.println() work. out is a static field in the java.lang.System class.

245. What is static initializer code?

Answer: A class can have a block of initializer code that is simply surrounded by curly braces and labeled as

```
static e.g.
public class Demo{
static int =10;
static{
System.out.println("Hello world');
}

}
```

And this code is executed exactly once at the time of class load.

246. Can an anonymous class implement an interface and extend a class at the same time?

Answer: No, an anonymous class can either implement an interface or extend a class at a particular time but not both at the same time.

247. What are the differences between JIT and HotSpot?

Answer: The Hotspot VM is a collection of techniques, the most significant of which is called "adaptive optimization.

The original JVMs interpreted byte codes one at a time. Second-generation JVMs added a JIT compiler, which compiles each method to native code upon first execution, then executes the native code. Thereafter, whenever the method is called, the native code is executed. The adaptive optimization technique used by Hotspot is a hybrid approach, one that combines byte code interpretation and run-time compilation to native code.

Hotspot, unlike a regular JIT compiling VM, doesn't do "premature optimization".

248. How Java enabled High Performance?

Answer: Java uses Just-In-Time compiler to enable high performance. Just-In-Time compiler is a program that turns Java bytecode, which is a program that contains instructions that must be interpreted into instructions that can be sent directly to the processor.

249. What is a memory footprint? How can you specify the lower and upper limits of the RAM used by the JVM? What happens when the JVM needs more memory?

Answer: When JVM needs more memory then it does the garbage collection, and sweeps all the memory which is not being used.

250. What is the difference amongst JVM Spec, JVM Implementation, and JVM Runtime?

Answer: The JVM spec is the blueprint for the JVM generated and owned by Sun. The JVM implementation is the actual implementation of the spec by a vendor and the JVM runtime is the actual running instance of a JVM implementation.

251. What is JIT compiler?

Answer: **Just-In-Time (JIT) compiler:** It is used to improve the performance. JIT compiles parts of the byte code that have similar functionality at the same time, and hence reduces the amount of time needed for compilation. Here the term "compiler" refers to a translator from the instruction set of a Java virtual machine (JVM) to the instruction set of a specific CPU.

252. What is Java Virtual Machine and how it is considered in context of Java's platform independent feature?

Answer: When Java is compiled, it is not compiled into platform specific machine, rather into platform independent byte code. This byte code is distributed over the web and interpreted by virtual Machine (JVM) on whichever platform it is being run.

253. What is the main difference between Java platform and other platforms?

Answer: The Java platform differs from most other platforms in the sense that it's a software-based platform that runs on top of other hardware-based platforms. It has two components:

1. Runtime Environment
2. API(Application Programming Interface)

254. What gives Java its 'write once and run anywhere' nature?

Answer: Java is compiled to be a byte code which is the intermediate language between source code and machine code. This byte code is not platform specific and hence can be fed to any platform. After being fed to the JVM, which is specific to a particular operating system, the code platform specific machine code is generated thus making java platform independent.

255. Describe what happens when an object is created in Java?

Answer: Several things happen in a particular order to ensure the object is constructed properly:

1. Memory is allocated from heap to hold all instance variables and implementation-specific data of the object and its superclasses. Implemenation-specific data includes pointers to class and method data.
2. The instance variables of the objects are initialized to their default values.
3. The constructor for the most derived class is invoked. The first thing a constructor does is call the constructor for its superclasses. This process continues until the constructor for java.lang.Object is called, as java.lang.Object is the base class for all objects in java.
4. Before the body of the constructor is executed, all instance variable initializers and initialization blocks are executed. Then the body of the constructor is executed. Thus, the constructor for the base class completes first and constructor for the most derived class completes last.

256. Can we declare multiple main() methods in multiple classes. ie can we have each main method in its class in our program?

Answer: YES

257. Can you run the product development on all operating systems?

Answer: The product which was developed in java can run on all platforms if there exists a Platform specific JVM.

258. What is polymorphism?

Answer: Polymorphism is the feature of OOPs. One interfaces multiple implementations. Designing a generic interface for a group of related activities. This helps reduce Complexity by allowing the same interface to be used to specify a general class of action. Polymorphism is achieved in a class by method overloading. Run time Polymorphism is achieved in a class hierarchy by method overriding.

259. Suppose if we have variable ' I ' in run method, if I can?

Answer: Create one or more thread each thread will occupy a separate copy or same variable will be shared?

Threads will share the data and code. So if 'I' is instance variable then it will be shared by all threads. If 'I' is a static variable then it will have a same copy it.

260. What are native methods? How do you use them?

Answer: Native methods are methods written in other languages like C, C++, or even assembly language. You can call native methods from Java using JNI. Native methods are used when the implementation of a particular method is present in language other than Java say C, C++. To use the native methods in java we use the keyword native public native method_a().

This native keyword is signal to the java compiler that the implementation of this method is in a language other than java. Native methods are used when we realize that it would take up a lot of rework to write that piece of already existing code in other language to Java.

261. What are the four corner stone's of OOP?

Answer: Abstraction, Encapsulation, Polymorphism and Inheritance.

262. What do you understand by private, protected and public?

Answer: These are accessibility modifiers. Private is the most restrictive, while public is the least restrictive. There is no real difference between protected and the default type (also known as package protected) within the context of the same package; however the protected keyword allows visibility to a derived class in a different package.

263. Difference between a Class and an Object?

Answer: A class is a definition or prototype whereas an object is an instance or living representation of the prototype.

264. What is Down casting?

Answer: Down casting is the casting from a general to a more specific type, i.e. casting down the hierarchy.

265. Can a top level class be private or protected?

Answer: No, a top level class cannot be private or protected. It can have either "public" or no modifier.

266. What is the difference between method overriding and overloading?

Answer: Overriding is a method with the same name and arguments as in a parent, whereas overloading is the same method name but different arguments.

267. What is the restriction on an Overridden methods' accessibility?

Answer: Overriding methods cannot reduce accessibility - they can either have same or greater accessibility.

268. Can a method be overloaded based on different return type but same argument type?

Answer: No, because the methods can be called without using their return type in which case there is ambiquity for the compiler.

269. What is a "stateless" protocol?

Answer: Without getting into lengthy debates, it is generally accepted that protocols like HTTP are stateless i.e. there is no retention of state between a transaction which is a single request response combination.

270. What happens to a static var that is defined within a method of a class?

Answer: Can't do it. You'll get a compilation error.

271. What is constructor chaining and how is it achieved in Java?

Answer: A child object constructor always first needs to construct its parent (which in turn calls its parent constructor.). In Java it is done via an implicit call to the no-args constructor as the first statement.

272. How many static init can you have?

Answer: As many as you want, but the static initializers and class variable initializers are executed in textual order and may not refer to class variables declared in the class whose declarations appear textually after the use, even though these class variables are in scope.

273. What is passed by ref and what by value?

Answer: All Java method arguments are passed by value. However, Java does manipulate objects by reference, and all object variables themselves are references.

274. How do you ensure size of a primitive data type?

Answer: You can't.

275. Where and how can you use a private constructor?

Answer: Private constructor is used if you do not want other classes to instantiate the object and to prevent subclassing.

276. What is Dynamic Binding (late binding)?

Answer: Binding refers to the linking of a procedure call to the code to be executed in response to the call. Dynamic binding means that the code associated with a given procedure call is not known until the time of the call at run-time.

277. What is the difference amongst JVM Spec, JVM Implementation, JVM Runtime?

Answer: The JVM spec is the blueprint for the JVM generated and owned by Sun. The JVM implementation is the actual implementation of the spec by a vendor and the JVM runtime is the actual running instance of a JVM implementation.

278. Give a few reasons for using Java?

Answer: Java is a fun language. Let's look at some of the reasons:

- Built-in support for multi-threading, socket communication and memory management (automatic garbage collection).
- Object Oriented (OO).
- Better portability than other languages across operating systems.
- Supports Web based applications (applet, Servlet, JSP), distributed applications (sockets, RMI, EJB etc) and network protocols (HTTP, JRMP etc) with the help of extensive standardized APIs (Application Programming Interfaces).

279. What are the advantages of Object Oriented Languages (OOPL)?

Answer: The Object Oriented Languages directly represents the real life objects like car, Jeep, Account, Customer etc. The features of the OO programming languages like **polymorphism**, **inheritance** and **encapsulation** makes it powerful.

280. Which would be faster - an application developed in Java or an application developed in C++?

Answer: An application developed in C++ would be about 30 times faster than Java.

281. How is Java different from C++?

Answer: Java is a platform independent, object oriented language while C++ is having some of its features from C, which is a procedural language so it is not pure object oriented. Even Java is not 100% pure object oriented.

1. Pointers are supported in C++ while not in Java. The memory management is done automatically with help of part of JVM called Garbage Colector.
2. Multiple inheritances is not supported in Java but supported in C++.
3. There are no structures and unions in Java.
4. There is no scope resolution operator in Java (::).
5. There are no destructors in Java like C++.
6. There is no virtual keyword in Java because all non-static method uses dynamic binding.

282. How can an animation using images be created with the help of Java?

Answer: An animation can be created by loading all the images in a browser and displaying them one by one in the paint function.

283. What is the difference between Java and HTML?

Answer: Java is a full-fledged object oriented programming language. It is derived from C++ and shares the same basic syntax with that language. HTML (HyperText Markup Language) is not a programming language. It is simply used as a scripting tool to develop web pages. It is not an editor - it is a simple scripting language that defines how the text and images will appear on the web page. Java is used to create small applications (called applets) that run in the browser. It can also be used to develop full-fledged applications.

284. What software is needed to learn Java?

Answer: A Java compiler/development environment such as VJ++ is needed to learn Java.

285. What are the different int data types provided by Java?

Answer: The different data types supported by Java are-- int, short, long and byte. The byte wise representations are as follows:

- byte-8 byte
- short-16 byte
- int-32 byte
- long-64 byte.

286. Does Java support virtual functions?

Answer: No, Java does not support virtual functions directly as supported by C++. Virtual functions can be implemented in Java using abstract classes and interfaces. Abstract class is a class with declaration of methods, but without their implementation. The implementation of the methods takes place in the subclasses. Another example of virtual functions is interfaces. The only difference between an abstract class and an interface is that abstract classes can be used only when they are superclasses and the subclass implements their methods. Whereas in an interface the methods can be implemented even by classes, which are not inherited.

287. How JAVA achieves platform independence?

Answer: Java is platform independent because of the consistent data sizes at all the platforms on which Java code is run. The output of a Java compiler is not an executable code it is bytecode. bytecode is highly optimized set of instructions designed to be executed by a virtual machine that the Java run-time system emulates. As Java programs are interpreted, rather than compiled it is much easier to run them in a variety of run-time environments.

288. What is a Java Virtual Machine (JVM)?

Answer: A Java Virtual Machine is a runtime environment required for execution of a Java application. Every Java application runs inside a runtime instance of some concrete implementation of abstract specifications of JVM. It is JVM which is crux of 'platform independent' nature of the language.

289. What is a JVM consisted of?

Answer: Each time a Java Application is executed then an instance of JVM, responsible for its running, is created. A JVM instance is described in terms of subsystems, memory areas, data types, and instructions.

290. What is a class loader and what are its responsibilities?

Answer: The Class loader is a subsystem of a JVM which is responble, predominantly for loading classes and interfaces in the system. Apart from this, a class loader is responsible for the following activities:

- Verification of imported types (classes and interfaces)
- Allocating memory for class variables and initializing them to default values. Static fields for a class are created and these are set to standard default values but they are not explicitly initialized. The method tables are constructed for the class.

291. What is heap and stack?

Answer: The heap is the part of memory of JVM where all objects reside.

The stack is consisted of stack frames. When a thread invokes a method, the JVM pushes a new frame onto that thread's Java stack. Each stack frame is consisted of operand stack and the local variable array. All arguments, local variables, intermediate computations and return values if any are kept in this stack corresponding to the method invoked. The stack frame on the top of the stack is called the active stack frame, which is the current place of execution. When the method completes, the virtual machine pops and discards the frame for that method.

292. How is your Java program executed inside JVM?

Answer: When JVM executes a Java application, a runtime instance of JVM is born. This runtime instance invoke main() method of Java application. The main() method of an application serves as the starting point for that application's initial thread. The initial thread can in turn fire off other threads.This thread has a program counter (PC) and Java stack. Whenever main() method is invoked, a stack frame is pushed onto the stack, this then becomes the active tack frame. The program counter in the new Java stack frame will point to the beginning of the method.

If there are more method invocations within main() method then this process of pushing new stack frame onto the stack for each method call is repeated as and when they are invoked. When a method returns, the active frame is popped from the stack and the one below becomes the active stack frame. The PC is set to the instruction after the method call and the method continues.

There is only one heap corresponding to an instance of JVM and all objects created are stored here. This heap is shared by all threads created in an application.

Inside the Java virtual machine, threads come in two flavors: daemon and non-daemon. A daemon thread is ordinarily a thread used by the virtual machine itself, such as a thread that performs garbage collection. The application, however, can mark any threads it creates as daemon threads. The initial thread of an application--the one that begins at main()--is a non- daemon thread.

A Java application continues to execute (the virtual machine instance continues to live) as long as any non-daemon threads are still running. When all non-daemon threads of a Java application terminate, the virtual machine instance will exit. If permitted by the security manager, the application can also cause its own demise by invoking the exit() method of class Runtime or System.

When main() returns, it terminates the application's only non-daemon thread, which causes the virtual machine instance to exit.

293. What is Java class file's magic number?

Answer: A Magic Number of a class file is a unique identifier for tools to quickly differentiate class files from non class files. The first four bytes of each Java class file has the magic value as 0xCAFEBABE.And the answer to why this number, I do not actually know but there may be very few sensible and acceptable options possible constructed from letters A-F which can surely not be 'CAFEFACE' or 'FADECAFE'....

294. How JVM performs Thread Synchronization?

Answer: JVM associates a lock with an object or a class to achieve multithreading. A lock is like a token or privilege that only one thread can "possess" at any one time. When a thread wants to lock a particular object or class, it asks the JVM.

JVM responds to thread with a lock maybe very soon, maybe later, or never. When the thread no longer needs the lock, it returns it to the JVM. If another thread has requested the same lock, the JVM passes the lock to that thread. If a thread has a lock, no other thread can access the locked data until the thread that owns the lock releases it.

295. How JVM performs Garbage Collection?

Answer: One of the most frequently asked questions during interviews and it seeks a precise and clear understanding of the concept. Whenever a reference to an object on heap lies dangling or no longer in use by an active program then it becomes eligible for being garbage collected by JVM.JVM specifications do not force any specific kind of garbage collection algorithm though there are several algorithms like reference.

296. How to profile heap usage?

Answer: Try using -Xaprof to get a profile of the allocations (objects and sizes) of your application.

Also try -agentlib:hprof=heap=all (or other option, try -agentlib:hprof=help for a list)

What will you do if VM exits while printing "OutOfMemoryError" and increasing max heap size doesn't help?

The Java HotSpot VM cannot expand its heap size if memory is completely allocated and no swap space is available. This can occur, for example, when several applications are running simultaneously. When this happens, the VM will exit after printing a message similar to the following.

Exception java. lang. Out Of Memory Error: requested bytes

If you see this symptom, consider increasing the available swap space by allocating more of your disk for virtual memory and/or by limiting the number of applications you run simultaneously. You may also be able to avoid this problem by setting the command-line flags -Xmx and -Xms to the same value to prevent the VM from trying to expand the heap. Note that simply increasing the value of -Xmx will not help when no swap space is available.

297. What is Java virtual machine?

Answer: It is the component of the Java technology responsible for Java's cross-platform delivery, the small size of its compiled code, and Java's ability to protect users from malicious programs. The Java Virtual Machine is an abstract computing machine. Like a real computing machine, it has an instruction set and uses various memory areas. It is reasonably common to implement a programming language using a virtual machine.

The Java Virtual machine does not assume any particular implementation technology or host platform. It is not inherently interpreted, and it may just as well be implemented by compiling its instruction set to that of a real CPU, as for a conventional programming language. It may also be implemented in microcode, or directly in silicon.

The Java Virtual Machine knows nothing of the Java programming language, only of a particular file format, the class file format. A class file contains Java Virtual Machine instructions (or bytecodes) and a symbol table, as well as other ancillary information.

For the sake of security, the Java Virtual Machine imposes strong format and structural constraints on the code in a class file. However, any language with functionality that can be expressed in terms of a valid class file can be hosted by the Java Virtual Machine.

298. What is class loader?

***Answer:* The basics of Java class loaders:**

Class loaders are one of the cornerstones of the Java virtual machine (JVM) architecture. They enable the JVM to load classes without knowing anything about the underlying file system semantics, and they allow applications to dynamically load Java classes as extension modules.

Describes the behavior of converting a named class into the bits responsible for implementing that class.

299. What is Byte code verification?

Answer: The Byte Code Verification Process

What about the concept of a "hostile compiler"? Although the Java compiler ensures that Java source code doesn't violate the safety rules, when an application such as the HotJava Browser imports a code fragment from anywhere, it doesn't actually know if code fragments follow Java language rules for safety: the code may not have been produced by a known-to-be trustworthy Java compiler. In such a case, how is the Java run-time system on your machine to trust the incoming byte code stream? The answer is simple: the Java run-time system doesn't trust the incoming code, but subjects it to *byte code verification.*

The tests range from simple verification that the format of a code fragment is correct, to passing each code fragment through a simple theorem prover to establish that it plays by the rules:

- it doesn't forge pointers,
- it doesn't violate access restrictions,
- it accesses objects as what they are (for example, InputStream objects are always used as InputStreams and never as anything else).

A language that is safe, plus run-time verification of generated code, establishes a base set of guarantees that interfaces cannot be violated.

The Byte Code Verifier:

The *byte code verifier* traverses the byte codes, constructs the type state information, and verifies the types of the parameters to all the byte code instructions.

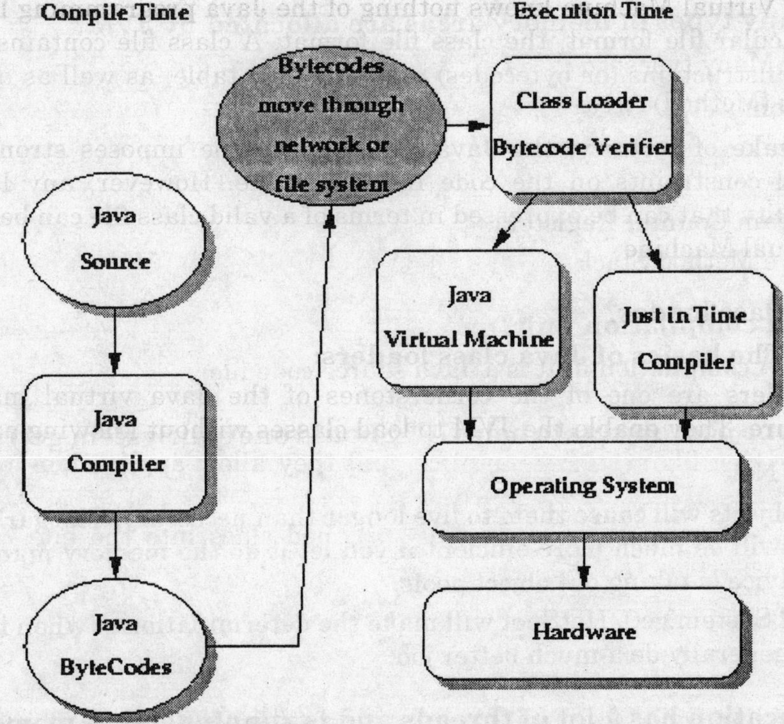

The illustration shows the flow of data and control from Java language source code through the Java compiler, to the class loader and bytecode verifier and hence on to the Java virtual machine, which contains the interpreter and runtime system. The important issue is that the Java class loader and the bytecode verifier make no assumptions about the primary source of the bytecode stream--the code may have come from the local system, or it may have travelled halfway around the planet. The bytecode verifier acts as a sort of gatekeeper: it ensures that code passed to the Java interpreter is in a fit state to be executed and can run without fear of breaking the Java interpreter. Imported code is not allowed to execute by any means until after it has passed the verifier's tests. Once the verifier is done, a number of important properties are known:

- There are no operand stack overflows or underflows
- The types of the parameters of all bytecode instructions are known to always be correct
- Object field accesses are known to be legal--private, public, or protected

While all this checking appears excruciatingly detailed, by the time the bytecode verifier has done its work, the Java interpreter can proceed, knowing that the code will run securely. Knowing these properties makes the Java interpreter much faster, because it doesn't have to check anything. There are no operand type checks and no stack overflow checks. The interpreter can thus function at full speed without compromising reliability.

300. How many types of memory areas are allocated by JVM?

Answer: Many types:

- Class (Method) Area
- Heap
- Stack
- Program Counter Register
- Native Method Stack

301. What is a compilation unit?

Answer: A compilation unit is a Java source code file.

302. Should one pool objects to help GC? Should one call System.gc() periodically?

Answer: No!

Pooling objects will cause them to live longer than necessary. The garbage collection methods will be much more efficient if you let it do the memory management. The strong advice is taking out object pools.

Don't call System.gc(), HotSpot will make the determination of when its appropriate and will generally do a much better job.

303. An application has a lot of threads and is running out of memory, why?

Answer: You may be running into a problem with the default stack size for threads. In Java SE 6, the default on Sparc is 512k in the 32-bit VM, and 1024k in the 64-bit VM. On x86 Solaris/Linux it is 320k in the 32-bit VM and 1024k in the 64-bit VM.

On Windows, the default thread stack size is read from the binary (java.exe). As of Java SE 6, this value is 320k in the 32-bit VM and 1024k in the 64-bit VM.

You can reduce your stack size by running with the -Xss option. For example:
java -server -Xss64k

Note that on some versions of Windows, the OS may round up thread stack sizes using very coarse granularity. If the requested size is less than the default size by 1K or more, the stack size is rounded up to the default; otherwise, the stack size is rounded up to a multiple of 1 MB.

64k is the least amount of stack space allowed per thread.

304. If your program is I/O bound or running in native methods, do these activities engage JVM?

Answer: The answer is 'No'. If the program is I/O bound or running in native methods, then the VM is not involved in the consumption of CPU time. The VM technology will engage CPU for running byte codes. Typical examples of time spent not running byte code are graphical operations that make heavy use of native methods, and I/O operations such as reading and writing data to network sockets or database files.

305. What is the difference between interpreted code and compiled code?

Answer: An interpreter produces a result from a program, while a compiler produces a program written in assembly language and in case of Java from byte codes. The scripting languages like JavaScript,Python etc. require Interpreter to execute them. So a program written in scripting language will directly be executed with interpreter installed on that computer, if it is absent then this program will not execute. While in case of compiled code, an assembler or a virtual machine in case of Java is required to convert assembly level code or byte codes into machine level instructions/commands. Generally, interpreted programs are slower than compiled programs, but are easier to debug and revise.

306. Why Java based GUI intensive program has performance issues?

Answer: GUI intensive Java application mostly runs underlying OS specific native libraries which is time and more CPU cycles consuming.

The overall performance of a Java application depends on four factors:

- The design of the application
- The speed at which the virtual machine executes the Java bytecodes
- The speed at which the libraries that perform basic functional tasks execute (in native code)
- The speed of the underlying hardware and operating system

The virtual machine is responsible for byte code execution, storage allocation, thread synchronization, etc. Running with the virtual machine are native code libraries that handle input and output through the operating system, especially graphics operations through the window system. Programs that spend significant portions of their time in those native code libraries will not see their performance on HotSpot improved as much as programs that spend most of their time executing byte codes.

307. What is 64 bit Java?

Answer: A 64-bit version of Java has been available to Solaris SPARC users since the 1.4.0 release of J2SE. A 64-bit capable J2SE is an implementation of the Java SDK (and the JRE along with it) that runs in the 64-bit environment of a 64-bit OS on a 64-bit processor. The primary advantage of running Java in a 64-bit environment is the larger address space.

This allows for a much larger Java heap size and an increased maximum number of Java Threads, which is needed for certain kinds of large or long-running applications. The primary complication in doing such a port is that the sizes of some native data types are changed. Not surprisingly the size of pointers is increased to 64 bits. On Solaris and most Unix platforms, the size of the C language long is also increased to 64 bits. Any native code in the 32-bit SDK implementation that relied on the old sizes of these data types is likely to require updating.

Within the parts of the SDK written in Java things are simpler, since Java specifies the sizes of its primitive data types precisely. However even some Java code needs updating, such as when a Java int is used to store a value passed to it from a part of the implementation written in C.

308. What is the difference between JVM and JRE?

Answer: A Java Runtime Environment (JRE) is a prerequisite for running Java applications on any computer. A JRE contains a Java Virtual Machine (JVM), all standard, core java classes and runtime libraries. It does not contain any development tools such as compiler, debugger, etc. JDK (Java Development Kit) is a whole package required to Java Development which essentially contains JRE+JVM, and tools required to compile and debug, execute Java applications.

309. What is Hot Java?

Answer: Hot Java is a Browser provided by Sun. It is a modular, applet-aware, extensible World Wide Web browser written entirely in Java. The security in Hot Java provides a safe environment for the execution of imported code. The security is based on interlocking layers of security that range from the design of the Java language at the base to the file and network access protections at the top.

310. What are the differences between JRE And JVM AND JDK?

Answer: The "JDK" is the Java Development Kit. I.e., the JDK is bundle of software that you can use to develop Java based software. The "JRE" is the Java Runtime Environment. I.e., the JRE is an implementation of the Java Virtual Machine which actually executes Java programs. Typically, each JDK contains one (or more) JRE's along with the various development tools like the Java source compilers, bundling and deployment tools, debuggers, development libraries, etc.

311. Give a simplest way to find out the time a method takes for execution without using any profiling tool?

Answer: Read the system time just before the method is invoked and immediately after method returns. Take the time difference, which will give you the time taken by a method for execution.

To put it in code...

```
long start = System.currentTimeMillis ();
method ();
long end = System.currentTimeMillis ();
```

System.out.println ("Time taken for execution is" + (end - start));

Remember that if the time taken for execution is too small, it might show that it is taking zero milliseconds for execution. Try it on a method which is big enough, in the sense the one which is doing considerable amount of processing.

312. What is a package?

Answer: A package stores a group of related classes and interfaces. They eliminate the conflicts in class names in different group of classes.

313. When can an object reference be cast to an interface reference?

Answer: An object reference is cast to an interface reference when the object implements the referenced interface.

314. Which class is extended by all other classes?

Answer: The Object class is extended by all other classes.

315. Can an object be garbage collected while it is still reachable?

Answer: A reachable object cannot be garbage collected. Only unreachable objects may be garbage collected.

316. Is the ternary operator written x : y ? z or x ? y : z ?

Answer: It is written x ? y : z.

317. How is rounding performed under integer division?

Answer: The fractional part of the result is truncated. This is known as rounding toward zero.

318. What is the purpose of the System class?

Answer: The purpose of the System class is to provide access to system resources.

319. Is &&= a valid Java operator?

Answer: No, it is not.

320. What modifiers may be used with an interface declaration?

Answer: An interface may be declared as public or abstract.

321. Is a class a subclass of itself?

Answer: A class is a subclass of itself.

322. What modifiers can be used with a local inner class?

Answer: A local inner class may be final or abstract.

323. What is the difference between static and non-static variables?

Answer: A static variable is associated with the class as a whole rather than with specific instances of a class. Non-static variables take on unique values with each object instance.

324. Which Math method is used to calculate the absolute value of a number?

Answer: The abs() method is used to calculate absolute values.

325. When does the compiler supply a default constructor for a class?

Answer: The compiler supplies a default constructor for a class if no other constructors are provided.

326. If a method is declared as protected, where may the method be accessed?

Answer: A protected method may only be accessed by classes or interfaces of the same package or by subclasses of the class in which it is declared.

327. Which non-Unicode letter characters may be used as the first character of an identifier?

Answer: The non-Unicode letter characters $ and _ may appear as the first character of an identifier.

328. What restrictions are placed on method overloading?

Answer: Two methods may not have the same name and argument list but different return types.

329. What is casting?

Answer: There are two types of casting, casting between primitive numeric types and casting between object references. Casting between numeric types is used to convert larger values, such as double values, to smaller values, such as byte values. Casting between object references is used to refer to an object by a compatible class, interface, or array type reference.

330. What is the return type of a program's main() method?

Answer: A program's main() method has a void return type.

331. What if the static modifier is removed from the signature of the main method?

Answer: Program compiles. But at runtime throws an error "NoSuchMethodError".

332. What is the difference between a field variable and a local variable?

Answer: A field variable is a variable that is declared as a member of a class. A local variable is a variable that is declared local to a method.

333. Under what conditions is an object's finalize() method invoked by the garbage collector?

Answer: The garbage collector invokes an object's finalize() method when it detects that the object has become unreachable.

334. How are this () and super () used with constructors?

Answer: this() is used to invoke a constructor of the same class. super() is used to invoke a superclass constructor.

335. What are the legal operands of the instanceof operator?

Answer: The left operand is an object reference or null value and the right operand is a class, interface, or array type.

336. How are this and super used?

Answer: this is used to refer to the current object instance. super is used to refer to the variables and methods of the superclass of the current object instance.

337. What is a compilation unit?

Answer: A compilation unit is a Java source code file.

338. What restrictions are placed on method overriding?

Answer: Overridden methods must have the same name, argument list, and return type. The overriding method may not limit the access of the method it overrides. The overriding method may not throw any exceptions that may not be thrown by the overridden method.

339. Can an abstract class be final?

Answer: An abstract class may not be declared as final.

340. What is numeric promotion?

Answer: Numeric promotion is the conversion of a smaller numeric type to a larger numeric type, so that integer and floating-point operations may take place. In numerical promotion, byte, char, and short values are converted to int values. The int values are also converted to long values, if necessary. The long and float values are converted to double values, as required.

341. What is the difference between a public and a non-public class?

Answer: A public class may be accessed outside of its package. A non-public class may not be accessed outside of its package.

342. What is a pointer? Does Java support pointers?

Answer:

- Pointer means a reference handle to a memory location.
- Java doesn't support the use of pointers as their improper handling causes memory leaks and compromises the reliability.

343. Differentiate between Path and Classpath?

Answer:

- Path and Classpath both are operating system level environment variables.
- Path tells where the system can find the executable (.exe) files while classpath provides the location .class files.

344. Is it necessary to declare main() method compulsorily in all java classes?

Answer:

- No, it is not.
- main() method needs to be defined only if the source class is a java application.

345. What modifiers may be used with a top-level class?

Answer: A top-level class may be public, abstract, or final.

346. What are the Object and Class classes used for?

Answer: The Object class is the highest-level class in the Java class hierarchy. The Class class is used to represent the classes and interfaces that are loaded by a Java program.

347. Can an unreachable object become reachable again?

Answer: An unreachable object may become reachable again. This can happen when the object's finalize() method is invoked and the object performs an operation which causes it to become accessible to reachable objects.

348. Is a class a subclass of itself?

Answer: A class is a subclass of itself.

349. What modifiers can be used with a local inner class?

Answer: A local inner class may be final or abstract.

350. How would you pass a java integer by reference to another function?

Answer: Passing by reference is impossible in JAVA but Java support the object reference so. Object is the only way to pass the integer by reference.

351. What is data encapsulation? What does it buy you?

Answer: The most common example I can think of is a javabean. Encapsulation may be used by creating 'get' and 'set' methods in a class which are used to access the fields of the object. Typically the fields are made private while the get and set methods are public.

Encapsulation can be used to validate the data that is to be stored, to do calculations on data that is stored in a field or fields, or for use in introspection (often the case when using javabeans in Struts, for instance).

352. Can we declare multiple main() methods in multiple classes. I.e. can we have each main method in its class in our program?

Answer: YES

353. Why is multiple inheritances not possible in Java?

Answer: It depends on how you understand "inheritance". Java can only "extends" one super class, but can "implements" many interfaces; that doesn't mean the multiple inheritance is not possible. You may use interfaces to make inheritance work for you. Or you may need to work around. For example, if you cannot get a feature from a class because your class has a super class already, you may get that class's feature by declaring it as a member field or getting an instance of that class. So the answer is that multiple inheritance in Java is possible.

354. Can Java code be compiled to machine dependent executable file?

Answer: Yes. There are many tools out there. If you did so, the generated exe file would be run in the specific platform, not cross-platform.

355. What are the drawbacks of inheritance? (donated by RS in Mar. 2005)

Answer: Since inheritance inherits everything from the super class and interface, it may make the subclass too clustering and sometimes error-prone when dynamic overriding or dynamic overloading in some situation. In addition, the inheritance may make peers hardly understand your code if they don't know how your super-class acts.

Usually, when you want to use a functionality of a class, you may use subclass to inherit such function or use an instance of this class in your class. Which is better, depends on your specification.

356. Is there any other way that you can achieve inheritance in Java

Answer: There are a couple of ways. As you know, the straight way is to "extends" and/or "implements". The other way is to get an instance of the class to achieve the inheritance. That means to make the supposed-super-class be a field member. When you use an instance of the class, actually you get every function available from this class, but you may lose the dynamic features of OOP.

357. Can a private method of a superclass be declared within a subclass?

Answer: Sure. A private field or method or inner class belongs to its declared class and hides from its subclasses. There is no way for private stuff to have a runtime overloading or overriding (polymorphism) features.

358. What is a platform?

Answer: A platform is the hardware or software environment in which a program runs. Most platforms can be described as a combination of the operating system and hardware, like Windows 2000/XP, Linux, Solaris, and MacOS.

359. What is the main difference between Java platform and other platforms?

Answer: The Java platform differs from most other platforms in that it's a software-only platform that runs on top of other hardware-based platforms.

The Java platform has two components:

a) The Java Virtual Machine (Java VM)

b) The Java Application Programming Interface (Java API)

360. What is the Java Virtual Machine?

Answer: The Java Virtual Machine is software that can be ported onto various hardware-based platforms.

361. What is the Java API?

Answer: The Java API is a large collection of ready-made software components that provide many useful capabilities, such as graphical user interface (GUI) widgets.

362. What is native code?

Answer: The native code is code that after you compile it, the compiled code runs on a specific hardware platform.

363. Is Java code slower than native code?

Answer: Not really. As a platform-independent environment, the Java platform can be a bit slower than native code. However, smart compilers, well-tuned interpreters, and just-in-time bytecode compilers can bring performance close to that of native code without threatening portability.

364. Can main() method be overloaded?

Answer: Yes. the main() method is a special method for a program entry. You can overload main() method in any ways. But if you change the signature of the main method, the entry point for the program will be gone. For example:

```
//the following are legal methods for entry point
public static void main(String[] args) {} // standard
static public void main(String[] args) {} // unconventional
private static void main(String[] args) {} // unconventional
//the following are legal overloaded methods
public static int main(String arg) {}
public void main(String str1, string str2) {}
public String main(String arg, int i) {}
```

For a good practice, don't overload main method or use a similar main method in a class which is not served as an entry point for your program.

365. How does Java handle integer overflows and underflows?

Answer: It uses those low order bytes of the result that can fit into the size of the type allowed by the operation.

366. What modifiers may be used with an inner class that is a member of an outer class?

Answer: A (non-local) inner class may be declared as public, protected, private, static, final, or abstract.

367. If a method is declared as protected, where may the method be accessed?

Answer: A protected method may only be accessed by classes or interfaces of the same package or by subclasses of the class in which it is declared.

368. What are wrapped classes?

Answer: Wrapped classes are classes that allow primitive types to be accessed as objects.

369. If I don't provide any arguments on the command line, then the String array of Main method will be empty or null?

Answer: It is empty. But not null.

370. What is the difference between the Boolean & operator and the && operator?

Answer: If an expression involving the Boolean & operator is evaluated, both operands are evaluated. Then the & operator is applied to the operand. When an expression involving the && operator is evaluated, the first operand is evaluated. If the first operand returns a value of true then the second operand is evaluated. The && operator is then applied to the first and second operands. If the first operand evaluates to false, the evaluation of the second operand is skipped. Operator & has no chance to skip both sides evaluation and && operator does. If asked why, give details as above.

371. What is the purpose of the Runtime class?

Answer: The purpose of the Runtime class is to provide access to the Java runtime system.

372. What is the purpose of the System class?

Answer: The purpose of the System class is to provide access to system resources.

373. What must a class do to implement an interface?

Answer: It must provide all of the methods in the interface and identify the interface in its implements clause.

374. What is a static method?

Answer: A static method is a method that belongs to the class rather than any object of the class and doesn't apply to an object or even require that any objects of the class have been instantiated.

375. What is a protected method?

Answer: A protected method is a method that can be accessed by any method in its package and inherited by any subclass of its class.

376. What is the difference between a static and a non-static inner class?

Answer: A non-static inner class may have object instances that are associated with instances of the class's outer class. A static inner class does not have any object instances.

377. When can an object reference be cast to an interface reference?

Answer: An object reference be cast to an interface reference when the object implements the referenced interface.

378. What if the main method is declared as private?

Answer: The program compiles properly but at runtime it will give "Main method not public." message.

379. What if the static modifier is removed from the signature of the main method?

Answer: Program compiles. But at runtime throws an error "NoSuchMethodError".

380. What if I write static public void instead of public static void?

Answer: Program compiles and runs properly.

381. What if I do not provide the String array as the argument to the method?

Answer: Program compiles but throws a runtime error "NoSuchMethodError".

382. What is the first argument of the String array in main method?

Answer: The String array is empty. It does not have any element. This is unlike C/ C++ where the first element by default is the program name.

383. If I do not provide any arguments on the command line, then the String array of Main method will be empty or null?

Answer: It is empty. But not null.

384. How can one prove that the array is not null but empty using one line of code?

Answer: Print args.length. It will print 0. That means it is empty. But if it would have been null then it would have thrown a NullPointerException on attempting to print args.length.

385. What environment variables do I need to set on my machine in order to be able to run Java programs?

Answer: CLASSPATH and PATH are the two variables.

386. Can an application have multiple classes having main method?

Answer: Yes it is possible. While starting the application we mention the class name to be run. The JVM will look for the Main method only in the class whose name you have mentioned. Hence there is not conflict amongst the multiple classes having main method.

387. Can I have multiple main methods in the same class?

Answer: No the program fails to compile. The compiler says that the main method is already defined in the class.

388. Do I need to import java.lang package any time? Why?

Answer: No. It is by default loaded internally by the JVM.

389. Can I import same package/class twice? Will the JVM load the package twice at runtime?

Answer: One can import the same package or same class multiple times. Neither compiler nor JVM complains about it. And the JVM will internally load the class only once no matter how many times you import the same class.

390. If a class is declared without any access modifiers, where may the class be accessed?

Answer: A class that is declared without any access modifiers is said to have package or friendly access. This means that the class can only be accessed by other classes and interfaces that are defined within the same package.

391. Does a class inherit the constructors of its superclass?

Answer: A class does not inherit constructors from any of its superclasses.

392. Which class should you use to obtain design information about an object?

Answer: The Class class is used to obtain information about an object's design.

393. What are the problems faced by Java programmers who don't use layout managers?

Answer: Without layout managers, Java programmers are faced with determining how their GUI will be displayed across multiple windowing systems and finding a common sizing and positioning that will work within the constraints imposed by each windowing system.

394. What is the difference between static and non-static variables?

Answer: A static variable is associated with the class as a whole rather than with specific instances of a class. Non-static variables take on unique values with each object instance.

395. What restrictions are placed on method overloading?

Answer: Two methods may not have the same name and argument list but different return types.

396. What restrictions are placed on method overriding?

Answer: Overridden methods must have the same name, argument list, and return type. The overriding method may not limit the access of the method it overrides. The overriding method may not throw any exceptions that may not be thrown by the overridden method.

397. What is casting?

Answer: There are two types of casting, casting between primitive numeric types and casting between object references. Casting between numeric types is used to convert larger values, such as double values, to smaller values, such as byte values. Casting between object references is used to refer to an object by a compatible class, interface, or array type reference.

398. How are this() and super() used with constructors?

Answer: this() is used to invoke a constructor of the same class. super() is used to invoke a superclass constructor.

399. How is it possible for two String objects with identical values not to be equal under the == operator?

Answer: The == operator compares two objects to determine if they are the same object in memory. It is possible for two String objects to have the same value, but located indifferent areas of memory.

400. Does importing a package imports the subpackages as well? e.g. Does importing com.MyTest.* also import com.MyTest.UnitTests.*?

Answer: No you will have to import the subpackages explicitly. Importing com.

MyTest.* will import classes in the package MyTest only. It will not import any class in any of its subpackage.

401. What is the difference between declaring a variable and defining a variable?

Answer: In declaration we just mention the type of the variable and its name. We do not initialize it. But defining means declaration + initialization. e.g String s; is just a declaration while String s = new String ("abcd"); Or String s = "abcd"; are both definitions.

402. What is the default value of an object reference declared as an instance variable?

Answer: null unless we define it explicitly.

403. Can a top level class be private or protected?

Answer: No. A top level class cannot be private or protected. It can have either "public" or no modifier. If it does not have a modifier it is supposed to have a default access. If a top level class is declared as private the compiler will complain that the "modifier private is not allowed here". This means that a top level class cannot be private. Same is the case with protected.

404. What type of parameter passing does Java support?

Answer: In Java the arguments are always passed by value.

405. Primitive data types are passed by reference or pass by value?

Answer: Primitive data types are passed by value.

406. Objects are passed by value or by reference?

Answer: Java only supports pass by value. With objects, the object reference itself is passed by value and so both the original reference and parameter copy both refer to the same object.

407. What is a Java package and how is it used?

Answer: A Java package is a naming context for classes and interfaces. A package is used to create a separate name space for groups of classes and interfaces. Packages are also used to organize related classes and interfaces into a single API unit and to control accessibility to these classes and interfaces.

408. What are the Object and Class classes used for?

Answer: The Object class is the highest-level class in the Java class hierarchy. The Class class is used to represent the classes and interfaces that are loaded by a Java program.

409. How the object oriented approach helps us keep complexity of software development under control?

Answer: We can discuss such issue from the following aspects:

- Objects allow procedures to be encapsulated with their data to reduce potential interference.
- Inheritance allows well-tested procedures to be reused and enables changes to make once and have effect in all relevant places.
- The well-defined separations of interface and implementation allow constraints to be imposed on inheriting classes while still allowing the flexibility of overriding and overloading.

410. What is design by contract?

Answer: The design by contract specifies the obligations of a method to any other methods that may use its services and also theirs to it. For example, the preconditions specify what the method required to be true when the method is called. Hence making sure that preconditions are. Similarly, post conditions specify what must be true when the method is finished, thus the called method has the responsibility of satisfying the post conditions.

In Java, the exception handling facilities support the use of design by contract, especially in the case of checked exceptions. The assert keyword can be used to make such contracts.

411. What is the benefit of subclass?

Answer: Generally:

- The sub class inherits all the public methods and the implementation.
- The sub class inherits all the protected methods and their implementation.
- The sub class inherits all the default(non-access modifier) methods and their implementation.
- The sub class also inherits all the public, protected and default member variables from the super class.
- The constructors are not part of this inheritance model.

412. Where and how can you use a private constructor.

Answer: Private constructor can be used if you do not want any other class to instanstiate it by using new. The instantiation is done from a static public method, which is used when dealing with the factory method pattern.

413. In System.out.println(),what is System,out and println,pls explain?

Answer: System is a predefined final class,out is a PrintStream object acting as a field member and println is a built-in overloaded method in the out object.

414. What is meant by "Abstract Interface"?

Answer: First, an interface is abstract. That means you cannot have any implementation in an interface. All the methods declared in an interface are abstract methods or signatures of the methods.

415. Can you make an instance of an abstract class? For example - java.util. Calender is an abstract class with a method getInstance() which returns an instance of the Calender class.

Answer: No! You cannot make an instance of an abstract class. An abstract class has to be sub-classed. If you have an abstract class and you want to use a method which has been implemented, you may need to subclass that abstract class, instantiate your subclass and then call that method.

416. What is the output of x<y? a:b = p*q when x=1,y=2,p=3,q=4?

Answer: When this kind of question has been asked, find the problems you think is necessary to ask back before you give an answer. Ask if variables a and b have been declared or initialized. If the answer is yes. You can say that the syntax is wrong. If the statement is rewritten as: x<y? a:(b=p*q); the return value would be variable a because the x is 1 and less than y = 2; the x < y statement return true and variable a is returned.

417. Why Java does not support pointers?

Answer: Because pointers are unsafe. Java uses reference types to hide pointers and programmers feel easier to deal with reference types without pointers. This is why Java and C# shine.

418 Why can't I say just abs() or sin() instead of Math.abs() and Math.sin()?

Answer: The import statement does not bring methods into your local name space. It lets you abbreviate class names, but not get rid of them altogether. That's just the way it works, you'll get used to it. It's really a lot safer this way.

However, there is actually a little trick you can use in some cases that gets you what you want. If your top-level class doesn't need to inherit from anything else, make it inherit from java.lang.Math. That *does* bring all the methods into your local name space. But you can't use this trick in an applet, because you have to inherit from java.awt.Applet. And actually, you can't use it on java.lang.Math at all, because Math is a "final" class which means it can't be extended.

418. Why are there no global variables in Java?

Answer: Global variables are considered bad form for a variety of reasons: Adding state variables breaks referential transparency (you no longer can understand a statement or expression on its own: you need to understand it in the context of the settings of the global variables), State variables lessen the cohesion of a program:

you need to know more to understand how something works. A major point of Object-Oriented programming is to break up global state into more easily understood collections of local state, when you add one variable; you limit the use of your program to one instance. What you thought was global, someone else might think of as local: they may want to run two copies of your program at once. For these reasons, Java decided to ban global variables.

419. What does it mean that a class or member is final?

Answer: A final class can no longer be subclassed. Mostly this is done for security reasons with basic classes like String and Integer. It also allows the compiler to make some optimizations, and makes thread safety a little easier to achieve. Methods may be declared final as well. This means they may not be overridden in a subclass. Fields can be declared final, too. However, this has a completely different meaning. A final field cannot be changed after it's initialized, and it must include an initializer statement where it's declared. For example, public final double c = 2.998; It's also possible to make a static field final to get the effect of C++'s const statement or some uses of C's #define, e.g. public static final double c = 2.998;

420. What does it mean that a method or class is abstract?

Answer: An abstract class cannot be instantiated. Only its subclasses can be instantiated. You indicate that a class is abstract with the abstract keyword like this:

```
public abstract class Container extends Component {
Abstract classes may contain abstract methods. A method declared
abstract is not actually implemented in the current class. It exists
only to be overridden in subclasses. It has no body. For example,
public abstract float price();
```

Abstract methods may only be included in abstract classes. However, an abstract class is not required to have any abstract methods, though most of them do. Each subclass of an abstract class must override the abstract methods of its superclasses or itself be declared abstract.

421. Describe what happens when an object is created in Java?

Answer: Several things happen in a particular order to ensure the object is constructed properly: Memory is allocated from heap to hold all instance variables and implementation-specific data of the object and its superclasses. Implementation-specific data includes pointers to class and method data. The instance variables of the objects are initialized to their default values. The constructor for the most derived class is invoked. The first thing a constructor does is call the constructor for its superclasses. This process continues until the constructor for java.lang.Object is called, as java.lang.Object is the base class for all objects in java. Before the body of the constructor is executed, all instance variable initializers and initialization blocks are executed. Then the body of the constructor is executed. Thus, the constructor for the base class completes first and constructor for the most derived class completes last.

422. What is the difference between instanceof and isInstance?

Answer: instanceof is used to check to see if an object can be cast into a specified type without throwing a cast class exception. isInstance() Determines if the specified Object is assignment-compatible with the object represented by this Class. This method is the dynamic equivalent of the Java language instanceof operator. The method returns true if the specified Object argument is non-null and can be cast to the reference type represented by this Class object without raising a ClassCastException. It returns false otherwise.

423. Why there are no global variables in Java?

Answer: Global variables are globally accessible. Java does not support globally accessible variables due to following reasons:

- The global variables breaks the referential transparency
- Global variables creates collisions in namespace.

424. What is heap in Java?

Answer: JAVA is fully Object oriented language. It has two phases first one is Compilation phase and second one is interpretation phase. The Compilation phase convert the java file to class file (byte code is only readable format of JVM) than Interpretation phase interoperate the class file line by line and give the proper result.

425. How are memory leaks possible in Java?

Answer: If any object variable is still pointing to some object which is of no use, then JVM will not garbage collect that object and object will remain in memory creating memory leak

426. What would happen if you say this = null

Answer: this will give a compilation error as follows

cannot assign value to final variable this

427. How would you pass a java integer by reference to another function?

Answer: Passing by reference is impossible in JAVA but Java supports the object reference so object is the only way to pass the integer by reference.

428. Do multiple inheritance in Java

Answer: It's not possible directly. That means this feature is not provided by Java, but it can be achieved with the help of Interface. By implementing more than one interface.

429. What is data encapsulation? What does it buy you?

Answer: The most common example I can think of is a javabean. Encapsulation may be used by creating 'get' and 'set' methods in a class which are used to access the fields of the object. Typically the fields are made private while the get and set methods are public.

dEncapsulation can be used to validate the data that is to be stored, to do calculations on data that is stored in a field or fields, or for use in introspection (often the case when using javabeans in Struts, for instance).

430. Can we define a class inside the interface?

Answer: Yes, of course! If we define a class inside the interface, java compiler creates a static nested class. Let's see how can we define a class within the interface:

```
interface M{
      class A{}
}
```

431. How all can you free memory?

Answer: With the help of finalize() method.

If a programmer really wants to explicitly request a garbage collection at some point, System.gc() or Runtime.gc() can be invoked, which will fire off a garbage collection at that time.

432. Does java do reference counting?

Answer: It is more likely that the JVMs you encounter in the real world will use a tracing algorithm in their garbage-collected heaps.

433. What does a static inner class mean? How is it different from any other static member?

Answer: A static inner class behaves like any "outer" class. It may contain methods and fields.

It is not necessarily the case that an instance of the outer class exists even when we have created an instance of the inner class. Similarly, instantiating the outer class does not create any instances of the inner class.

The methods of a static inner class may access all the members (fields or methods) of the inner class but they can access only static members (fields or methods) of the outer class. Thus, f can access the field x, but it cannot access the field y.

434. How do you declare constant values in java?

Answer: Using Final keyword we can declare the constant values. Final member can be instantiate only at the time of declaration. Null.

435. Can we declare a static variable inside a method?

Answer: No, static variables can't be declared inside a method otherwise the class will not compile.

436. Tell us something about different types of casting?

Answer: There are two types of casting:

a) Casting between primitive numeric types

b) Casting between object references.

- Casting between numeric types is used to convert larger values into smaller values. For e.g. double values to byte values.
- Casting between object references helps you refer to an object by a compatible class, interface, or array type reference.

437. What is Downcasting?

Answer: Downcasting means casting from a general to a more specific type.

438. What do you mean by order of precedence and associativity?

Answer:

- Order of precedence: It determines the order in which the operators in an expression should be evaluated.
- Associativity: It determines whether an expression should be evaluated left-to-right or right-to-left.

439. If a class is declared without any access modifiers, where can the class be accessed?

Answer:

- Class declared without any access modifiers is said to have package access.
- Such a class can only be accessed by other classes and interfaces defined within the same package.

440. How do constructors use this() and super()?

Answer:

- this() is used to refer to another constructor in the same class with a different parameter list.
- super() is used to invoke the superclass's constructor.

441. Explain numeric promotion?

Answer:

- Conversion of a smaller numeric type to a larger numeric type is called numeric promotion.

- This helps in carrying out integer and floating-point operations.
- Byte, char, and short values are converted to int values in numeric promotion.
- int values are converted to long values, if required.
- The long and float values are converted to double values, if required.

442. What is final modifier?

Answer: The final modifier keyword that the programmer cannot change the value anymore.

Following is what happens when it is applied on classes, variables or methods.

- final Classes- A final class cannot have subclasses.
- final Variables- Once initialized, a final variable cannot be changed.
- final Methods- A final method cannot be overridden by subclasses.

443. What are the restrictions imposed on method overriding?

Answer:

- Overridden methods must have the same name, argument list, and return type.
- The overriding method cannot limit the access of the method overridden.
- The overriding method cannot throw any exceptions that overridden method doesn't throw.

444. What restrictions are placed on method overriding?

Answer: The restriction on method overloading is the signature of the method.

- The signature is the number, type, and order of the arguments passed to a method.
- Overridden methods must have the same name, argument list, and return type.
- Any method which has the same name cannot have the same signature.
- They can have the same return types in the same scope.
- The compiler uses the signature to detect which overloaded method to refer when a overloaded method is called.
- If two methods have the same name and signature the compiler will throw a runtime error.

445. Can I import same package/class twice? Will the JVM load the package twice at runtime?

Answer: One can import the same package or same class multiple times. Neither compiler nor JVM complains about it. But the JVM will internally load the class only once no matter how many times you import the same class.

446. What is static import?

Answer: By static import, we can access the static members of a class directly, there is no to qualify it with the class name.

Static Import:

The static import feature of Java 5 facilitates the java programmer to access any static member of a class directly. There is no need to qualify it by the class name.

Advantage of static import:

- Less coding is required if you have access any static member of a class oftenly.

Disadvantage of static import:

- If you overuse the static import feature, it makes the program unreadable and unmaintainable.

Simple Example of static import

```
import static java.lang.System.*;
class StaticImportExample{
public static void main(String args[]){
        out.println("Hello");//Now no need of System.out
        out.println("Java");
    }
}
```

Output: Hello
Java

447. What is the difference between import and static import?

Answer: The import allows the java programmer to access classes of a package without package qualification whereas the static import feature allows to access the static members of a class without the class qualification. The import provides accessibility to classes and interface whereas static import provides accessibility to static members of the class.

448. Name few Design Patterns used for designing Java applications?

Answer: Singleton, Factory, Abstract Factory, Proxy, Command, Builder.

449. Explain the use of "Native" keyword?

Answer: Used in method declarations to specify that the method is not implemented in the same Java source file, but rather in another language.

450. Difference between implicit and explicit type casting?

Answer: An explicit conversion is where you use some syntax to tell the program to do a conversion whereas in case of implicit type casting you need not provide the data type.

451. What is reflection?

Answer: Reflection is the process of examining or modifying the runtime behaviour of a class at runtime.It is used in:

- IDE (Integrated Development Environment) e.g. Eclipse, MyEclipse, NetBeans.
- Debugger
- Test Tools etc.

452. Can you access the private method from outside the class?

Answer: Yes, by changing the runtime behaviour of a class if the class is not secured.

453. What will happen if static modifier is removed from the signature of the main method?

Answer: Program throws "NoSuchMethodError" error at runtime.

454. Name Wrapper classes available for primitive types?

Answer:

boolean	:	java.lang.Boolean
byte	:	java.lang.Byte
char	:	java.lang.Character
double	:	java.lang.Double
float	:	java.lang.Float
int	:	java.lang.Integer
long	:	java.lang.Long
short	:	java.lang.Short
void	:	java.lang.Void

455. Why do we need wrapper classes?

Answer: It is sometimes easier to deal with primitives as objects. Moreover most of the collection classes store objects and not primitive data types. And also the wrapper classes provide many utility methods also. Because of these reasons we need wrapper classes. And since we create instances of these classes we can store them in any of the collection classes and pass them around as a collection. Also we can pass them around as method parameters where a method expects an object.

456. What is an immutable class?

Answer: Immutable class is a class which once created; its contents cannot be changed. Immutable objects are the objects whose state cannot be changed once constructed. E.g. String class.

457. How to create an immutable class?

Answer: To create an immutable class following steps should be followed:

1. Create a final class.
2. Set the values of properties using constructor only.
3. Make the properties of the class final and private
4. Do not provide any setters for these properties.
5. If the instance fields include references to mutable objects, don't allow those objects to be changed:
   1. Don't provide methods that modify the mutable objects.
   2. Don't share references to the mutable objects. Never store references to external, mutable objects passed to the constructor; if necessary, create copies, and store references to the copies. Similarly, create copies of your internal mutable objects when necessary to avoid returning the originals in your methods.

E.g.

```
public final class FinalPersonClass {
private final String name;
private final int age;
public FinalPersonClass(final String name, final int age) {
super();
this.name = name;
this.age = age;
}
public int getAge() {
return age;
}
public String getName() {
              return name;
}
}
```

458. Immutable objects are automatically thread-safe –true/false?

Answer: True. Since the state of the immutable objects cannot be changed once they are created they are automatically synchronized/thread-safe.

459. Which classes in java are immutable?

Answer: All wrapper classes in java.lang are immutable – String, Integer, Boolean, Character, Byte, Short, Long, Float, Double, BigDecimal, BigInteger

460. What are the advantages of immutability?

Answer: The advantages are:

1) Immutable objects are automatically thread-safe; the over ad caused due to use of synchronization is avoided.
2) Once created the state of the immutable object cannot be changed so there is no possibility of them getting into an inconsistent state.
3) The references to the immutable objects can be easily shared or cached without having to copy or clone them as there state cannot be changed ever after construction.
4) The best use of the immutable objects is as the keys of a map.

461. How does Java allocate stack and heap memory?

Answer: Each time an object is created in Java it goes into the area of memory known as heap. The primitive variables like int and double are allocated in the stack, if they are local method variables and in the heap if they are member variables (i.e. fields of a class).

In Java methods local variables are pushed into stack when a method is invoked and stack pointer is decremented when a method call is completed.

In a multi-threaded application each thread will have its own stack but will share the same heap. This is why care should be taken in your code to avoid any concurrent access issues in the heap space. The stack is thread safe (each thread will have its own stack) but the heap is not thread safe unless guarded with synchronization through your code.

4

String Handling

1. **What is String in Java? String is a data type?**

   Answer: String is a Class in java and defined in java.lang package. It's not a primitive data type like int and long. String class represents character Strings. String is used in almost all the Java applications and there are some interesting facts we should know about String. String in immutable and final in Java and JVM uses String Pool to store all the String objects. Some other interesting things about String is the way we can instantiate a String object using double quotes and overloading of "+" operator for concatenation.

2. **What are different ways to create String Object?**

   Answer: We can create String object using new operator like any normal java class or we can use double quotes to create a String object. There are several constructors available in String class to get String from char array, byte array, StringBuffer and StringBuilder.

```
String str = new String("abc");
String str1 = "abc";
```

   When we create a String using double quotes, JVM looks in the String pool to find if any other String is stored with same value. If found, it just returns the reference to that String object else it creates a new String object with given value and stores it in the String pool.

   When we use new operator, JVM creates the String object but don't store it into the String Pool. We can useintern() method to store the String object into String pool or return the reference if there is already a String with equal value present in the pool.

3. Write a method to check if input String is Palindrome?

Answer: A String is said to be Palindrome if it's value is same when reversed. For example "aba" is a Palindrome String.

String class doesn't provide any method to reverse the String but StringBuffer and StringBuilder class has reverse method that we can use to check if String is palindrome or not.

```
private static boolean isPalindrome(String str) {
if (str == null)
        return false;
        StringBuilder strBuilder = new StringBuilder(str);
        strBuilder.reverse();
        return strBuilder.toString().equals(str);
}
```

Sometimes interviewer asks not to use any other class to check this, in that case we can compare characters in the String from both ends to find out if it's palindrome or not.

```
private static boolean isPalindromeString(String str) {
        if (str == null)
                return false;
                int length = str.length();
                System.out.println(length / 2);
        for (int i = 0; i < length / 2; i++) {

                if (str.charAt(i) != str.charAt(length - i - 1))
                return false;
        }
        return true;
}
```

4. Write a method that will remove given character from the String?

Answer: We can use replaceAll method to replace all the occurance of a String with another String. The important point to note is that it accepts String as argument, so we will use Character class to create String and use it to replace all the characters with empty String.

```
private static String removeChar(String str, char c) {
        if (str == null)
                return null;
```

```
    return str.replaceAll(Character.toString(c), "");
}
```

5. How can we make String upper case or lower case?

Answer: We can use String class toUpperCase and toLowerCase methods to get the String in all upper case or lower case. These methods have a variant that accepts Locale argument and use that locale rules to convert String to upper or lower case.

6. What is String subSequence method?

Answer: Java 1.4 introduced CharSequence interface and String implements this interface, this is the only reason for the implementation of subSequence method in String class. Internally it invokes the String substring method.

7. How to compare two Strings in java program?

Answer: Java String implements Comparable interface and it has two variants of compareTo() methods.

compareTo(String anotherString) method compares the String object with the String argument passed lexicographically. If String object precedes the argument passed, it returns negative integer and if String object follows the argument String passed, it returns positive integer. It returns zero when both the String have same value, in this case equals(String str) method will also return true.

compareToIgnoreCase(String str): This method is similar to the first one, except that it ignores the case. It uses String CASE_INSENSITIVE_ORDER Comparator for case insensitive comparison. If the value is zero thenequalsIgnoreCase(String str) will also return true.

8. How to convert String to char and vice versa?

Answer: This is a tricky question because String is a sequence of characters, so we can't convert it to a single character. We can use use charAt method to get the character at given index or we can use toCharArray()method to convert String to character array.

Check this post for sample program on converting String to character array to String.

9. How to convert String to byte array and vice versa?

Answer: We can use String getBytes() method to convert String to byte array and we can use String constructor new String(byte[] arr) to convert byte array to String.

10. Can we use String in switch case?

Answer: This is a tricky question used to check your knowledge of current Java developments. Java 7 extended the capability of switch case to use Strings also, earlier java versions doesn't support this.

If you are implementing conditional flow for Strings, you can use if-else conditions and you can use switch case if you are using Java 7 or higher versions.

11. Write a program to print all permutations of String?

Answer: This is a tricky question and we need to use recursion to find all the permutations of a String, for example "AAB" permutations will be "AAB", "ABA" and "BAA".

We also need to use Set to make sure there are no duplicate values.

12. Write a function to find out longest palindrome in a given string?

Answer: A String can contain palindrome strings in it and to find longest palindrome in given String is a programming question.

13. Difference between String, StringBuffer and StringBuilder?

Answer: String is immutable and final in java, so whenever we do String manipulation, it creates a new String. String manipulations are resource consuming, so java provides two utility classes for String manipulations – StringBuffer and StringBuilder.

StringBuffer and StringBuilder are mutable classes. StringBuffer operations are thread-safe and synchronized where StringBuilder operations are not thread-safe. So when multiple threads are working on same String, we should use StringBuffer but in single threaded environment we should use StringBuilder.

StringBuilder performance is fast than StringBuffer because of no overhead of synchronization.

14. Why String is immutable or final in Java

Answer: There are several benefits of String because it's immutable and final.

- String Pool is possible because String is immutable in java.
- It increases security because any hacker can't change its value and it's used for storing sensitive information such as database username, password etc.
- Since String is immutable, it's safe to use in multi-threading and we don't need any synchronization.
- Strings are used in java classloader and immutability provides security that correct class is getting loaded by Classloader.

15. How to Split String in java?

Answer: We can use split(String regex) to split the String into String array based on the provided regular expression.

16. Why Char array is preferred over String for storing password?

Answer: String is immutable in java and stored in String pool. Once it's created it stays in the pool until unless garbage collected, so even though we are done with password it's available in memory for longer duration and there is no way to avoid it. It's a security risk because anyone having access to memory dump can find the password as clear text.

If we use char array to store password, we can set it to blank once we are done with it. So we can control for how long it's available in memory that avoids the security threat with String.

17. How do you check if two Strings are equal in Java?

Answer: There are two ways to check if two Strings are equal or not – using "==" operator or using equals method. When we use "==" operator, it checks for value of String as well as reference but in our programming, most of the time we are checking equality of String for value only. So we should use equals method to check if two Strings are equal or not.

There is another function equalsIgnoreCase that we can use to ignore case.

```
String s1 = "abc";
String s2 = "abc";
String s3= new String("abc");
System.out.println("s1 == s2 ? "+(s1==s2)); //true
System.out.println("s1 == s3 ? "+(s1==s3)); //false
System.out.println("s1 equals s3 ? "+(s1.equals(s3))); //true
```

18. What is String Pool?

Answer: As the name suggests, String Pool is a pool of Strings stored in Java heap memory. We know that String is special class in java and we can create String object using new operator as well as providing values in double quotes.

19. What does String intern() method do?

Answer: When the intern method is invoked, if the pool already contains a string equal to this String object as determined by the equals(Object) method, then the string from the pool is returned. Otherwise, this String object is added to the pool and a reference to this String object is returned.

This method always return a String that has the same contents as this string, but is guaranteed to be from a pool of unique strings.

20. Does String is thread-safe in Java?

Answer: Strings are immutable, so we can't change its value in program. Hence it's thread-safe and can be safely used in multi-threaded environment.

21. Why String is popular HashMap key in Java?

Answer: Since String is immutable, its hashcode is cached at the time of creation and it doesn't need to be calculated again. This makes it a great candidate for key in a Map and its processing is fast than other HashMap key objects. This is why String is mostly used Object as HashMap keys.

22. What is Contract between hashcode and equal method?

Answer: The Java super class java.lang.Object has two very important methods defined.

```
public boolean equals(Object obj)
public int hashCode()
```

It is very important to understand the contract between equals and hashcode. The general contract of hashCode is:

Whenever hashCode method is invoked on the same object more than once during the execution of the application, the hashCode method consistently return same integer value.

- If two objects are equal according to the equals(Object) method, then calling the hashCode method on each of the two objects must produce the same integer result.
- It is not required that if two objects are unequal according to the equals(java.lang.Object)method, then calling the hashCode method on each of the two objects must produce distinct integer results. However, the programmer should be aware that producing distinct integer results for unequal objects may improve the performance of hashtables.

23. What is Hash Code collision?

Answer: The idea of hashing is to store an element into array at a position index computed as below.

- obtain element_hash_code of the element by processing the element's data and generating an integer value.
- use a simple mod operation to map into the array's range: index = hash(element) = abs(element_hash_code % array_capacity)

The hashcode collision occurs when the index calculated by hash function results same for two or more elements.

24. Why StringBuffer is called mutable?

Answer: The String class is considered as immutable; so that once it is created a String object cannot be changed. If there is a necessity to make a lot of modifications to Strings of characters then StringBuffer should be used.

25. What is the difference between StringBuffer and StringBuilder class?

Answer: Use StringBuilder whenever possible because it is faster than StringBuffer. But, if thread safety is necessary then use StringBuffer objects.

26. Define immutable object?

Answer: An immutable object can't be changed once it is created.

27. Explain the scenarios to choose between String, StringBuilder and StringBuffer?

Answer:

- If the Object value will not change in a scenario use String Class because a String object is immutable.
- If the Object value can change and will only be modified from a single thread, use a StringBuilder because StringBuilder is unsynchronized (means faster).
- If the Object value may change, and can be modified by multiple threads, use a StringBuffer because StringBuffer is thread safe (synchronized).

28. Difference between String, StringBuffer and StringBuilder?

Answer:

String	StringBuffer	StringBuilder
String is a immutable class	StringBuffer is a mutable class	StringBuilder is a mutable class
New object is created every time when modified	No new object is created, modification is done in existing one	No new object is created, modification is done in existing one
Syntax - String s1="hello";	Syntax - StringBuffer sf=new StringBuffer("hello");	Syntax - StringBuilder sb=new StringBuilder("hello");
-	StringBuffer methods are synchronized.	StringBuilder methods are non-synchronized and added in jdk 5.
Use String if you require immutability	use Stringbuffer in java if you need mutable + thread-safety.	use StringBuilder in Java if you require mutable + without thread-safety..

5

Exception Handling

1. What is Exception in Java?

Answer: Exception is an error event that can happen during the execution of a program and disrupts it's normal flow. Exception can arise from different kind of situations such as wrong data entered by user, hardware failure, network connection failure etc.

Whenever any error occurs while executing a java statement, an exception object is created and then JREtries to find exception handler to handle the exception. If suitable exception handler is found then the exception object is passed to the handler code to process the exception, known as catching the exception. If no handler is found then application throws the exception to runtime environment and JRE terminates the program.

Java Exception handling framework is used to handle runtime errors only, compile time errors are not handled by exception handling framework.

2. What are the different kinds of exceptions? How do you catch a Runtime exception

Answer: There are 2 types of exceptions.

1. Checked exception
2. Unchecked exception.

Checked exception is cached at the compile time while unchecked exception is checked at run time.

1. **Checked Exceptions:** Environmental error that cannot necessarily be detected by testing; e.g. disk full, broken socket, database unavailable, etc.
2. **Unchecked exception. Errors:** Virtual machine error: class not found, out of memory, no such method, illegal access to private field, etc.

Runtime Exceptions: Programming errors that should be detected in testing: index out of bounds, null pointer, illegal argument, etc.

Checked exceptions must be handled at compile time. Runtime exceptions do not need to be. Errors often cannot be.

3. What are the Exception Handling Keywords in Java?

Answer: There are four keywords used in java exception handling.

- throw: Sometimes we explicitly want to create exception object and then throw it to halt the normal processing of the program. throw keyword is used to throw exception to the runtime to handle it.
- throws: When we are throwing any checked exception in a method and not handling it, then we need to use throws keyword in method signature to let caller program know the exceptions that might be thrown by the method. The caller method might handle these exceptions or propagate it to it's caller method using throws keyword. We can provide multiple exceptions in the throws clause and it can be used with main() method also.
- try-catch: We use try-catch block for exception handling in our code. try is the start of the block and catch is at the end of try block to handle the exceptions. We can have multiple catch blocks with a try and try-catch block can be nested also. catch block requires a parameter that should be of type Exception.
- finally: finally block is optional and can be used only with try-catch block. Since exception halts the process of execution, we might have some resources open that will not get closed, so we can use finally block. finally block gets executed always, whether exception occurrs or not.

4. Explain Java Exception Hierarchy?

Answer: Java Exceptions are hierarchical and inheritance is used to categorize different types of exceptions. Throwable is the parent class of Java Exceptions Hierarchy and it has two child objects – Error and Exception. Exceptions are further divided into checked exceptions and runtime exception.

Errors are exceptional scenarios that are out of scope of application and it's not possible to anticipate and recover from them, for example hardware failure, JVM crash or out of memory error.

Checked Exceptions are exceptional scenarios that we can anticipate in a program and try to recover from it, for example FileNotFoundException. We should catch this exception and provide useful message to user and log it properly for debugging purpose. Exception is the parent class of all Checked Exceptions.

Runtime Exceptions are caused by bad programming, for example trying to retrieve an element from the Array. We should check the length of array first before trying to retrieve the element otherwise it might throw ArrayIndexOutOfBoundException at runtime. RuntimeException is the parent class of all runtime exceptions.

5. What are important methods of Java Exception Class?

Answer: Exception and all of its subclasses doesn't provide any specific methods and all of the methods are defined in the base class Throwable.

- String getMessage() – This method returns the message String of Throwable and the message can be provided while creating the exception through it's constructor.
- String getLocalizedMessage() – This method is provided so that subclasses can override it to provide locale specific message to the calling program. Throwable class implementation of this method simply use getMessage() method to return the exception message.
- synchronized Throwable getCause() – This method returns the cause of the exception or null id the cause is unknown.
- String toString() – This method returns the information about Throwable in String format, the returned String contains the name of Throwable class and localized message.
- void printStackTrace() – This method prints the stack trace information to the standard error stream, this method is overloaded and we can pass PrintStream or PrintWriter as argument to write the stack trace information to the file or stream.

6. What is the difference between exception and error?

Answer: The exception class defines mild error conditions that your program encounters.

Ex: ArithmeticException, FileNotFound exception

Exceptions can occur when try to open the file, which does not exist

- the network connection is disrupted
- operands being manipulated are out of prescribed ranges
- the class file you are interested in loading is missing

The error class defines serious error conditions that you should not attempt to recover from. In most cases it is advisable to let the program terminate when such an error is encountered.

Ex: Running out of memory error, Stack overflow error.

7. Explain Java 7 ARM Feature and multi-catch block?

Answer: If you are catching a lot of exceptions in a single try block, you will notice that catch block code looks very ugly and mostly consists of redundant code to log the error, keeping this in mind Java 7 one of the feature was multi-catch block where we can catch multiple exceptions in a single catch block. The catch block with this feature looks like below:

```
catch(IOException | SQLException | Exception ex){
logger.error(ex);
     throw new MyException(ex.getMessage());
}
```

Most of the time, we use finally block just to close the resources and sometimes we forget to close them and get runtime exceptions when the resources are exhausted. These exceptions are hard to debug and we might need to look into each place where we are using that type of resource to make sure we are closing it. So java 7 one of the improvement was try-with-resources where we can create a resource in the try statement itself and use it inside the try-catch block. When the execution comes out of try-catch block, runtime environment automatically close these resources. Sample of try-catch block with this improvement is:

```
try (MyResource mr = new MyResource()) {
     System.out.println("MyResource created in try-with-resources");
} catch (Exception e) {
     e.printStackTrace();
}
```

8. What is difference between Checked and Unchecked Exception in Java?

Answer:

- Checked Exceptions should be handled in the code using try-catch block or else main() method should use throws keyword to let JRE know about these exception that might be thrown from the program. Unchecked Exceptions are not required to be handled in the program or to mention them in throws clause.
- Exception is the super class of all checked exceptions whereas RuntimeException is the super class of all unchecked exceptions.
- Checked exceptions are error scenarios that are not caused by program, for example FileNotFoundException in reading a file that is not present, whereas Unchecked exceptions are mostly caused by poor programming, for example NullPointerException when invoking a method on an object reference without making sure that it's not null.

9. What is difference between throw and throws keyword in Java?

Answer: throws keyword is used with method signature to declare the exceptions that the method might throw whereas throw keyword is used to disrupt the flow of program and handing over the exception object to runtime to handle it.

10. How to write custom exception in Java?

Answer: We can extend Exception class or any of its subclasses to create our custom exception class. The custom exception class can have its own variables and methods that we can use to pass error codes or other exception related information to the exception handler.

A simple example of custom exception is shown below.

MyException.java

```
package com.journaldev.exceptions;
import java.io.IOException;
public class MyException extends IOException {
    private static final long serialVersionUID = 4664456874499611218L;
    private String errorCode="Unknown_Exception";
    public MyException(String message, String errorCode){
        super(message);
        this.errorCode=errorCode;
    }
    public String getErrorCode(){
        return this.errorCode;
    }
}
```

11. What is OutOfMemoryError in Java?

Answer: OutOfMemoryError in Java is a subclass of java.lang.VirtualMachineError and its thrown by JVM when it ran out of heap memory, and no more memory could be made available by the garbage collector. We can fix this error by providing more memory to run the java application through java options.

```
$>java MyProgram -Xms1024m -Xmx1024m -XX:PermSize=64M
-XX:MaxPermSize=256m
```

12. What are different scenarios causing "Exception in thread main"?

Answer: Some of the common main thread exception scenarios are:

- Exception in thread main java.lang.UnsupportedClassVersionError: This exception comes when your java class is compiled from another JDK version and you are trying to run it from another java version.
- Exception in thread main java.lang.NoClassDefFoundError: There are two variants of this exception. The first one is where you provide the class full name with .class extension. The second scenario is when Class is not found.

- Exception in thread main java.lang.NoSuchMethodError: main: This exception comes when you are trying to run a class that doesn't have main method.
- Exception in thread "main" java.lang.ArithmeticException: Whenever any exception is thrown from main method, it prints the exception is console. The first part explains that exception is thrown from main method, second part prints the exception class name and then after a colon, it prints the exception message.

13. What happens when exception is thrown by main method?

Answer: When exception is thrown by main() method, Java Runtime terminates the program and print the exception message and stack trace in system console.

14. Can an exception be rethrown?

Answer: Yes, an exception can be rethrown.

15. When is the finally clause of a try-catch-finally statement executed?

Answer: The finally clause of the try-catch-finally statement is always executed unless the thread of execution terminates or an exception occurs within the execution of the finally clause.

16. What class of exceptions are generated by the Java run-time system?

Answer: The Java runtime system generates RuntimeException and Error exceptions.

17. What is the relationship between a method's throws clause and the exceptions that can be thrown during the method's execution?

Answer: A method's throws clause must declare any checked exceptions that are not caught within the body of the method.

18. What classes of exceptions may be thrown by a throw statement?

Answer: A throw statement may throw any expression that may be assigned to the Throwable type.

19. What happens if an exception is not caught?

Answer: An uncaught exception results in the uncaughtException() method of the thread's ThreadGroup being invoked, which eventually results in the termination of the program in which it is thrown.

20. What happens if a try-catch-finally statement does not have a catch clause to handle an exception that is thrown within the body of the try statement?

Answer: The exception propagates up to the next higher level try-catch statement (if any) or results in the program's termination.

21. Can try statements be nested?

Answer: Try statements may be tested.

22. How does a try statement determine which catch clause should be used to handle an exception?

Answer: When an exception is thrown within the body of a try statement, the catch clauses of the try statement are examined in the order in which they appear. The first catch clause that is capable of handling the exception is executed. The remaining catch clauses are ignored.

23. What is the purpose of the finally clause of a try-catch-finally statement?

Answer: The finally clause is used to provide the capability to execute code no matter whether or not an exception is thrown or caught.

24. Is it necessary that each try block must be followed by a catch block?

Answer: It is not necessary that each try block must be followed by a catch block. It should be followed by either a catch block OR a finally block. And whatever exceptions are likely to be thrown should be declared in the throws clause of the method

25. What classes of exceptions may be caught by a catch clause?

Answer: A catch clause can catch any exception that may be assigned to the Throwable type. This includes the Error and Exception types. Errors are generally irrecoverable conditions.

26. Can we have an empty catch block?

Answer: We can have an empty catch block but it's the example of worst programming. We should never have empty catch block because if the exception is caught by that block, we will have no information about the exception and it will be a nightmare to debug it. There should be at least a logging statement to log the exception details in console or log files.

Provide some Java Exception Handling Best Practices?

Some of the best practices related to Java Exception Handling are:

- Use Specific Exceptions for ease of debugging.
- Throw Exceptions Early (Fail-Fast) in the program.
- Catch Exceptions late in the program, let the caller handle the exception.
- Use Java 7 ARM feature to make sure resources are closed or use finally block to close them properly.
- Always log exception messages for debugging purposes.
- Use multi-catch block for cleaner close.
- Use custom exceptions to throw single type of exception from your application API.

- Follow naming convention, always end with Exception.
- Document the Exceptions Thrown by a method using @throws in javadoc.
- Exceptions are costly, so throw it only when it makes sense. Else you can catch them and provide null or empty response.

27. What is the use of the finally block?

Answer: Finally is the block of code that is always executed even when an exception has occurred.

28. Does the code in finally block get executed if there is an exception and a return statement in a catch block?

Answer: If an exception occurs and there is a return statement in catch block, the finally block is still executed. The finally block will not be executed when the System.exit(1) statement is executed earlier or the system shut down earlier or the memory is used up earlier before the thread goes to finally block.

29. Does the code in finally block get executed if there is an exception and a return statement in a catch block?

Or

What is the purpose of the finally clause of a try-catch-finally statement?

Answer: The finally clause is used to provide the capability to execute code no matter whether or not an exception is thrown or caught. If an exception occurs and there is a return statement in catch block, the finally block is still executed. The finally block will not be executed when the System.exit(0) statement is executed earlier or on system shut down earlier or the memory is used up earlier before the thread goes to finally block.

```
try{
      //some statements
}
catch{
//statements when exception is caught
}
finally{
//statements executed whether exception occurs or not
}
```

30. Does the order of placing catch statements matter in the catch block?

Answer: Yes, it does. The FileNoFoundException is inherited from the IOException. So FileNoFoundException is caught before IOException. Exception's subclasses have to be caught first before the General Exception

31. Explain the user defined Exceptions?

Answer: User defined Exceptions are custom Exception classes defined by the user for specific purpose. A user defined exception can be created by simply sub-classing an Exception class or a subclass of an Exception class. This allows custom exceptions to be generated (using throw clause) and caught in the same way as normal exceptions.

Example:

```
class CustomException extends Exception {
}
```

32. When is finally block NOT called?

Answer:

- Finally block is NOT called in following cases: If the JVM exits while the try or catch code is being executed. This may happen due to System.exit() call.
- If the thread executing the try or catch code gets interrupted or killed. In this case, the finally block may not execute although the application keeps working.
- If an exception is thrown in finally block is not handled. In this case, the remaining code in finally block may not execute.

33. What is the difference between final, finally and finalize()?

Answer:

final:

- It is a modifier which can be applied to a class, method or variable.
- It is not possible to inherit the final class, override the final method and change the final variable.

finally:

- It is an exception handling code section.
- It gets executed whether an exception is raised or not by the try block code segment.

```
finalize()
```

- It is a method of Object class.
- It is executed by the JVM just before garbage collecting object to give a final chance for resource releasing activity.

Out of the three, only finally is related to java exception handling.

34. What is difference between throw and throws?

Answer:

throw keyword	throws keyword
1) throw is used to explicitly throw an exception.	throws is used to declare an exception.
2) checked exceptions cannot be propagated with throw only.	checked exception can be propagated with throws.
3) throw is followed by an instance.	throws is followed by class.
4) throw is used within the method.	throws is used with the method signature.
5) You cannot throw multiple exception	You can declare multiple exception e.g. public void method() throws IOException,SQLException.

35. What things should be kept in mind while creating your own exceptions in Java?

Answer: While creating your own exception:

- All exceptions must be a child of Throwable.
- If you want to write a checked exception that is automatically enforced by the Handle or Declare Rule, you need to extend the Exception class.
- You want to write a runtime exception, you need to extend the RuntimeException class.

36. What is NullPointerException?

Answer: A NullPointerException is thrown when calling the instance method of a null object, accessing or modifying the field of a null object etc.

37. Does it matter in what order catch statements for FileNotFoundException and IOException are written?

Answer: Yes, it does. The FileNoFoundException is inherited from the IOException. Exception's subclasses have to be caught first.

38. When is the ArrayStoreException thrown?

Answer: When copying elements between different arrays, if the source or destination arguments are not arrays or their types are not compatible, an ArrayStoreException will be thrown.

39. When ArithmeticException is thrown?

Answer: The ArithmeticException is thrown when integer is divided by zero or taking the remainder of a number by zero. It is never thrown in floating-point operations.

40. What will happen if static modifier is removed from the signature of the main method?

Answer: Program throws "NoSuchMethodError" error at runtime.

41. If System.exit (0); is written at the end of the try block, will the finally block still execute?

Answer: No in this case the finally block will not execute because when you say System.exit (0); the control immediately goes out of the program, and thus finally never executes.

42. When is the ArrayStoreException thrown?

Answer: When copying elements between different arrays, if the source or destination arguments are not arrays or their types are not compatible, an ArrayStoreException will be thrown.

43. What is the problem with following code?

```
If (x == null && x.getMethod() == true)
```

Answer: It will throw NPE in case x is null.

44. What is an Assertion and why using assertion in your program is a good idea?

Answer: In a Java program, several times, one would like to make certain assumptions for executing a program. For example, while taking a square root of a numeric value it has to be assumed that this value should not be negative. An assertion is a statement in the Java programming language that enables to test assumptions about one's program. Assertions are supported from J2SE1.4 and later. A simple example of assertion can be checking of an employee object from being null: Employee employee = null;

45. Explain Assertions with a code example.

Answer: The main reason of introducing assertions in Java from R1.4 onwards is to reduce the chances of bugs which otherwise would have gone unnoticed, in one's code. In fact, finding and removing bugs is one tedious and not so exciting task. Assertions should be used for scenarios which ideally should never happen in the lifecycle of a program, check assumptions about data structures (such as ensuring that an array is of the correct length), or enforcing constraints on arguments of private methods. Assertions help in a way to block these bugs at the beginning of writing actual logic inside your code that saves lot of efforts, time and most significantly, costs. A simple assertion facility provides a limited form of design-by-contract programming. In design-by-contract programming identification of preconditions and post conditions to a program are must before even starting the coding itself.

Here is simple Java code which uses assertions; here the task is to determine the gender of a person. We have used a *switch-case* statement to define the overall flow of the logic.

46. How many forms of assertions we have?

Answer: There are two forms of assertions:

The ***first, simpler form*** is:

assert *Expression1* ;

where Expression1 is a boolean expression.

When the system runs the assertion, it evaluates Expression1 and if it is false throws an AssertionError with no detail message.

While the ***second form*** of the assertion statement is:

assert *Expression1* : *Expression2* ;

where: Expression1 is a boolean expression.

Expression2 is an expression that has a value. (It cannot be an invocation of a method that is declared void.)

This form is used when the assert statement has to provide a detail message for the *AssertionError*. The system passes the value of Expression2 to the appropriate AssertionError constructor, and this constructor uses the string representation of the value as the error's detail message. This detail message helps in analyzing and diagnosing the assertion failure which ultimately helps in resolving the error.

47. When assertions should be avoided?

Answer: In following situations the assertions should be avoided:

- When assertion becomes a performance issue. It means an assertion should not include too complex logic equaling implementation of a method.
- Do not use assertions in argument checking of public methods. As argument checking is part of a method implementation and if these arguments are erroneous then it will throw runtime exception and assertion failure will not result in any error.

48. What situations are best suitable for implementing assertions?

Answer: Assertions can best be implemented:

- As Internal Invariants
- As Control flow Invariants
- As Pre conditions and Post conditions
- As Class Invariants

49. If my class already extends from some other class what should I do if I want an instance of my class to be thrown as an exception object?

Answer: One cannot do anything in this scenario. Because Java does not allow multiple inheritance and does not provide any exception interface as well.

50. How does an exception permeate through the code?

Answer: An unhandled exception moves up the method stack in search of a matching When an exception is thrown from a code which is wrapped in a try block followed by one or more catch blocks, a search is made for matching catch block. If a matching type is found then that block will be invoked. If a matching type is not found then the exception moves up the method stack and reaches the caller method. Same procedure is repeated if the caller method is included in a try catch block. This process continues until a catch block handling the appropriate type of exception is found. If it does not find such a block then finally the program terminates.

51. What are the different ways to handle exceptions?

Answer: There are two ways to handle exceptions,

1. By wrapping the desired code in a try block followed by a catch block to catch the exceptions. And
2. List the desired exceptions in the throws clause of the method and let the caller of the method handle those exceptions.

52. What is the basic difference between the 2 approaches to exception handling?

1. try catch block and

2. Specifying the candidate exceptions in the throws clause?

When should you use which approach?

Answer: In the first approach as a programmer of the method, you urself are dealing with the exception. This is fine if you are in a best position to decide should be done in case of an exception. Whereas if it is not the responsibility of the method to deal with its own exceptions, then do not use this approach. In this case use the second approach. In the second approach we are forcing the caller of the method to catch the exceptions that the method is likely to throw. This is often the approach library creator's use. They list the exception in the throws clause and we must catch them. You will find the same approach throughout the java libraries we use.

53. Is it necessary that each try block must be followed by a catch block?

Answer: It is not necessary that each try block must be followed by a catch block. It should be followed by either a catch block OR a finally block. And whatever exceptions are likely to be thrown should be declared in the throws clause of the method.

54. If I write return at the end of the try block, will the finally block still execute?

Answer: Yes even if you write return as the last statement in the try block and no exception occurs, the finally block will execute. The finally block will execute and then the control return.

6

Multithreading

1. **What is a thread?**

   Answer: A thread is a set of instructions executing apart from other threads (with its own stack) but sharing the same memory space (with the same heap).

2. **What is the difference between Process and Thread?**

   Answer: Process is a program in execution whereas thread is a separate path of execution in a program.

   A process can contain multiple threads. In most multithreading operating systems, a process gets its own memory address space; a thread doesn't. Threads typically share the heap belonging to their parent process.

   For instance, a JVM runs in a single process in the host O/S. Threads in the JVM share the heap belonging to that process; that's why several threads may access the same object.

   Typically, even though they share a common heap, threads have their own stack space. This is how one thread's invocation of a method is kept separate from another's.

   This is all a gross oversimplification, but it's accurate enough at a high level. Lots of details differ between operating systems.

   Java runtime environment runs as a single process which contains different classes and programs as processes. Thread can be called lightweight process. Thread requires less resource to create and exists in the process, thread shares the process resources.

Process	Thread
A program	Similar to a sequential program
Can run on its own	Cannot run on its own
Unit of allocation	Unit of execution
Have its own memory space	Share with others

Process	Thread
Each process has one or more threads	Each thread belongs to one process
Expensive, need to context switch	Cheap, can use process memory and may not need to context switch
More secure. One process cannot corrupt another process	Less secure. A thread can write the memory used by another thread

3. What are the benefits of multi-threaded programming?

Answer: In Multi-Threaded programming, multiple threads are executing concurrently that improves the performance because CPU is not idle incase some thread is waiting to get some resources. Multiple threads share the heap memory, so it's good to create multiple threads to execute some task rather than creating multiple processes. For example, Servlets are better in performance than CGI because Servlet support multi-threading but CGI doesn't.

4. Difference between multithreading and multitasking?

Answer: A Web Server understands and supports only HTTP protocol whereas an Application Server supports HTTP, TCP/IP and many more protocols. Also many more features such as Caches,Clusters, Load Balancing are there in Application Servers which are not available in Web Servers. We can also Configure Application Servers to work as Web Server. In short, Applicaion Server is a super set of which Web Server is a sub set.

5. How does multithreading take place on a computer with a single CPU?

Answer: The operating system's task scheduler allocates execution time to multiple tasks. By quickly switching between executing tasks, it creates the impression that tasks execute sequentially.

6. What is the difference between a lightweight and a heavyweight process?

Answer: [Short ***answer:*** threads are lightweight, programs (aka processes or tasks) are heavyweight.]

Lightweight and heavyweight processes refer the mechanics of a multi-processing system.

In a lightweight process, threads are used to divvy up the workload. Here you would see one process executing in the OS (for this application or service.) This process would posess 1 or more threads. Each of the threads in this process shares the same address space. Because threads share their address space, communication between the threads is simple and efficient. Each thread could be compared to a process in a heavyweight scenario.

In a heavyweight process, new processes are created to perform the work in parallel. Here (for the same application or service), you would see multiple processes running.

Each heavyweight process contains its own address space. Communication between these processes would involve additional communications mechanisms such as sockets or pipes.

The benefits of a lightweight process come from the conservation of resources. Since threads use the same code section, data section and OS resources, less overall resources are used. The drawback is now you have to ensure your system is thread-safe. You have to make sure the threads don't step on each other. Fortunately, Java provides the necessary tools to allow you to do this.

7. What is difference between user Thread and daemon Thread?

Answer: When we create a Thread in java program, it's known as user thread. A daemon thread runs in background and doesn't prevent JVM from terminating. When there are no user threads running, JVM shutdown the program and quits. A child thread created from daemon thread is also a daemon thread.

8. How can we create a Thread in Java?

Answer: There are two ways to create Thread in Java – first by implementing Runnable interface and then creating a Thread object from it and second is to extend the Thread Class. Read this post to learn more about creating threads in java.

9. What are different states in lifecycle of Thread?

Answer: When we create a Thread in java program, its state is New. Then we start the thread that change it's state to Runnable. Thread Scheduler is responsible to allocate CPU to threads in Runnable thread pool and change their state to Running. Other Thread states are Waiting, Blocked and Dead. Read this post to learn more about life cycle of thread.

10. What is atomic operation? What are atomic classes in Java Concurrency API?

Answer: Atomic operations are performed in a single unit of task without interference from other operations. Atomic operations are necessity in multi-threaded environment to avoid data inconsistency.

int++ is not an atomic operation. So by the time one threads read its value and increment it by one, other thread has read the older value leading to wrong result.

To solve this issue, we will have to make sure that increment operation on count is atomic, we can do that using Synchronization but Java 5 java.util.concurrent. atomic provides wrapper classes for int and long that can be used to achieve this atomically without usage of Synchronization. Go to this article to learn more about atomic concurrent classes.

11. What is Lock interface in Java Concurrency API? What are its benefits over synchronization?

Answer: Lock interface provide more extensive locking operations than can be obtained using synchronized methods and statements. They allow more flexible structuring, may have quite different properties, and may support multiple associated Condition objects.

The advantages of a lock are

- It's possible to make them fair
- It's possible to make a thread responsive to interruption while waiting on a Lock object.
- It's possible to try to acquire the lock, but return immediately or after a timeout if the lock can't be acquired
- It's possible to acquire and release locks in different scopes, and in different orders

12. What is Executors Framework?

Answer: In Java 5, Executor framework was introduced with the java.util.concurrent. Executor interface.

The Executor framework is a framework for standardizing invocation, scheduling, execution, and control of asynchronous tasks according to a set of execution policies.

Creating a lot many threads with no bounds to the maximum threshold can cause application to run out of heap memory. So, creating a ThreadPool is a better solution as a finite number of threads can be pooled and reused. Executors framework facilitate process of creating Thread pools in java. Check out this post to learn with example code to create thread pool using Executors framework.

13. What is BlockingQueue? How can we implement Producer-Consumer problem using Blocking Queue?

Answer: java.util.concurrent.BlockingQueue is a Queue that supports operations that wait for the queue to become non-empty when retrieving and removing an element, and wait for space to become available in the queue when adding an element.

BlockingQueue doesn't accept null values and throw NullPointerException if you try to store null value in the queue.

BlockingQueue implementations are thread-safe. All queuing methods are atomic in nature and use internal locks or other forms of concurrency control.

BlockingQueue interface is part of java collections framework and it's primarily used for implementing producer consumer problem.

14. What is Callable and Future?

Answer: Java 5 introduced java.util.concurrent.Callable interface in concurrency package that is similar to Runnable interface but it can return any Object and able to throw Exception.

Callable interface use Generic to define the return type of Object. Executors class provide useful methods to execute Callable in a thread pool. Since callable tasks run in parallel, we have to wait for the returned Object. Callable tasks return java.util. concurrent.Future object. Using Future we can find out the status of the Callable task and get the returned Object. It provides get() method that can wait for the Callable to finish and then return the result.

15. What is FutureTask Class?

Answer: FutureTask is the base implementation class of Future interface and we can use it with Executors for asynchronous processing. Most of the time we don't need to use FutureTask class but it comes real handy if we want to override some of the methods of Future interface and want to keep most of the base implementation. We can just extend this class and override the methods according to our requirements. Check out Java FutureTask Example post to learn how to use it and what are different methods it has.

16. What are Concurrent Collection Classes?

Answer: Java Collection classes are fail-fast which means that if the Collection will be changed while some thread is traversing over it using iterator, the iterator.next() will throw ConcurrentModificationException.

Concurrent Collection classes support full concurrency of retrievals and adjustable expected concurrency for updates.

Major classes are ConcurrentHashMap, CopyOnWriteArrayList and CopyOnWriteArraySet, check this post to learn how to avoid ConcurrentModificationException when using iterator.

17. What is Executors Class?

Answer: Executors class provide utility methods for Executor, ExecutorService, ScheduledExecutorService, ThreadFactory, and Callable classes.

Executors class can be used to easily create Thread Pool in java, also this is the only class supporting execution of Callable implementations.

18. What are some of the improvements in Concurrency API in Java 8?

Answer: Some important concurrent API enhancements are:

- ConcurrentHashMap compute(), forEach(), forEachEntry(), forEachKey(), forEachValue(), merge(), reduce() and search() methods.
- CompletableFuture that may be explicitly completed (setting its value and status).
- Executors newWorkStealingPool() method to create a work-stealing thread pool using all available processors as its target parallelism level.

19. Explain Java Thread Life cycle.

Answer: The life cycle of threads in Java is very similar to the life cycle of processes running in an operating system. During its life cycle the thread moves from one state to another depending on the operation performed by it or performed on it. A Java thread can be in one of the following states:

- NEW: A thread that is just instantiated is in new state. When a start () method is invoked, the thread moves to the ready state from which it is automatically moved to runnable state by the thread scheduler.
- RUNNABLE (ready_running) A thread executing in the JVM is in running state.
- BLOCKED A thread that is blocked waiting for a monitor lock is in this state. This can also occur when a thread performs an I/O operation and moves to next (runnable) state.
- WAITING A thread that is waiting indefinitely for another thread to perform a particular action is in this state.
- TIMED_WAITING (sleeping) A thread that is waiting for another thread to perform an action up to a specified waiting time is in this state.
- TERMINATED (dead) A thread that has exited is in this state.

20. What are the states associated in the thread?

Answer: Thread contains ready, running, waiting and dead states.

21. What state is a thread in when it is executing?

Answer: An executing thread is in the running state.

22. How can a dead thread be restarted?

Answer: A dead thread cannot be restarted.

23. What are the different ways of creating thread?

Answer: There are two ways of creating thread.

- Implementing Runnable: The Runnable interface defines a single method, run, meant to contain the code executed in the thread. The Runnable object is passed to the Thread constructor, as in the HelloRunnable example

```
public class HelloRunnable implements Runnable {
public void run() {
System.out.println("Hello from a thread!");
}
public static void main(String args[]) {
(new Thread(new HelloRunnable())).start();
}
}
```

- Subclass Thread: The Thread class itself implements Runnable interface, though it runs method does nothing. An application can subclass Thread, and provides its own implementation of run, as in the HelloThread example:

```
public class HelloThread extends Thread {
public void run() {
System.out.println("Hello from a thread!");.
}
public static void main(String args[])
{
•   (new HelloThread()).start();
}
}
```

24. What are the differences between extending the Thread class and implementing the Runnable interface?

Answer: Extending the Thread class will make your class unable to extend other classes, because of the single inheritence feature in JAVA. However, this will give you a simpler code structure. If you implement runnable, you can gain better object-oriented design and consistency and also avoid the single inheritance problems.

25. When is a thread created?

Answer: A thread is created by the VM behind the scenes during a call to the start() method. It begins its life inside the run() method of the thread subclass instance whose start() method was called.

26. How do I create a new thread and have it start running?

Answer: Creating a thread involves creating a new Thread and invoking its start() method. Calling start() causes the run() method of the Thread subclass or the Runnable object passed to the Thread constructor to execute.

```
Thread t1 = new Thread() {
      public void run() {
            for (int i=0; i<100; i++) {
                  System.out.println("Tastes Great");
            }
      }
};
Runnable r = new Runnable() {
      public void run() {
            for (int i=0; i<100; i++) {
```

```
                System.out.println("Less Filling");
            }
        }
    };
    Thread t2 = new Thread(r);
    t1.start();
    t2.start();
```

27. What is the use of start() function in starting a thread? Why we don't use the run(0 function directly to run the thread?

Answer: The start() method tells the Java Virtual Machine that it needs to create a system specific thread. After creating the system resource, it passes the Runnable object to it to execute its run() method. Calling the run() method directly has the "Thread" execute in the same thread as the calling object, not in a separate thread of execution, as intended.

In other words, calling run() is just like a normal method call. Whereas, calling start() tells the thread to create the necessary system resources and then execute the run() method asynchronously.

28. Can each Java object keep track of all the threads that want to exclusively access to it?

Answer: Yes.

29. What is the use of start() function in starting a thread? Why we do not use the run() function directly to run the thread?

Answer: The start() method tells the Java Virtual Machine that it needs to create a system specific thread. After creating the system resource, it passes the Runnable object to it to execute its run() method. Calling the run() method directly has the "Thread" execute in the same thread as the calling object, not in a separate thread of execution, as intended.

In other words, calling run() is just like a normal method call. Whereas, calling start() tells the thread to create the necessary system resources and then execute the run() method asynchronously.

30. What method must be implemented by all threads?

Answer: All tasks must implement the run() method, whether they are a subclass of Thread or implement the Runnable interface.

31. Where can I find a set of data structures to deal with many of the concurrent programming concepts?

Answer: Doug Lea has produced a utility library in conjunction with his Concurrent

Programming in Java that includes many common classes needed to help you synchronize your data access, like mutex and semaphore.

32. Which way a developer should use for creating thread, i.e. Sub classing Thread or implementing Runnable.

Answer: There are two ways of creating Thread in java (i.e. sub classing or implementing Runnable). It is very important to understand the implication of using these two approaches.

There are two different points about using these two approaches.

- By extending the thread class, the derived class itself is a thread object and it gains full control over the thread life cycle. Implementing the Runnable interface does not give developers any control over the thread itself, as it simply defines the unit of work that will be executed in a thread.
- Another important point is that when extending the Thread class, the derived class cannot extend any other base classes because Java only allows single inheritance. By implementing the Runnable interface, the class can still extend other base classes if necessary.

To summarize, if developer needs a full control over the Thread life cycle, sub classing Thread class is a good choice, and if programs need more flexibility by extending other class developer, should go with implementing Runnable interface.

33. How to create multithreaded program? Explain different ways of using thread? When a thread is created and started, what is its initial state?

Or

Extending Thread class or implementing Runnable Interface. Which is better?

Answer: You have two ways to do so. First, making your class "extends" Thread class. The other way is making your class implement "Runnable" interface. The latter is more advantageous, cause when you are going for multiple inheritance, then only interface can help. . If you are already inheriting a different class, then you have to go for Runnable Interface. Otherwise you can extend Thread class. Also, if you are implementing interface, it means you have to implement all methods in the interface. Both Thread class and Runnable interface are provided for convenience and use them as per the requirement. But if you are not extending any class, better extend Thread class as it will save few lines of coding. Otherwise performance wise, there is no distinguishable difference. A thread is in the ready state after it has been created and started.

34. What are three ways in which a thread can enter the waiting state?

Answer: A thread can enter the waiting state by invoking its sleep() method, by blocking on I/O, by unsuccessfully attempting to acquire an object's lock, or by invoking an object's wait() method. It can also enter the waiting state by invoking its (deprecated) suspend() method.

35. What's new with the stop(), suspend() and resume() methods in JDK 1.2?

Answer: The stop(), suspend() and resume() methods have been deprecated in JDK 1.2.

36. How would you implement a thread pool?

Answer: public class ThreadPool extends java.lang.Object implements ThreadPoolInt

This class is a generic implementation of a thread pool, which takes the following input

a) Size of the pool to be constructed

b) Name of the class which implements Runnable (which has a visible default constructor) and constructs a thread pool with active threads that are waiting for activation. Once the threads have finished processing they come back and wait once again in the pool.

This thread pool engine can be locked i.e. if some internal operation is performed on the pool then it is preferable that the thread engine be locked. Locking ensures that no new threads are issued by the engine. However, the currently executing threads are allowed to continue till they come back to the passivePool

37. What is the class and interface in java to create thread and which is the most advantageous method?

Answer: Thread class and Runnable interface can be used to create threads and using Runnable interface is the most advantageous method to create threads because we need not extend thread class here.

38. What is the use of Join method?

Answer: The join method allows one thread to wait for the completion of another. If " t " is a Thread object whose thread is currently executing,

t.join();

Causes the current thread to pause execution until t's thread terminates. Overloads of join allow the programmer to specify a waiting period. However, as with sleep, join is dependent on the OS for timing, so you should not assume that join will wait exactly as long as you specify.

Like sleep, join responds to an interrupt by exiting with an InterruptedException.

39. What is the difference between sleep(), wait() and suspend()?

Answer: Thread.sleep() sends the current thread into the "Not Runnable" state for some amount of time. The thread keeps the monitors it has aquired -- i.e. if the thread is currently in a synchronized block or method no other thread can enter this block or method. If another thread calls t.interrupt() it will wake up the sleeping thread.

Note that sleep is a static method, which means that it always affects the current thread (the one that is executing the sleep method). A common mistake is to call t.sleep() where t is a different thread; even then, it is the current thread that will sleep, not the t thread.

t.suspend() is deprecated. Using it is possible to halt a thread other than the current thread. A suspended thread keeps all its monitors and since this state is not interruptable it is deadlock prone.

object.wait() sends the current thread into the "Not Runnable" state, like sleep(), but with a twist. Wait is called on a object, not a thread; we call this object the "lock object." Before lock.wait() is called, the current thread must synchronize on the lock object; wait() then releases this lock, and adds the thread to the "wait list" associated with the lock. Later, another thread can synchronize on the same lock object and call lock.notify(). This wakes up the original, waiting thread. Basically, wait()/notify() is like sleep()/interrupt(), only the active thread does not need a direct pointer to the sleeping thread, but only to the shared lock object.

40. What is the difference between yielding and sleeping?

Answer: When a task invokes its yield() method, it returns to the ready state. When a task invokes its sleep() method, it returns to the waiting state.

41. What happens when you invoke a thread's interrupt method while it is sleeping or waiting?

Answer: When a task's interrupt() method is executed, the task enters the ready state. The next time the task enters the running state, an InterruptedException is thrown.

42. What are three ways in which a thread can enter the waiting state?

Or

What are different ways in which a thread can enter the waiting state?

Answer: A thread can enter the waiting state by the following ways:

1. Invoking its sleep() method,
2. By blocking on I/O
3. By unsuccessfully attempting to acquire an object's lock
4. By invoking an object's wait() method.
5. It can also enter the waiting state by invoking its (deprecated) suspend() method.

43. How can one thread wait for another thread to die before it continues execution?

Answer: The thread's join() method allows you to wait for another thread to finish execution.

```
Thread t1 = new Thread(runnable);
t1.start();
// do stuff
...
// wait for t1 to finish
t1.join()
```

44. How do I get a thread to pause?

Answer: The static sleep() method of the Thread class will let your thread sleep for a set number of milliseconds (or nanoseconds). When the thread wakes up, it will be scheduled to execute in the future. It may not start executing immediately after the timeout.

```
try {
Thread.sleep(3000); // 3 seconds
} catch (InterruptedException e) {
            System.err.prinlnt("You interrupted me");
     }
```

[You can have another thread wake up the sleeping thread prematurely by calling t.interrupt() (where "t" is a pointer to the thread object).

Note that since Thread.sleep() is a static method, the following code will not do what you expect it to:

```
Thread t = new MyThread();
t.start();
try {
            t.sleep(3000);
} catch (InterruptedException e) {
            System.err.prinlnt("You interrupted me");
}
```

It will pause the **current** thread, meaning the thread executing the shown code, not the child thread (t/MyThread).

45. What are daemon thread and which method is used to create the daemon thread?

Answer: Daemon thread is a low priority thread which runs intermittently in the back ground doing the garbage collection operation for the java runtime system. setDaemon method is used to create a daemon thread.

46. How can a daemon thread be implemented?

Answer: After creating an object of a Thread class and before starting the thread, call the setDeamon () function of the Thread class with parameter as true. This will mark the thread as a daemon thread.

47. Is there any limitation on the number of daemon threads in an application?

Answer: No, there is no limitation on the number of daemon threads in an application.

48. What is a daemon thread? What is the use of deamon thread?

Answer: Daemon term is mainly used in UNIX. In Java, this is used to indicate a special type of thread. Normally when a thread is created in Java, by default it is a non-daemon thread. Whenever a Java Program is executed, the Java Virtual Machine (JVM) will not exit until any non-daemon threads are still running. This means if the main thread of an application ends and the remaining threads left are Daemon threads, then the JVM will exit killing all the daemon threads without warning.

A daemon thread should be used for some background task that might provide a service to the applications. E.g. a Server threads listening on a port for the clients` requests. A thread for which an exit method is not provided or which does not have an exit mechanism can be marked as a daemon thread.

49. How do I have one thread wait for another thread to finish before continuing?

Answer: You can wait for a thread to finish by calling its join() method. For instance, in the following code, the current thread will wait until thread2 finishes before printing “Done”.

```
thread2.start();
// do more stuff here
thread2.join();
System.out.println("Done");
```

50. How can I catch exceptions thrown in secondary threads I create?

Answer: You need to create the secondary threads in a custom `ThreadGroup`. Subclass `ThreadGroup` and override `public void uncaughtException(Thread source, Throwable throwable)`. This method would then be notified when an uncaught exception is thrown.

51. How do I create a variable local to a Thread?

Answer: The Java 1.2 release introduced the concept of thread local variables as a standard class. Previously, they existed in the sun.server.util package of the Java

WebServer product. Now, you get them in the java.lang.ThreadLocal and java.lang.InheritableThreadLocal classes. These classes permit individual threads to have independent copies of variables. With ThreadLocal, only a particular thread sees the variable, with InheritableThreadLocal a thread and all its descendents can see it. Here's an example,

```
public class LocalThreadVars implements Runnable {
static private class MyThreadLocal extends ThreadLocal {
        protected Object initialValue() {
                return new Double (Math.random() * 1000.0);
        }
    }
    static ThreadLocal threadLocal = new MyThreadLocal();
    static int counter = 0;
    private LocalThreadVars() {
        counter++;
    }
    public void run() {
        LocalThreadVars myLTV = new LocalThreadVars();
        displayValues();
        try {
                Thread.currentThread().sleep (((Double)
threadLocal.get()).longValue());
                myLTV.displayValues();
        } catch (InterruptedException e) {
                e.printStackTrace();
        }
    }
    private void displayValues() {
        System.out.println (threadLocal.get() + "\t" + counter +
"\t" + Thread.currentThread().getName());
    }
    public static void main (String args[]) {
        LocalThreadVars ltv = new LocalThreadVars();
        ltv.displayValues();
        for (int i=0;i<5;i++) {
                Thread t = new Thread (ltv);
                t.start();
        }
    }
}
```

52. Is there a separate stack for each thread in Java?

Answer: No

53. What is the main difference between a preemptive scheduler and a non-preemptive scheduler?

Answer: A preemptive scheduler interrupts a thread of execution when its time slice runs out. A non-preemptive (or "cooperative") scheduler waits for the thread to yield control.

[Java native thread implementations are usually preemptive; the green-threads implementation is cooperative but priority-preemptive, which means that when a high-priority thread becomes runnable, it immediately becomes active.]

54. How does a preemptive scheduler manage a thread's time slice?

Answer: The lowest level preemptive scheduler (kernel layer) uses the system timer interrupt and context switching to manage time slices. When any CPU interrupt occurs, the CPU makes a note of where it was, and what it was doing (pushes all registers onto the stack). The CPU then processes the interrupt and returns to what it was previously doing (pops all registers from the stack). The thread context in this sense, is the information the CPU needs to start or resume execution in any section of code. The scheduler is invoked by the timer interrupt routine (it can also be part of the timer interrupt). The scheduler checks to see if the current time slice has expired; if so, the current thread context is stored and the next valid thread context is restored. The most basic implementation is a stack swap, as each thread has its own stack. When a thread is created, it gets a new context with an empty stack. The new context directs the CPU to the thread's run() member at the beginning of its time slice. A thread's context is destroyed when the thread returns from the run() member, or its stop() member is successfully invoked.

55. Why are resources tied to ThreadGroups?

Answer: Every thread of execution on any given platform has its own context, which contains an execution state, and a set of access rights (among other things). A thread's access rights are equal to that of the parent thread, minus rights denied by the parent. In Java, all threads of execution, and thread groups within an applet (or application) belong to a parent ThreadGroup object. A thread's access to Java resources is therefore determined by its parent ThreadGroup object (including the thread of execution that passes through init(), start(), stop(), processEvent(...),

56. How can I create ThreadGroups in applets running in Netscape 4.7 without generating security exceptions?

Answer: Sign your code and enable UniversalThreadGroupAccess
PrivilegeManager.enablePrivilege("UniversalThreadGroupAccess");

57. How can multiple threads be controlled simultanesously?

Answer: If you create threads in a ThreadGroup object, they may be controlled simultaneously with the member functions of said object.

58. What is synchronization?

Answer: Synchronization is the mechanism that ensures that only one thread is accessed the resources at a time.

59. When you will synchronize a piece of your code?

Answer: When you expect your code will be accessed by different threads and these threads may change a particular data causing data corruption.

60. What is deadlock?

Answer: When two threads are waiting each other and can't precede the program is said to be deadlock.

61. What is the Difference between synchronized and synchronized block?

Answer: In case of a Synchronized method a thread may need to have the lock for a longer time as compared to the synchronized block.

Another difference between synchronized method and block is that we don't specify the particular object whose monitor is required to be obtained by thread for entering a synchronized method, whereas we can specify the particular object in case of synchronized block.

62. What are synchronized methods and synchronized statements?

Answer: Synchronized methods are methods that are used to control access to an object. A thread only executes a synchronized method after it has acquired the lock for the method's object or class. Synchronized statements are similar to synchronized methods. A synchronized statement can only be executed after a thread has acquired the lock for the object or class referenced in the synchronized statement195. What are the two basic ways in which classes that can be run as threads may be defined? A thread class may be declared as a subclass of Thread, or it may implement the Runnable interface.

63. Static Synchronization vs Instance Synchronization?

Answer: When a static synchronized method is called, the program obtains the class lock before calling the method. This mechanism is identical to the case in which method is non-static, it is just a different lock, and this lock is solely for static method. Apart from the functional relationship between the two locks, they are not operationally related at all.

64. Multiple Threads can access a class method at the same time. To avoid this we use SYNCHRONIZED. However, using SYNCHRONIZED can lock that method until released by the particular thread. Is there a way to avoid this locking?

Answer: Use SYNCHRONIZE with the object to be locked within the method.

65. Will there be a performance penalty if you make a method synchronized? If so, can you make any design changes to improve the performance.

Answer: yes, the performance will be down if we use synchronization. One can minimize the penalty by including garbage collection algorithm, which reduces the cost of collecting large numbers of short- lived objects. And also by using improved thread synchronization for invoking the synchronized methods, the invoking will be faster.

66. How does serialization work?

Answer: It's like FIFO method (first in first out)

67. Can a method be static and synchronized?

Answer: No a static method can't be synchronized.

68. What is synchronization and why is it important?

Answer: With respect to multithreading, synchronization is the capability to control the access of multiple threads to shared resources. Without synchronization, it is possible for one thread to modify a shared object while another thread is in the process of using or updating that object's value. This often causes dirty data and leads to significant errors.

69. Different uses of synchronized keyword?

Answer: The keyword synchronized is used to acquire a exclusive monitor lock on an object. It can be used to mark either a method or a block of code. In both cases, it means to acquire a lock for the duration of the method or block, and to release the lock at the end. It also takes a parameter, which names the object whose lock will be acquired. (The parameter is implicit when marking a method, as shown below.)

```
synchronized (foo) {
  ...
}
```

Acquires a lock on the object instance "foo" at the open brace, and releases the lock at the close brace.

```
synchronized (this) {
  ...
```

```
}
Acquires a lock on the current object instance ("this") at the open
brace, and releases the lock at the close brace.

synchronized void bar() {
  ...
}
Acquires a lock on the current object instance at the open brace, and
releases it at the close brace. This is equivalent (*) to
void bar() {
 synchronized (this) {
   ...
 }
}

class Foo {
  synchronized static void bar() {
    ...
  }
}
```

Acquires and releases a lock on the class instance of class Foo. Every class, when loaded, is given an instance of class Class. That means that no matter who invokes method Foo.bar(), the lock will be on the static instance, and not on any specific instance of class Foo.

I know this sounds confusing, but it has the same semantics as any other use of static: all statics (methods, variables, etc) are essentially global, interact with all other statics of the same class, and do not interact with non-static instance data.

Whether a method is public or not makes no difference to the semantics of synchronized.

(* Actually, there is a very small, technical difference between void bar() { synchronized (this) { ... } } and synchronized void bar() { ... }: the VM may be able to very slightly optimize the latter case, since the synchronization is marked in the method signature and not in code. However, this is not important in practice.)

70. What will happen if non-synchronized method calls a static synchronized method and what kind of lock it acquires?

Answer: If non-static synchronized method calls a static synchronized method it acquires both lock i.e. lock on the object and lock on the class level.

Class lock does not actually exist the class lock, is the object lock of the "Class" object that models the class. Since there is only one "Class" object per class, using this object achieves the synchronization for static method.

- Only one thread can execute a synchronized static method per class.
- Only one thread per instance of the class can execute a non-static synchronized method.
- Any number of threads can execute a non-synchronized method static or non-static method.

71. What object does non-static synchronized methods use for locking?

Answer: Non-static synchronized methods synchronize on the instance (`this`) of the class.

72. What are the different uses of the synchronized keyword?

Answer: The keyword synchronized is used to acquire an exclusive monitor lock on an object. It can be used to mark either a method or a block of code. In both cases, it means to acquire a lock for the duration of the method or block, and to release the lock at the end. It also takes a parameter, which names the object whose lock will be acquired. (The parameter is implicit when marking a method, as shown below.)

```
synchronized (foo) {
  ...
}
Acquires a lock on the object instance "foo" at the open brace, and
releases the lock at the close brace.
synchronized (this) {
  ...
}
Acquires a lock on the current object instance ("this") at the open
brace, and releases the lock at the close brace.
synchronized void bar() {
  ...
}
Acquires a lock on the current object instance at the open brace, and
releases it at the close brace. This is equivalent (*) to
void bar() {
      synchronized (this) {
    ...
      }
}
class Foo {
      synchronized static void bar() {
      ...
}
}
```

Acquires and releases a lock on the class instance of class Foo. Every class, when loaded, is given an instance of class Class. That means that no matter who invokes method Foo.bar(), the lock will be on the static instance, and **not** on any specific instance of class Foo.

I know this sounds confusing, but it has the same semantics as any other use of static: all statics (methods, variables, etc) are essentially global, interact with all other statics of the same class, and do not interact with non-static instance data.

Whether a method is public or not makes no difference to the semantics of synchronized.

(* Actually, there is a very small, technical difference between void bar() { synchronized (this) { ... } } and synchronized void bar() { ... }: the VM may be able to very slightly optimize the latter case, since the synchronization is marked in the method signature and not in code. However, this is not important in practice.)

73. What object does static synchronized methods use for locking?

Answer: Static synchronized methods synchronize on the class object (this. getClass()) of the class.

74. Can a lock be acquired on a class?

Answer: Yes, a lock can be acquired on a class. This lock is acquired on the class's Class object.

75. What is the use of volatile in Java?

Answer: Threads are allowed to hold the values of variables in local memory (e.g. in a machine register).

If a variable is marked as volatile, every time when the variable is used, it must be read from the main memory, similarly every time the variable is written, the value must be stored in main memory.

76. What are the ways in which a thread can enter the waiting state?

Answer: A thread can enter the waiting state by invoking its sleep() method, by blocking on IO, by unsuccessfully attempting to acquire an object's lock, or by invoking an object's wait() method. It can also enter the waiting state by invoking its (deprecated) suspend() method.

77. How does multi-threading take place on a computer with a single CPU?

Answer: The operating system's task scheduler allocates execution time to multiple tasks. By quickly switching between executing tasks, it creates the impression that tasks execute sequentially.

78. What invokes a thread's run() method?

Answer: After a thread is started, via its start() method of the Thread class, the JVM invokes the thread's run() method when the thread is initially executed.

79. What is the difference between yielding and sleeping?

Answer: When a task invokes its yield() method, it returns to the ready state. When a task invokes its sleep() method, it returns to the waiting state.

80. What's the difference between the methods sleep() and wait()?

Answer: The code sleep(2000); puts thread aside for exactly two seconds. The code wait(2000), causes a wait of up to two second. A thread could stop waiting earlier if it receives the notify() or notifyAll() call. The method wait() is defined in the class Object and the method sleep() is defined in the class Thread.

81. What is a transient variable?

Answer: A transient variable is a variable that may not be serialized during Serialization and which is initialized by its default value during de-serialization.

82. What is daemon thread?

Answer: Daemon thread is a low priority thread, which runs intermittently in the back ground doing the garbage collection operation for the java runtime system.

83. Is there any limitation on the number of daemon threads in an application?

Answer: No, there is no limitation on the number of daemon threads in an application.

84. How can a daemon thread be implemented?

Answer: After creating an object of a Thread class and before starting the thread, call the setDeamon () function of the Thread class with parameter as true. This will mark the thread as a daemon thread.

85. When should I use setDaemon() and why?

Answer: Use setDaemon() to tell the JVM to make the thread a daemon thread. According to Webster's, a daemon (variant of demon) is an attendant power or spirit. Daemon threads are typically used to perform services for your application/applet (such as loading the "fiddley bits"). The core difference between user threads and daemon threads is that the JVM will only shut down a program when all user threads have terminated or starved to death (See the "Starvation" FAQ, #41875). Daemon threads are terminated by the JVM when there are no longer any user threads running, including the main thread of execution. Use daemons as the minions they are.

[In short: daemon threads do not keep the program from quitting; user threads do.]

86. Which method is used to create the daemon thread?

Answer: setDaemon method is used to create a daemon thread.

87. Which method must be implemented by all threads?

Answer: All tasks must implement the run() method

88. What is multithreading and what are the methods for inter-thread communication and what is the class in which these methods are defined?

Answer: Multithreading is the mechanism in which more than one thread run independent of each other within the process.

wait (), notify () and notifyAll() methods can be used for inter-thread communication and these methods are in Object class.

wait( ) : When a thread executes a call to wait( ) method, it surrenders the object lock and enters into a waiting state.

notify( ) or notifyAll( ) : To remove a thread from the waiting state, some other thread must make a call to notify( ) or notifyAll( ) method on the same object.

89. Why are the methods wait() and notify() defined in the Object class when they are used with Threads?

Answer: The wait() and notify() methods are object-specific. The wait() method suspends the current thread of execution, and tells the object to keep track of the suspended thread. The notify() method tells the object to wake up the suspended threads that it is currently keeping track of. Since wait() and notify() are object specific, they must be used within code that is synchronized on the object in question. It is also important to use state variables when using wait() and notify(), as threads can be woken up by conditions other than notify().

90. What is the purpose of the wait(), notify(), and notifyAll() methods?

Answer: - The wait(),notify(), and notifyAll() methods are used to provide an efficient way for threads to wait for a shared resource. When a thread executes an object's wait() method, it enters the waiting state. It only enters the ready state after another thread invokes the object's notify() or notifyAll() methods.

91. What is "starvation" when used in the context of the Java threading model?

Answer: Starvation is when the Java runtime (JVM) doesn't allocate time to a thread to execute. This may be due to a poor scheduling algorithm (like green Threads under Solaris, where a for loop from 1 to 1 million doing something CPU intensive wouldn't yield the CPU under Solaris but would under Windows), poor programming practice (not returning from the paint() method in an applet), or a hostile attack (like hitting a host with a denial of service attack where the CPU is busy outside the Java process).

92. What happens when a thread cannot acquire a lock on an object?

Answer: If a thread attempts to execute a synchronized method or synchronized statement and is unable to acquire an object's lock, it enters the waiting state until the lock becomes available.

93. What is the meaning of calling a method or object "thread-safe?"

Answer: Basically, calling a method "thread-safe" means that even if multiple threads try to access it simultaneously, nothing bad happens. Here "bad" usually means that due to race conditions, or deadlock, or other pitfalls, the object's state gets corrupted, or its methods produce unreliable results. A method usually achieves thread-safety by protecting access to shared resources. This usually translates to using the Java synchronized keyword to protect blocks of code that access instance variables, or other shared variables.

For an object to be thread-safe, it must be possible for multiple threads to simultaneously access the same method, or multiple methods, in that object. Usually this is achieved by assuring that each method is thread-safe, but this doesn't always suffice, since methods can call each other in strange ways, leading to deadlock and other weirdness.

It is very difficult to prove that an object is thread-safe. The main rule of thumb for making thread-safe objects is, "Make all the instance variables private, and all the public accessor methods synchronized." However, this is sometimes difficult to achieve in practice, due to exigencies of performance, architecture, or implementation. Accurate multithreaded programming is a true art, and very difficult to master. Read "Java Threads" by Oaks and Wong, and "Concurrent Programming in Java" by Lea, for inspiration in your quest to become a thread-safe programmer.

94. What is the keyword volatile used for? What sort of situations should I use volatile when developing a multi-threaded application?

Answer: Volatile modifiers tells the compiler that the variable can be changed unexpectedly by other part of programme. When you have nore than one thread and you expect any thread can change the variable you should use volatile. This will tell the compiler to check for the master copy of this variable. Mostly used for boolean flags.

95. When and why IllegalMonitorStateException throw?

Answer: Thrown to indicate that a thread has attempted to wait on an object's monitor or to notify other threads waiting on an object's monitor without owning the specified monitor.

According to the JavaDoc, IllegalMonitorStateException is thrown "to indicate that a thread has attempted to wait on an object's monitor or to notify other threads waiting on an object's monitor without owning the specified monitor."

As explained in How do wait and notify really work? , in order to call foo.wait() or foo. notify(), the calling thread must own a lock on object foo. This exception is thrown if you call it without a preceding synchronized (foo).

96. What is the relationship between synchronized and volatile keyword?

Answer: The JVM is guaranteed to treat reads and writes of data of 32 bits or less as atomic.(Some JVM might treat reads and writes of data of 64 bits or less as atomic in future) For long or double variable, programmers should take care in multi-threading environment. Either put these variables in a synchronized method or block, or declare them volatile.

97. What factors are used to decide using synchronized or volatile?

Answer: Whether you use volatile or synchronized depends on several factors.

a). If you are not updating many variables often in a multithread environment, consider using volatile.

b). If you are updating many variables, consider using synchronized, because using volatile might be slower.

98. Two methods have key words static synchronized and synchronized separately. What is the difference between them?

Answer: Both are synchronized methods. One is instance method, the other is class method. Method with static modifier is a class method. That means the method belongs to class itself and can be accessed directly with class name and is also called Singleton design. The method without static modifier is an instance method. That means the instance method belongs to its object. Every instance of the class gets its own copy of its instance method.

Since both methods are synchronized methods, you are not asked to explain what is a synchronized method. You are asked to tell the difference between instance and class method. Of course, your explanation to how synchronized keyword works doesn't hurt. And you may use this opportunity to show your knowledge scope.

When synchronized is used with a static method, a lock for the entire class is obtained. When synchronized is used with a non-static method, a lock for the particular object (that means instance) of the class is obtained.

99. What is mutual exclusion? How can you take care of mutual exclusion using Java threads?

Answer: Mutual exclusion is a phenomenon where no two processes can access critical regions of memory at the same time. Using Java multithreading we can arrive at mutual exclusion. For mutual exclusion, you can simply use the synchronized keyword and explicitly or implicitly provide an Object, any Object, to synchronize on. The synchronized keyword can be applied to a class, to a method, or to a block of code. There are several methods in Java used for communicating mutually exclusive threads such as wait( ), notify( ), or notifyAll( ). For example, the notifyAll( ) method wakes up all threads that are in the wait list of an object.

100. Can Java object be locked down for exclusive use by a given thread?

Or

what happens when a thread cannot acquire a lock on an object?

Answer: Yes. You can lock an object by putting it in a "synchronized" block. The locked object is inaccessible to any thread other than the one that explicitly claimed it. If a thread attempts to execute a synchronized method or synchronized statement and is unable to acquire an object's lock, it enters the waiting state until the lock becomes available.

101. What do you understand by Synchronization?

Or

What is synchronization and why is it important?

Or

Describe synchronization in respect to multithreading?

Or

What is synchronization?

Answer: With respect to multithreading, Synchronization is a process of controlling the access of shared resources by the multiple threads in such a manner that only one thread can access a particular resource at a time. In non synchronized multithreaded application, it is possible for one thread to modify a shared object while another thread is in the process of using or updating the object's value. Synchronization prevents such type of data corruption which may otherwise lead to dirty reads and significant errors.

```
E.g. synchronizing a function:
public synchronized void Method1 () {
// method code.
}
E.g. synchronizing a block of code inside a function:
public Method2 (){
synchronized (this) {
// synchronized code here.
}
}
```

102. When you will synchronize a piece of your code?

Answer: When you expect that your shared code will be accessed by different threads and these threads may change a particular data causing data corruption, then they are placed in a synchronized construct or a synchronized method.

7

Garbage Collector

1. **What do you know about the garbage collector?**

   Answer: In Java, memory management is done automatically by JVM. A programmer is free of this responsibility of handling memory. A garbage collector is a part of JVM responsible for removing objects from heap, which is no longer in use. The garbage collector typically runs in a background thread, periodically scanning the heap, identifying garbage objects, and releasing the memory they occupy so that the memory is available for future objects.

2. **What is Garbage Collection and how to call it explicitly?**

   Answer: When an object is no longer referred to by any variable, java automatically reclaims memory used by that object. This is known as garbage collection.

   System.gc() method may be used to call it explicitly.

3. **What is finalize() method ?**

   Answer: finalize () method is used just before an object is destroyed and can be called just prior to garbage collection.

4. **What is final, finalize() and finally?**

   Answer: **final:** final keyword can be used for class, method and variables.

   A final class cannot be subclassed and it prevents other programmers from subclassing a secure class to invoke insecure methods.

   A final method can't be overridden

   A final variable can't change from its initialized value.

   finalize( ) : finalize( ) method is used just before an object is destroyed and can be called just prior to garbage collection.

finally: finally, a key word used in exception handling, creates a block of code that will be executed after a try/catch block has completed and before the code following the try/catch block. The finally block will execute whether or not an exception is thrown.

For example, if a method opens a file upon exit, then you will not want the code that closes the file to be bypassed by the exception-handling mechanism. This finally keyword is designed to address this contingency.

5. Explain the keywords - native, transient, volatile, finally.

Answer:

native: to use methods which written in other language.

transient: if u declare state of class as transient then it's not saved in persistent area.

volatile: this is not optimized at the time of optimization because it's value may be changed implicitly or explicitly.

finally: finally is used to do work prior of closing the program because of exception. It's always called by compiler either exception generated or not.

6. What is phantom memory?

Answer: Phantom memory is false memory. Memory that does not exist in reality.

7. What is garbage Collection?

Answer: If no reference to an object, that object is assumed to be no longer needed, and the memory occupied by the object can be reclaimed. This is known as garbage collection.

8. Does garbage collection guarantee that a program will not run out of memory?

Answer: Garbage collection does not guarantee that a program will not run out of memory. As garbage collection is JVM dependent then It is possible for programs to use memory resources faster than they are garbage collected. Moreover garbage collection cannot be enforced, it is just suggested. Java guarantees that the finalize method will be run before an object is Garbage collected, it is called by the garbage collector on an object when garbage collection determines that there are no more references to the object.

The garbage collection is uncontrolled, it means you cannot predict when it will happen, you thus cannot predict exactly when the finalize method will run. Once a variable is no longer referenced by anything it is available for garbage collection. You can suggest garbage collection with System.gc(), but this does not guarantee when it will happen.

9. **Can an object's finalize() method be invoked while it is reachable?**

   Answer: An object's finalize() method cannot be invoked by the garbage collector while the object is still reachable. However, an object's finalize() method may be invoked by other objects.

10. **What are the disadvantages of reference counting in garbage collection?**

    Answer: An advantage of this scheme is that it can run in small chunks of time closely interwoven with the execution of the program. This characteristic makes it particularly suitable for real-time environments where the program can't be interrupted for very long. A disadvantage of reference counting is that it does not detect cycles. A cycle is two or more objects that refer to one another, for example, a parent object that has a reference to its child object, which has a reference back to its parent. These objects will never have a reference count of zero even though they may be unreachable by the roots of the executing program. Another disadvantage is the overhead of incrementing and decrementing the reference count each time. Because of these disadvantages, reference counting currently is out of favor.

11. **Is it advisable to depend on finalize for all cleanups?**

    Answer: The purpose of finalization is to give an opportunity to an unreachable object to perform any clean up before the object is garbage collected, and it is advisable.

12. **Describe the Garbage Collection process in Java?**

    Answer: The JVM spec mandates automatic garbage collection outside of the programmer's control. The System.gc() or Runtime.gc() is merely a suggestion to the JVM to run the GC process but is NOT guaranteed.

13. **When is an object subject to garbage collection?**

    Answer: An object is subject to garbage collection when it becomes unreachable to the program in which it is used.

14. **What is the purpose of garbage collection?**

    Answer: The purpose of garbage collection is to identify and discard objects that are no longer needed by a program so that their resources may be reclaimed and reused.

15. **What class of exceptions are generated by the Java run-time system?**

    Answer: The Java runtime system generates RuntimeException and Error exceptions.

16. **If an object is garbage collected, can it become reachable again?**

    Answer: Once an object is garbage collected, it ceases to exist. It can no longer become reachable again.

17. How does garbage collection work?

Answer: There are several basic strategies for garbage collection: reference counting, mark-sweep, mark-compact, and copying. In addition, some algorithms can do their job incrementally (the entire heap need not be collected at once, resulting in shorter collection pauses), and some can run while the user program runs (concurrent collectors). Others must perform an entire collection at once while the user program is suspended (so-called stop-the-world collectors). Finally, there are hybrid collectors, such as the generational collector employed by the 1.2 and later JDKs, which use different collection algorithms on different areas of the heap.

18. How all can you free memory?

Answer: With the help of finalize() method.

If a programmer really wants to explicitly request a garbage collection at some point, System.gc() or Runtime.gc() can be invoked, which will fire off a garbage collection at that time.

19. What is the purpose of finalization?

Answer: The purpose of finalization is to give an unreachable object the opportunity to perform any cleanup processing before the object is garbage collected.

20. Explain garbage collection?

Or

How you can force the garbage collection?

Or

What is the purpose of garbage collection in Java, and when is it used?

Or

What is Garbage Collection and how to call it explicitly?

Or

Explain Garbage collection mechanism in Java?

Answer: Garbage collection is one of the most important features of Java. The purpose of garbage collection is to identify and discard objects that are no longer needed by a program so that their resources can be reclaimed and reused. A Java object is subject to garbage collection when it becomes unreachable to the program in which it is used. Garbage collection is also called automatic memory management as JVM automatically removes the unused variables/objects (value is null) from the memory. Every class inherits finalize() method from java.lang.Object, the finalize() method is called by garbage collector when it determines no more references to the object exists. In Java, it is good idea to explicitly assign null into a variable when no more in use. In Java on calling System.gc() and Runtime.gc(), JVM tries to recycle the unused objects, but there is no guarantee when all the objects will garbage collected. Garbage collection is an automatic process and can't be forced. There is no guarantee that Garbage collection will start immediately upon request of System.gc().

21. What kind of thread is the Garbage collector thread?

Answer: It is a daemon thread.

22. What is gc()?

Answer: gc() is a daemon thread.gc() method is defined in System class that is used to send request to JVM to perform garbage collection.

23. Can an unrefrenced objects be refrenced again?

Answer: Yes.

24. How will you invoke any external process in Java?

Answer: By Runtime.getRuntime().exec(?) method.

25. Does Java have destructors?

Answer: Garbage collector does the job working in the background. Java does not have destructors; but it has finalizers that do a similar job.

The syntax is:

```
public void finalize(){
}
if an object has a finalizer, the method is invoked before the system
garbage collects the object.
```

26. What is the difference between Serial and Throughput Garbage collector?

Answer: The throughput garbage collector uses a parallel version of the young generation collector and is meant to be used with applications that have medium to large data sets. On the other hand, the serial collector is usually adequate for most small applications (those requiring heaps of up to approximately 100MB on modern processors).

8

Iostream

1. **What is a stream and what are the types of Streams and classes of the Streams?**

   Answer: A Stream is an abstraction that either produces or consumes information. There are two types of Streams and they are:

   Byte Streams: Provide a convenient means for handling input and output of bytes.

   Character Streams: Provide a convenient means for handling input & output of characters.

   Byte Streams classes: Are defined by using two abstract classes, namely InputStream and OutputStream.

   Character Streams classes: Are defined by using two abstract classes, namely Reader and Writer.

2. **What is the difference between Reader/Writer and InputStream/Output Stream?**

   Answer: The Reader/Writer class is character-oriented and the InputStream/OutputStream class is byte-oriented.

3. **What is an I/O filter?**

   Answer: An I/O filter is an object that reads from one stream and writes to another, usually altering the data in some way as it is passed from one stream to another.

4. **What is serialization and deserialization?**

   Answer: Serialization is the process of writing the state of an object to a byte stream. Deserialization is the process of restoring these objects.

5. What is object serialization?

Answer: Serializing an object involves encoding its state in a structured way within a byte array. Once an object is serialized, the byte array can be manipulated in various ways; it can be written to a file, sent over a network using a socket-based connection or RMI, or persisted within a database as a BLOB.

The serialization process encodes enough information about the object type within the byte stream, allowing the original object to be easily recreated upon *deserialization*, at a later point in time.

6. Can I persist my objects using serialization instead of using a relational or object database?

Answer: No. While serialization is a highly versatile mechanism having numerous applications, your long term storage needs should continue to be addressed by conventional relational or object databases.

Note that serialization does not provide any features for transaction management and concurrency control. Nor does it provide typical database features like indexed access, caching and a query language.

7. What are the security ramifications of using the Externalizable interface?

Answer: The methods within the Externalizable interface, readExternal() and writeExternal() have public scope. This implies some client object could potentially bypass the Java sandbox mechanisms and overwrite or gain access to the state of an externalizable object.

As a general rule of thumb, a class should implement the Externalizable interface only if the object contains nonsensistive information.

8. Why am I having an InvalidClassException thrown during the serialization of my object which implements the Externalizable interface?

Answer: Unlike objects which implement the Serializable interface, it is mandatory for objects implementing the Externalizable interface to also implement a public no-arg constructor. This constructor is the very first thing that is invoked by readExternal() when reconstructing the object from the bytestream. If a public no-arg constructor is absent, then an InvalidClassException is immediately thrown.

9. Why doesn't serialization save the value of static variables?

Answer: Variables declared as static members are not considered part of the state of an object because they are shared by all instances of that class. Classes which need to preserve the value of static members during serialization should save and restore these values explicitly using private void readObject(ObjectInputStream) and private void writeObject(ObjectOutputStream).

10. What is the Stream Unique IDentifier (SUID) that is written out as part of the serial stream?

Answer: The serialization process uses a unique identification value to keep track of the persisted objects. When a Serializable or Externalizable object is saved, it's fully-qualified class name and the Stream Unique IDentifier (SUID) of the class is written out to the stream. The SUID is a unique 64-bit hash, and is obtained by applying the SHA-1 message digest algorithm to the serialized class, including its name, field types and method signatures.

This step is important as it prevents the data persisted by one class from being read by another class with the same name. For any class to be able to read successfully from an object stream, it is imperative that its SUID matches the SUID of the serialized data in the stream.

11. What are the advantages and disadvantags of serialization?

Answer: The advantages of serialization are:

- It is easy to use and can be customized.
- The serialized stream can be encrypted, authenticated and compressed, supporting the needs of secure Java computing.
- Serialized classes can support coherent versioning and are flexible enough to allow gradual evolution of your application's object schema.
- Serialization can also be used as a mechanism for exchanging objects between Java and C++ libraries, using third party vendor libraries (like RogueWave's Tools.h++) within C++.
- There are simply too many critical technologies that rely upon serialization, including RMI, JavaBeans and EJB.

However, serialization has some disadvantages too:

- It should ideally not be used with large-sized objects, as it offers significant overhead. Large objects also significantly increase the memory requirements of your application since the object input/output streams cache live references to all objects written to or read from the stream until the stream is closed or reset. Consequently, the garbage collection of these objects can be inordinately delayed.
- The Serializable interface does not offer fine-grained control over object access - although you can somewhat circumvent this issue by implementing the complex Externalizable interface, instead.
- Since serialization does not offer any transaction control mechanisms per se, it is not suitable for use within applications needing concurrent access without making use of additional APIs.

12. Does serialization depend on the browser, platform, or VM?

Answer: The serialization format is independent of browser, independent of JVM vendor, and independent of platform. So serialization should work with any combination of the above.

For example, a serialized object written by Windows can be read by Unix, and vice verse. This is generally true of all I/O in Java.

13. If an object is serialized by a 1.1.x VM, can it be de-serialized by a 1.2.x VM?

Answer: Yes. No special steps are needed for this to work.

14. What is a stream and what are the types of Streams and classes of the Streams?

Answer: A Stream is an abstraction that either produces or consumes information. There are two types of Streams and they are:

Byte Streams: Provide a convenient means for handling input and output of bytes.

Character Streams: Provide a convenient means for handling input & output of characters.

Byte Streams classes: Are defined by using two abstract classes, namely InputStream and OutputStream.

Character Streams classes: Are defined by using two abstract classes, namely Reader and Writer.

15. What is the purpose of the File class?

Answer: The File class is used to create objects that provide access to the files and directories of a local file system.

16. What class allows you to read objects directly from a stream?

Answer: The ObjectInputStream class supports the reading of objects from input streams.

17. What is the difference between the File and RandomAccessFile classes?

Answer: The File class encapsulates the files and directories of the local file system. The RandomAccessFile class provides the methods needed to directly access data contained in any part of a file.

18. What interface must an object implement before it can be written to a stream as an object?

Answer: An object must implement the Serializable or Externalizable interface before it can be written to a stream as an object.

19. What is the serialization?

Answer: The serialization is a kind of mechanism that makes a class or bean persistence by having its properties or fields and state information saved and restored to and from storage.

20. How to make a class or a bean serializable?

Answer: By implementing either the java.io.Serializable interface, or the java.io.Externalizable interface. As long as one class in a class's inheritance hierarchy implements Serializable or Externalizable, that class is serializable.

21. How many methods in the Serializable interface?

Answer: There is no method in the Serializable interface. The Serializable interface acts as a marker, telling the object serialization tools that your class is serializable.

22. How many methods in the Externalizable interface?

Answer: There are two methods in the Externalizable interface. You have to implement these two methods in order to make your class externalizable. These two methods are readExternal() and writeExternal().

23. What is the difference between Serializalble and Externalizable interface?

Answer: When you use Serializable interface, your class is serialized automatically by default. But you can override writeObject() and readObject() two methods to control more complex object serailization process. When you use Externalizable interface, you have a complete control over your class's serialization process.

24. What is a transient variable?

Answer: A transient variable is a variable that may not be serialized. If you don't want some field to be serialized, you can mark that field transient or static.

25. What is the difference between the Reader/Writer class hierarchy and the InputStream/OutputStream class hierarchy?

Answer: The Reader/Writer class hierarchy is character-oriented, and the InputStream/OutputStream class hierarchy is byte-oriented.

26. What class allows you to read objects directly from a stream?

Answer: The ObjectInputStream class supports the reading of objects from input streams.

27. What interface must an object implement before it can be written to a stream as an object?

Answer: An object must implement the Serializable or Externalizable interface before it can be written to a stream as an object.

28. What is the difference between Serializalble and Externalizable interface? How can you control over the serialization process i.e. how can you customize the seralization process?

Answer: When you use Serializable interface, your class is serialized automatically by default. But you can override writeObject() and readObject() two methods to control more complex object serailization process. When you use Externalizable interface, you have a complete control over your class's serialization process. This interface contains two methods namely readExternal and writeExternal. You shquld implement these methods and write the logic for customizing the serialization process.

29. How to make a class or a bean serializable? How do I serialize an object to a file?

Or

What interface must an object implement before it can be written to a stream as an object?

Answer: An object must implement the Serializable or Externalizable interface before it can be written to a stream as an object. The class whose instances are to be serialized should implement an interface Serializable. Then you pass the instance to the ObjectOutputStream which is connected to a fileoutputstream. This will save the object to a file.

30. What happens to the object references included in the object?

Answer: The serialization mechanism generates an object graph for serialization. Thus it determines whether the included object references are serializable or not. This is a recursive process. Thus when an object is serialized, all the included objects are also serialized along with the original object.

31. What is serialization?

Answer: The serialization is a kind of mechanism that makes a class or a bean persistent by having its properties or fields and state information saved and restored to and from storage. That is, it is a mechanism with which you can save the state of an object by converting it to a byte stream.

Common Usage of serialization.

Whenever an object is to be sent over the network or saved in a file, objects are serialized.

32. What happens to the static fields of a class during serialization?

Answer: There are three exceptions in which serialization doesn't necessarily read and write to the stream.

These are

1. Serialization ignores static fields, because they are not part of any particular state.
2. Base class fields are only handled if the base class itself is serializable.
3. Transient fields.

33. What one should take care of while serializing the object?

Answer: One should make sure that all the included objects are also serializable. If any of the objects is not serializable then it throws a NotSerializableException.

34. What is a transient variable?

Or

Explain the usage of the keyword transient?

Or

What are Transient and Volatile Modifiers

Answer: A **transient variable** is a variable that may not be serialized i.e. the value of the variable can't be written to the stream in a Serializable class. If you don't want some field to be serialized, you can mark that field transient or static. In such a case when the class is retrieved from the ObjectStream the value of the variable is null. **Volatile modifier** applies to variables only and it tells the compiler that the variable modified by volatile can be changed unexpectedly by other parts of the program.

35. What is Externalizable?

Answer: Externalizable is an interface which contains two methods readExternal() and writeExternal(). These methods give you a control over the serialization mechanism. Thus if your class implements this interface, you can customize the serialization process by implementing these methods.

36. What happens to the static fields of a class during serialization?

Answer: There are three exceptions in which serialization does not necessarily read and write to the stream. These are

1. Serialization ignores static fields, because they are not part of any particular state.
2. Base class fields are only handled if the base class itself is serializable.
3. Transient fields.

9

Abstract Windows Toolkit (AWT)

1. **What is meant by controls and what are different types of controls in AWT?**

   Answer: Controls are components that allow a user to interact with your application and the AWT supports the following types of controls:

   Labels, Push Buttons, Check Boxes, Choice Lists, Lists, Scrollbars, Text Components.

   These controls are subclasses of Component.

2. **What is the difference between choice and list?**

   Answer: A Choice is displayed in a compact form that requires you to pull it down to see the list of available choices and only one item may be selected from a choice.

   A List may be displayed in such a way that several list items are visible and it supports the selection of one or more list items.

3. **What is the difference between scrollbar and scrollpane?**

   Answer: A Scrollbar is a Component, but not a Container whereas Scrollpane is a Conatiner and handles its own events and perform its own scrolling.

4. **What is a layout manager and what are different types of layout managers available in java.awt?**

   Answer: A layout manager is an object that is used to organize components in a container. The different layouts are available are FlowLayout, BorderLayout, CardLayout, GridLayout and GridBagLayout.

5. **How are the elements of different layouts organized?**

   Answer: **FlowLayout:** The elements of a FlowLayout are organized in a top to bottom, left to right fashion.

   BorderLayout: The elements of a BorderLayout are organized at the borders (North, South, East and West)and the center of a container.

CardLayout: The elements of a CardLayout are stacked, on top of the other, like a deck of cards.

GridLayout: The elements of a GridLayout are of equal size and are laid out using the square of a grid.

GridBagLayout: The elements of a GridBagLayout are organized according to a grid.

However, the elements are of different size and may occupy more than one row or column of the grid. In addition, the rows and columns may have different sizes.

6. Which containers use a Border layout as their default layout?

Answer: Window, Frame and Dialog classes use a BorderLayout as their layout.

7. Which containers use a Flow layout as their default layout?

Answer: Panel and Applet classes use the FlowLayout as their default layout.

8. Why the container does not support multiple layout managers?

Answer: because when u r using a particular layout manager it use full frame for work you can use grid bag layout for this purpose.

9. What is clipping?

Answer: Clipping is the process of confining paint operations to a limited area or shape.

10. What is meant by controls and what are different types of controls in AWT?

Answer: Controls are components that allow a user to interact with your application and the AWT supports the following types of controls:

Labels, Push Buttons, Check Boxes, Choice Lists, Lists, Scrollbars, Text Components.

These controls are subclasses of Component.

11. What is the difference between choice and list?

Answer: A Choice is displayed in a compact form that requires you to pull it down to see the list of available choices and only one item may be selected from a choice.

A List may be displayed in such a way that several list items are visible and it supports the selection of one or more list items.

12. What is the difference between scrollbar and scrollpane?

Answer: A Scrollbar is a Component, but not a Container whereas Scrollpane is a Conatiner and handles its own events and perform its own scrolling.

13. What is a layout manager and what are different types of layout managers available in java.awt?

Answer: A layout manager is an object that is used to organize components in a container. The different layouts are available are FlowLayout, BorderLayout, CardLayout, GridLayout and GridBagLayout.

14. What is a Layout Manager and what are the different Layout Managers available in java.awt and what is the default Layout manager for the panel and the panel subclasses?

Answer: A layout Manager is an object that is used to organize components in a container. The different layouts available in java.awt are:

- FlowLayout: The elements of a FlowLayout are organized in a top to bottom, left to right fashion.
- BorderLayout: The elements of a BorderLayout are organized at the borders (North, South, East and West) and the center of a container.
- CardLayout: The elements of a CardLayout are stacked, one on top of the other, like a deck of cards.
- GridLayout: The elements of a GridLayout are of equal size and are laid out using the square of a grid.
- GridBagLayout:

The elements of a GridBagLayout are organized according to a grid. However, the elements are of different sizes and may occupy more than one row or column of the grid. In addition, the rows and columns may have different sizes.

The default Layout Manager of Panel and Panel sub classes is FlowLayout.

15. Which containers use a Border layout as their default layout?

Answer: Window, Frame and Dialog classes use a BorderLayout as their layout.

16. Which containers use a Flow layout as their default layout?

Answer: Panel and Applet classes use the FlowLayout as their default layout.

17. Assume that g is an object belonging to the Graphics class. What image would be produced by the following commands? Draw a picture as part of your answer.

```
g.setColor(Color.gray);
g.fillRect(0,0,40,40);
g.fillRect(50,50,0,0);
g.setColor(Color.black);
g.fillOval(50,0,40,40);
g.fillOval(0,50,40,40);
```

Answer: The method "g.fillRect(x,y,w,h)" draws a solid rectangle with its upper left corner at the point (x,y). The other two parameters, w and h, give the width and height of the rectangle. In the second line "g.fillRect(50,50,0,0)" doesn't produce any image at all, since the width and height are specified as zero. The method "g.fillOval(x,y,w,h)" draws a solid oval that just fits inside the rectangle with upper left corner at (x,y) and with width w and height h. So, the picture produced contains one gray square and two black circles, arranged like this:
(Note: I actually meant the second line to be "g.fillRect(50,50,40,40)." Without this typo, the picture would have another gray square.)

18. What is the use of the window class?

Answer: The window class can be used to create a plain, bare bones window that does not have a border or menu. The Window class can also be used to display introduction or welcome screens.

19. What are the benefits of Swing over AWT?

Answer: Swing components are light weight. We can have a pluggable look & feel feature which shows us how they appear in other platforms. We can add images to Swing components. We have tool bars and tooltips in Swing.

20. Where the CardLayout is used?

Answer: Card Layout is used where we need to have a bunch of panel or frames one laying over another. It is replaced by TabbedPane in Swing.

21. What is the difference between Grid and GridbagLayout ?

Answer: In Grid layout the size of each grid is constant where as in GridbagLayout grid size can Vareid.

22. How will you add panel to a Frame?

Answer: Frame.add(panel,BorderLayout.NORTH) or Frame.add(panel,"North").

23. What is the use of the window class?

Answer: The window class can be used to create a plain, bare bones window that does not have a border or menu. The Window class can also be used to display introduction or welcome screens.

24. What is the difference between a Window and a Frame?

Answer: The Frame class extends Window to define a main application window that can have a menu bar.

25. What is the difference between the Font and FontMetrics classes?

Answer: The FontMetrics class is used to define implementation-specific properties, such as ascent and descent, of a Font object.

26. For which statements does it make sense to use a label?

Answer: The only statements for which it makes sense to use a label are those statements that can enclose a break or continue statement.

27. Which TextComponent method is used to set a TextComponent to the read-only state?

Answer: setEditable()

28. How are the elements of a CardLayout organized?

Answer: The elements of a CardLayout are stacked, one on top of the other, like a deck of cards.

29. What advantage do Java's layout managers provide over traditional windowing systems?

Answer: Java uses layout managers to lay out components in a consistent manner across all windowing platforms. Since Java's layout managers aren't tied to absolute sizing and positioning, they are able to accommodate platform-specific differences among windowing systems.

30. What is the difference between the paint() and repaint() methods?

Answer: The paint() method supports painting via a Graphics object. The repaint() method is used to cause paint() to be invoked by the AWT painting thread.

31. Which class is the immediate superclass of the Container class?

Answer: Component

32. How can the Checkbox class be used to create a radio button?

Answer: By associating Checkbox objects with a CheckboxGroup.

33. Name four Container classes.

Answer: Window, Frame, Dialog, FileDialog, Panel, Applet, or ScrollPane

34. What Checkbox method allows you to tell if a Checkbox is checked?

Answer: getState()

35. How are the elements of a GridLayout organized?

Answer: The elements of a GridBad layout are of equal size and are laid out using the squares of a grid.

36. Which Component subclass is used for drawing and painting?

Answer: Canvas

37. What are the problems faced by Java programmers who don't use layout managers?

Answer: Without layout managers, Java programmers are faced with determining how their GUI will be displayed across multiple windowing systems and finding a common sizing and positioning that will work within the constraints imposed by each windowing system.

38. What is Double Buffering?

Answer: Double Buffering is a technique used to achieve smooth animations in Canvases or Panels. It is memory and CPU consuming but is unavoidable as soon as you want to animate something. This technique is not applicable for native components like Buttons, Lists, etc... Since the redisplay is handled by the underlying toolkits (Motif or MsWin).

To handle double buffering, one must first draw the widget's contents in an off-screen image and then transfer the contents of the image to the visible window.

```
class DoubleBufferedCanvas extends Canvas {

    public void update(Graphics g) {
     Graphics offgc;
     Image offscreen = null;
     Dimension d = size();

     // create the offscreen buffer and associated Graphics
     offscreen = createImage(d.width, d.height);
     offgc = offscreen.getGraphics();
     // clear the exposed area
     offgc.setColor(getBackground());
     offgc.fillRect(0, 0, d.width, d.height);
     offgc.setColor(getForeground());
     // do normal redraw
     paint(offgc);
     // transfer offscreen to window
     g.drawImage(offscreen, 0, 0, this);
    }
}
```

This method has one major drawback: it copies the whole buffer each time an update is required. This may consume a lot of time and CPU for a large window

Hopefully, a graphics contains a definition of the area that has to be redrawn: it is called **clip region**. The region, in Java Graphics has two meanings:

1. It tells which part needs to be drawn
2. It clips drawing orders inside this area that means if you draw outside the clip region, nothing will appear.

Using clip regions, we can define an optimized version of the DoubleBufferedCanvas:

```
class OptimizedDoubleBufferedCanvas extends Canvas {

    public void update(Graphics g) {
     Graphics offgc;
     Image offscreen = null;
     Rectangle box = g.getClipRect();

     // create the offscreen buffer and associated Graphics
     offscreen = createImage(box.width, box.height);
     offgc = offscreen.getGraphics();
     // clear the exposed area
     offgc.setColor(getBackground());
     offgc.fillRect(0, 0, box.width, box.height);
     offgc.setColor(getForeground());
     // do normal redraw
     offgc.translate(-box.x, -box.y);
     paint(offgc);
     // transfer offscreen to window
     g.drawImage(offscreen, box.x, box.y, this);
    }
}
```

39. What is the preferred size of a component?

Answer: The preferred size of a component is the minimum component size that will allow the component to display normally.

40. What method is used to specify a container's layout?

Answer: The setLayout() method is used to specify a container's layout.

41. Which containers use a FlowLayout as their default layout?

Answer: The Panel and Applet classes use the FlowLayout as their default layout.

42. Name Component subclasses that support painting.

Answer: The Canvas, Frame, Panel, and Applet classes support painting.

43. Can an anonymous class be declared as implementing an interface and extending a class?

Answer: An anonymous class may implement an interface or extend a superclass, but may not be declared to do both.

44. Which Container method is used to cause a container to be laid out and redisplayed?

Answer: validate()

45. What is the difference between a Window and a Frame?

Answer: The Frame class extends Window to define a main application window that can have a menu bar.

46. What do heavy weight components mean?

Answer: Heavy weight components like Abstract Window Toolkit (AWT), depend on the local windowing toolkit. For example, java.awt.Button is a heavy weight component, when it is running on the Java platform for Unix platform, it maps to a real Motif button. In this relationship, the Motif button is called the peer to the java.awt.Button. If you create two Buttons, two peers and hence two Motif Buttons are also created. The Java platform communicates with the Motif Buttons using the Java Native Interface. For each and every component added to the application, there is an additional overhead tied to the local windowing system, which is why these components are called heavy weight.

47. How are the elements of a GridBagLayout organized?

Answer: The elements of a GridBagLayout are organized according to a grid. However, the elements are of different sizes and may occupy more than one row or column of the grid. In addition, the rows and columns may have different sizes.

48. What advantage do Java's layout managers provide over traditional windowing systems?

Answer: Java uses layout managers to lay out components in a consistent manner across all windowing platforms. Since Java's layout managers aren't tied to absolute sizing and positioning, they are able to accommodate platform-specific differences among windowing systems

49. What is the difference between the paint() and repaint() methods?

Answer: The paint() method supports painting via a Graphics object. The repaint() method is used to cause paint() to be invoked by the AWT painting thread.

50. Name Container classes.

Answer: Window, Frame, Dialog, FileDialog, Panel, Applet, or ScrollPane

51. What is the difference between a Scrollbar and a ScrollPane?

Answer: A Scrollbar is a Component, but not a Container. A ScrollPane is a Container. A ScrollPane handles its own events and performs its own scrolling.

52. What is a Container in a GUI?

Answer: A Container contains and arranges other components (including other containers) through the use of layout managers, which use specific layout policies to determine where components should go as a function of the size of the container.

53. How to add menushortcut to menu item?

Answer: If you have a button instance called aboutButton, you may add menu short cut by calling aboutButton.setMnemonic('A'), so the user may be able to use Alt+A to click the button.

54. What is the difference between Swing and AWT components?

Answer: AWT components are heavy-weight, whereas Swing components are lightweight. Heavy weight components depend on the local windowing toolkit. For example, java.awt.Button is a heavy weight component, when it is running on the Java platform for Unix platform, it maps to a real Motif button.

55. What is meant by Controls and what are different types of controls?

Answer: Controls are components that allow a user to interact with your application. The AWT supports the following types of controls:

Labels, Push buttons, Check boxes, Choice lists, Lists, Scroll bars, Text components These controls are subclasses of Component.

56. How can we get all public methods of an object dynamically?

Answer: By using

getMethods(): It return an array of method objects corresponding to the public methods of this class.

getFields(): It returns an array of Filed objects corresponding to the public Fields(variables) of this class.

getConstructors(): It returns an array of constructor objects corresponding to the public constructors of this class.

57. What are the SubClass of Textcomponent Class?

Answer: TextField and TextArea

58. Which method of the component class is used to set the position and the size of a component?

Answer: setBounds()

59. Which TextComponent method is used to set a TextComponent to the read-only state?

Answer: setEditable()

60. How can the Checkbox class be used to create a radio button?

Answer: By associating Checkbox objects with a CheckboxGroup.

61. What Checkbox method allows you to tell if a Checkbox is checked?

Answer: getState()

62. Which Component method is used to access a component's immediate Container?

Answer: getParent()

63. What methods are used to get and set the text label displayed by a Button object?

Answer: getLabel( ) and setLabel( )

64. What is the difference between a Choice and a List?

Answer: **A Choice** is displayed in a compact form that requires you to pull it down to see the list of available choices. Only one item may be selected from a Choice.

A List may be displayed in such a way that several List items are visible. A List supports the selection of one or more List items.

65. Which Container method is used to cause a container to be laid out and redisplayed?

Answer: validate( )

66. What is the difference between a Scollbar and a Scrollpane?

Answer: A Scrollbar is a Component, but not a Container.

A Scrollpane is a Container and handles its own events and performs its own scrolling.

67. Which Component subclass is used for drawing and painting?

Answer: Canvas.

68. Which method is used to set the text of a Label object?

Answer: setText( )

69. Which method will cause a Frame to be displayed?

Answer:

a). show( )

b). setVisible( )

70. All the componenet classes and container classes are derived from ________ class.

Answer: Object.

71. Which method of the container class can be used to add components to a Panel?

Answer: add ( ) method.

72. What are the subclasses of the Container class?

Answer: The Container class has three major subclasses. They are:
Window, Panel, ScrollPane

73. Can the Choice component allow multiple selection.

Answer: No

74. Which components are used to get text input from the user.

Answer: TextField and TextArea.

75. Which object is needed to group Checkboxes to make them exclusive?

Answer: CheckboxGroup.

76. What are the types of Checkboxes and what is the difference between them?

Answer: Java supports two types of Checkboxes. They are:
Exclusive and Non-exclusive.

In case of exclusive Checkboxes, only one among a group of items can be selected at a time. I f an item from the group is selected, the checkbox currently checked is deselected and the new selection is highlighted. The exclusive Checkboxes are also called as Radio buttons.

The non-exclusive checkboxes are not grouped together and each one can be selected independent of the other.

77. What is a Layout Manager and what are the different Layout Managers available in java.awt and what is the default Layout manager for the panal and the panal subclasses?

Answer: A layout Manager is an object that is used to organize components in a container.

78. What are the different layouts available in java.awt :

Answer: FlowLayout, BorderLayout, CardLayout, GridLayout, GridBag Layout. The default Layout Manager of Panal and Panal sub classes is FlowLayout".

79. Can I exert control over the size and placement of components in my interface?

Answer: Yes.

80. Can I add the same component to more than one container?

Answer: No. Adding a component to a container automatically removes it from any previous parent (container).

81. How do I specify where a window is to be placed?

Answer: Use setBounds, setSize, or setLocation methods to implement this.

```
setBounds(int x, int y, int width, int height)
setBounds(Rectangle r)
setSize(int width, int height)
setSize(Dimension d)
setLocation(int x, int y)
setLocation(Point p)
```

82. How can we create a borderless window?

Answer: Create an instance of the Window class, give it a size, and show it on the screen.

Ex. Frame obj =......

```
Window WA = new Window(obj);
WA.setLayout(new FlowLayout());
WA.add(new Button("OK"));
WA.getBounds(50,50,200,200);
WA.show();
```

83. Can I create a non-resizable windows? If so, how?

Answer: Yes. By using setResizable() method in class Frame.

84. What is the default Layout Manager for the Window and Window subclasses (Frame,Dialog)?

Answer: BorderLayout().

85. Which containers use a BorderLayout as their default layout?

Answer: The Window, Frame and Dialog classes use a BorderLayout as their default layout.

86. Which containers use a FlowLayout as their default layout?

Answer: The Panel and the Applet classes use the FlowLayout as their default layout.

87. What is the preferred size of a component?

Answer: The preferred size of a component size that will allow the component to display normally.

88. Which method is method to set the layout of a container?

Answer: setLayout( )

89. Which method returns the preferred size of a component?

Answer: getPreferredSize( )

90. Which layout should you use to organize the components of a container in a tabular form?

Answer: GridLayout

91. What are the default layouts for a applet, a frame and a panel?

Answer: For an applet and a panel, Flow layout is the default layout, whereas Border layout is default layout for a frame.

92. How can you change the current layout manager for a container?

Answer: By using setLayout() method.

93. Which is the default layout for Applet?

Answer: The default layout manager for an Applet is FlowLayout, and The FlowLayout manager attempts to honor the preferred size of any components.

94. Which method does display the messages whenever there is an item selection or deselection of the CheckboxMenuItem menu?

Answer: itemStateChanged method.

95. Which is a dual state menu item?

Answer: CheckboxMenuItem.

96. Which container may contain a menu bar?

Answer: Frame

97. What is the difference between a MenuItem and a CheckboxMenuItem?

Answer: The CheckboxMenuItem class extends the MenuItem class to support a menu item that may be checked or unchecked.

98. What is the correct ordering for the import, class and package declarations when found in a single file?

Answer: package, import, class

99. What is the parameter specification for the public static void main method?

Answer:

1) String args []
2) String [] args

100. What is the sweep and paint algorithm?

Answer: The painting algorithm takes as input a source image and a list of brush sizes. sweep algo is that it computes the arrangement of n lines in the plane ... a correct algorithm,

101. What are the component and container classes?

Answer: A component is a graphical object. A few examples of components are: Button, Canvas, Checkbox, Choice etc.

102. Explain the purpose of invalidate and validate methods.

Answer: The invalidate method is called as a side effect of an addition or deleting some component. Calling invalidate() is however the first step of processing a COMPONENT_RESIZED event.

103. What are AWT peers? When are peers created and destroyed?

Answer: A Component is associated with a standard AWT button object, a peer object (hidden button object internal to the native GUI) and an interfacing button object constructed per the native GUI.

104. Show with an example the usage of FileDialog object.

Answer: class FileDialog extends from Dialog class.

It is used to display a dialog window from which the user can select a file.

105. Explain the purposes of component's requestFocus method.

Answer: The purpose of the requestFocus() is to get the focus on the particular component and also on the window that contains the component.

106. Which method of the Component class is used to set the position and size of a component?

Answer: The methods are:

setMaximumSize(Dimension maximumSize)

Sets the maximum size of this component to a constant value.

107. What interface is extended by AWT event listeners?

Answer: The java.util.EventListener interface is extended by all the AWT event listeners.

108. What is paint method? What should we put in paint method? When is it invoked?

Answer: The AWT uses a Callback mechanism for painting which is the same for heavyweight and lightweight components.

109. What is the purpose of repaint method? When should we use repaint method?

Answer: repaint() requests can erase and redraw (update) after a small time delay. When you invoke repaint().

110. Explain the use of update method. When is it invoked?

Answer: An update method is called on calling the repaint method. The default implementation of the update() method clears the screen and calls the paint() method.

111. How does the XOR drawing mode work? What are the properties of XOR drawing?

Answer: setXORMode(Color c1) sets the paint mode of this graphics context to alternate between a graphics context's current color and the new specified color.

112. Explain how to load an image from the net into my applet.

Answer: private ImageIcon image;

inside the init method

image = new ImageIcon(new URL(http://www.xyz.gif));

113. Explain how to load an image from a file in a java application.

Answer: ImageIcon icon = createImageIcon("images/xyz.gif", "text string");

114. What is the difference between a Window and a Frame?

Answer: A frame is a resizable, movable window with title bar and close button. Usually it contains Panels. It's derived from a window and has a borderlayout by default.

115. Explain how to draw text over a background image.

Answer: BufferedImage img = ImageIO.read(new File("xxx")); // xxx is the path

TextOnBackground test = new TextOnBackground(img);

116. Define canvas?

Answer: It is a simple drawing surface which is used for painting images or to perform other graphical operations.

10

Event Handling

1. What are the advantages of the model over the event-inheritance model?

Answer: The event-delegation model has two advantages over the event-inheritance model. They are:

a) It enables event handling by objects other than the ones that generate the events. This allows a clean separation between a component's design and its use.

b) It performs much better in applications where many events are generated. This performance improvement is due to the fact that the event-delegation model does not have to be repeatedly process unhandled events as is the case of the event-inheritance.

2. What is source and listener?

Answer: **Source:** A source is an object that generates an event. This occurs when the internal state of that object changes in some way.

Listener: A listener is an object that is notified when an event occurs. It has two major requirements. First, it must have been registered with one or more sources to receive notifications about specific types of events.

Second, it must implement methods to receive and process these notifications.

3. What is adapter class?

Answer: An adapter class provides an empty implementation of all methods in an event listener interface. Adapter classes are useful when you want to receive and process only some of the events that are handled by a particular event listener interface. You can define a new class to act listener by extending one of the adapter classes and implementing only those events in which you are interested.

For example, the MouseMotionAdapter class has two methods, mouseDragged( )and mouseMoved().

The signatures of these empty are exactly as defined in the MouseMotionListener interface. If you are interested in only mouse drag events, then you could simply extend MouseMotionAdapter and implement mouseDragged( ) .

4. What is an event and what are the models available for event handling?

Answer: An event is an event object that describes a state of change in a source. In other words, event occurs when an action is generated, like pressing button, clicking mouse, selecting a list, etc.

There are two types of models for handling events and they are:

a) event-inheritance model and

b) event-delegation model

5. What are the advantages of the model over the event-inheritance model?

Answer: The event-delegation model has two advantages over the event-inheritance model. They are:

a) It enables event handling by objects other than the ones that generate the events. This allows a clean separation between a component's design and its use.

b) It performs much better in applications where many events are generated. This performance improvement is due to the fact that the event-delegation model does not have to be repeatedly process unhandled events as is the case of the event-inheritance.

6. What is the difference between the JDK 1.02 event model and the event-delegation model introduced with JDK 1.1?

Answer: The JDK 1.02 event model uses an event inheritance or bubbling approach. In this model, components are required to handle their own events. If they do not handle a particular event, the event is inherited by (or bubbled up to) the component's container. The container then either handles the event or it is bubbled up to its container and so on, until the highest-level container has been tried. In the event-delegation model, specific objects are designated as event handlers for GUI components. These objects implement event-listener interfaces. The event-delegation model is more efficient than the event-inheritance model because it eliminates the processing required to support the bubbling of unhandled events.

7. What is the highest-level event class of the event-delegation model?

Answer: The java.util.EventObject class is the highest-level class in the event-delegation class hierarchy.

8. What event results from the clicking of a button?

Answer: The ActionEvent event is generated as the result of the clicking of a button.

9. How can a GUI component handle its own events?

Answer: A component can handle its own events by implementing the required event-listener interface and adding itself as its own event listener.

10. What is the difference between the JDK 1.02 event model and the event-delegation model introduced with JDK 1.1?

Answer: The JDK 1.02 event model uses an event inheritance or bubbling approach. In this model, components are required to handle their own events. If they do not handle a particular event, the event is inherited by (or bubbled up to) the component's container. The container then either handles the event or it is bubbled up to its container and so on, until the highest-level container has been tried. In the event-delegation model, specific objects are designated as event handlers for GUI components. These objects implement event-listener interfaces. The event-delegation model is more efficient than the event-inheritance model because it eliminates the processing required to support the bubbling of unhandled events.

11. What is the purpose of the enableEvents() method?

Answer: The enableEvents() method is used to enable an event for a particular object. Normally, an event is enabled when a listener is added to an object for a particular event. The enableEvents() method is used by objects that handle events by overriding their event-dispatch methods.

12. What interface is extended by AWT event listeners?

Answer: All AWT event listeners extend the java.util.EventListener interface.

13. How can a GUI component handle its own events?

A component can handle its own events by implementing the required event-listener interface and adding itself as its own event listener.

14. What is the purpose of the enableEvents() method?

Answer: The enableEvents() method is used to enable an event for a particular object. Normally, an event is enabled when a listener is added to an object for a particular event. The enableEvents() method is used by objects that handle events by overriding their event-dispatch methods.

11 Java Swing

1. **Why swing is not thread safe?**

   Answer: The Swing API was designed to be powerful, flexible, and easy to use. In particular, we wanted to make it easy for programmers to build new Swing components, whether from scratch or by extending components that we provide.

   For this reason, we do not require Swing components to support access from multiple threads. Instead, we make it easy to send requests to a component so that the requests run on a single thread.

2. **Which package has light weight components?**

   Answer: javax.Swing package. All components in Swing, except JApplet, JDialog, JFrame and JWindow are lightweight components.

3. **What are peerless components?**

   Answer: The peerless components are called light weight components.

4. **What is the difference between the Font and FontMetrics classes?**

   Answer: The FontMetrics class is used to define implementation-specific properties, such as ascent and descent, of a Font object.

5. **What is the difference between Swing and AWT components?**

   Answer: AWT components are heavy-weight, whereas Swing components are lightweight. Hence Swing works faster than AWT. Heavy weight components depend on the local windowing toolkit. For example, java.awt.Button is a heavy weight component. Pluggable look and feel possible using java Swing. Also, we can switch from one look and feel to another at runtime in swing which is not possible in AWT.

6. **Name the containers which use Border Layout as their default layout?**

Answer: window, Frame and Dialog classes.

7. **Name Container classes.**

Answer: Window, Frame, Dialog, FileDialog, Panel, Applet, or ScrollPane

8. **How can a GUI component handle its own events?**

Answer: A component can handle its own events by implementing the required event-listener interface and adding itself as its own event listener.

9. **What is the difference between the paint() and repaint() methods?**

Answer: The paint() method supports painting via a Graphics object. The repaint() method is used to cause paint() to be invoked by the AWT painting thread.

10. **Which package has light weight components?**

Answer: javax.Swing package contains light weight components. All components in Swing, except JApplet, JDialog, JFrame and JWindow are lightweight components.

11. **What are peerless components?**

Answer: The peerless components are called light weight components.

12. **What is a Container in a GUI?**

Answer: A Container contains and arranges other components (including other containers) through the use of layout managers, which use specific layout policies to determine where components should go as a function of the size of the container.

13. **How are the elements of a GridBagLayout organized?**

Or

What is a layout manager and what are different types of layout managers available in java Swing?

Or

How are the elements of different layouts organized?

Answer: A layout manager is an object that is used to organize components in a container. The different layouts available are FlowLayout, BorderLayout, CardLayout, GridLayout and GridBagLayout.

FlowLayout: The elements of a FlowLayout are organized in a top to bottom, left to right fashion.

BorderLayout: The elements of a BorderLayout are organized at the borders (North, South, East and West) and the center of a container.

CardLayout: The elements of a CardLayout are stacked, on top of the other, like a deck of cards.

GridLayout: The elements of a GridLayout are of equal size and are laid out using the square of a grid.

GridBagLayout: The elements of a GridBagLayout are organized according to a grid. However, the elements may be different sizes and may occupy more than one row or column of the grid. In addition, the rows and columns may have different sizes.

14. What advantage do Java's layout managers provide over traditional windowing systems?

Answer: Java uses layout managers to lay out components in a consistent manner across all windowing platforms. Since Java's layout managers aren't tied to absolute sizing and positioning, they are able to accommodate platform-specific differences among windowing systems.

15. What method is used to specify a container's layout?

Answer: The setLayout() method is used to specify a container's layout. For example, setLayout(new FlowLayout()); will be set the layout as FlowLayout.

16. Which Container method is used to cause a container to be laid out and redisplayed?

Answer: validate()

17. Name Component subclasses that support painting.

Answer: The Canvas, Frame, Panel, and Applet classes support painting.

18. What is the purpose of the enableEvents() method?

Answer: The enableEvents() method is used to enable an event for a particular component. Normally, an event is enabled when a listener is added to an object for a particular event. The enableEvents() method is used by objects that handle events by overriding their event-dispatch methods.

19. What is the difference between a Window and a Frame?

Answer: The Frame class extends Window to define a main application window that can have a menu bar.

20. What do heavy weight components mean?

Answer: Heavy weight components like Abstract Window Toolkit (AWT) depend on the local windowing toolkit. For example, java.awt .Button is a heavy weight component.

21. What is the difference between a Scrollbar and a ScrollPane?

Answer: A Scrollbar is just a Component, but not a Container. A ScrollPane is a Container. A ScrollPane handles its own events and performs its own scrolling.

22. What is the preferred size of a component?

Answer: The preferred size of a component is the minimum component size that will allow the component to display normally.

23. Which containers use a FlowLayout as their default layout?

Answer: The Panel and Applet classes use the FlowLayout as their default layout.

24. What is Event-Driven-Thread (EDT) in Swing?

Answer: Event-Driven-Thread or EDT is a special thread in Swing and AWT. Event-Driven Thread is used to draw graphics and listen for events in Swing. You will get a bonus point if you able to highlight that time consuming operations like connecting to database, opening a file or connecting to network should not be done on EDT thread because it could lead to freezing GUI because of blocking and time consuming nature of these operations instead they should be done on separate thread and EDT can just be used to spawn those thread on a button click or mouse click.

25. Does Swing is thread safe? What do you mean by swing is not thread-safe?

Answer: Since Swing components are not thread-safe it means you cannot update these components in any thread other than Event-Driven-Thread. If you do so you will get unexpected behavior. Some time interviewer will also ask what are thread-safe methods in swing which can be safely called from any thread only few like repaint() and revalidate().

26. What are differences between Swing and AWT?

Answer: There is couple of differences between swing and AWT:

1) AWT component are considered to be heavyweight while Swing component are lightweights
2) Swing has plug-gable look and feel.
3) AWT is platform depended same GUI will look different on different platform while Swing is developed in Java and is platform dependent.

27. Why Swing components are called lightweight component?

Answer: AWT components are associated with native screen resource and called heavyweight component while Swing components is uses the screen resource of an ancestor instead of having their own and that's why called lightweight or lighter component.

28. What is difference between invokeAndWait and invokeLater?

Answer: Some time the question is how do you update swing component from a thread other than EDT, for such kind of scenario we use SwingUtilities. invokeAndWait(Runnable r) and SwingUtilities.invokeLetter(Runnable r) though there are quite a few differences between these two, major one is invokeAndWait is a blocking call and wait until GUI updates while invokeLater is a non blocking asynchronous call. In my opinion these question has its own value and every swing developer should be familiar with these questions or concept not just for interview point of view but on application perspective. you can read more on my post How InvokeAndWait and InvokeLater works in Swing

29. Write code for JTable with custom cell editor and custom cell renderer?

Answer: JTable is one of favorite topic of all Swing interviews and most popular questions on swing interviews are from JTable why? Because here interviewer will directly asked you to write code another reason is JTable heavily used in all Electronic TRADING GUI. GUI used for online stock TRADING uses JTable to show data in tabular format so an in depth knowledge of JTable is required to work on ONLINE TRADING GUI developed in Swing. While this question is just an example questions around JTable are mostly centered around updating table, how do you handle large volume of data in table, using customize cell renderer and editor, sorting table data based on any column etc. so just make sure you have done quite a few handsone exercise on JTable before appearing for any java swing interview in IB.

30. Write code to print following layout (mainly focused on GridBag layout)?

Answer: GridBagLayout in swing is most powerful but at same time most complex layout and a clear cut experience and expertise around GridBagLayout is desired for developing Swing GUI for trading systems. No matter whether you are developing GUI for equities trading, futures or OPTIONS TRADING or forex trading you always required GridBagLayout. Swing interview question on GridBagLayout will be mostly on writing code for a particular layout just like an example shown here. In which six buttons A, B, C, D, E and F are organized in certain fashion.

31. How do you handle opening of database, file or network connection on a click of button?

Answer: You should not do this operation in EDT thread instead spawn a new thread from actionListener or button and disable the button until operation gets completed to avoid resubmitting request. Only condition is that your GUI should always be responsive no matter what happens on network connection or database connection because these operations usually take time.

12 Java Applet

1. **What is the difference between applications and applets?**

   Answer:

   a) Application must be run on local machine whereas applet needs no explicit installation on local machine.

   b) Application must be run explicitly within a java-compatible virtual machine whereas applet loads and runs itself automatically in a java-enabled browser.

   d) Application starts execution with its main method whereas applet starts execution with its init method.

   e) Application can run with or without graphical user interface whereas applet must run within a graphical user interface.

2. **How does applet recognize the height and width?**

   Answer: Using getParameters() method.

3. **When do you use codebase in applet?**

   Answer: When the applet class file is not in the same directory, codebase is used.

4. **What is the lifecycle of an applet?**

   Answer: init( ) method - Can be called when an applet is first loaded

   start( ) method - Can be called each time an applet is started

   paint( ) method - Can be called when the applet is minimized or maximized

   stop( ) method - Can be used when the browser moves off the applet's page

   destroy( ) method - Can be called when the browser is finished with the applet

5. **How do you set security in applets?**

   Answer: using setSecurityManager() method

6. **How will you initialize an Applet?**

   Answer: By including the initialization code in the init() method.

7. **What is the order of method invocation in an Applet?**

   Answer: init(), start(), paint(), stop(), destroy(),

8. **When is update method called?**

   Answer: Whenever we minimize, maximize, restart the applet and explicitly calling the repaint() method in the code.

   Repaint() method will implicitly call the update() method.

9. **How will you communicate between two Applets?**

   Answer: By creating URL object, URLConnection object and getting InputStream , OutputStream Using getInputStream(), getOutputStream().

10. **What is an applet?**

    Answer: Applet is a dynamic and interactive program that runs inside a web page displayed by a java capable browser.

11. **How does applet recognize the height and width?**

    Answer:Using getParameters() method.

12. **When do you use codebase in applet?**

    Answer:When the applet class file is not in the same directory, codebase is used.

13. **How do you set security in applets?**

    Answer: using setSecurityManager() method

14. **The definition of an applet named MyApplet would begin with the line**

```
class MyApplet extends Applet {
```

    What is going on here? What is "Applet"? What is the word "extends" doing there?

    Answer: Applet is the name of a class that is a standard part of Java. Here, MyApplet is a new class that is being defined as a subclass of Applet. The word "extends" is used to create subclasses in this way. The class MyApplet inherits everything that is in the class Applet. The rest of the definition of MyApplet will consist of additions and modifications to the stuff that is inherited from Applet.

    (Note: The Applet class is actually defined in the package java.applet, so the above line has to be preceded by "import java.applet.*" or "import java.applet.Applet;" to make the applet class available.)

15. An applet can define a method

public boolean keyDown(Event evt, int key)

What is the purpose of such a method? What is the key parameter for? Why is this method "public"?

Answer: This keyDown method will be called by the "system" when the user presses a key on the keyboard (assuming that the applet has the input focus at that time). You would write such a method to react to the user's keystrokes. The key parameter tells which key the user pressed. This method has to be public since it is called by the system, from outside the class that contains the method.

16. Is it possible to access the network resources through an Applet on the browser?

Answer: There is no way that an applet can access network resources. You have to implement a Java Query Server that will be running on the same machine from where you are receiving your applet (that is Internet Server). Your applet will communicate with that server which will fulfill all the requirement of the applet. You can communicate between applet and Java query server using sockets RMI (preferred, as this will return the whole object).

17. Java applets can be downloaded from anywhere and run on a client`s system. What are the restrictions imposed on Java applets that prevent them from causing system damage or security breaches?

Answer: The restrictions that are there for Java applets are: -

- Applets cannot read or write to the local file system where it is being executed.
- Applets can only communicate back to the server from where it was downloaded by the browser.
- Applets cannot execute any local program on the client`s system.

18. What is the sequence of interpretation, compilation of a java applet?

Answer: A java program is first compiled to bytecode which is stored in a '.class file'. This file is downloaded as an applet to a browser which then interprets it by converting it into machine code appropriate to the hardware platform on which it is running.

19. Is it possible to access the network resources through an Applet on the browser?

Answer: There is no way that an applet can access network resources. You have to implement a Java Query Server that will be running on the same machine from where you are receiving your applet (that is Internet Server). Your applet will communicate with that server which will fulfill all the requirement of the applet. You can communicate between applet and Java query server using sockets RMI (preferred, as this will return the whole object).

20. When we give the resize function within an applet then it does not reflect the changes when we see the applet in the IE. Why does this happen?

Answer: Applets are resized only in appletviewer, not in browsers. Change the applet height/width attributes in the HTML file and refresh IE.

21. What is the relationship between clipping and repainting?

Answer: When a window is repainted by the AWT painting thread, it sets the clipping regions to the area of the window that requires repainting.

22. How do I load a serialized applet?

Answer: Instead of specifying the CODE attribute of an <APPLET> tag, you use the OBJECT attribute, as in:

```
<APPLET
  OBJECT=TheApplet.ser
  WIDTH=300
  HEIGHT=300
>
</APPLET>
```

This allows you to pre-initialize your applet to some saved state, instead of having to reinitialize your applet each time it is loaded.

23. Why does it take so much time to access an Applet having Swing Components the first time?

Answer: Because behind every swing component are many Java objects and resources. This takes time to create them in memory. JDK 1.3 from Sun has some improvements which may lead to faster execution of Swing applications.

24. Which method is called by Applet class to load an image?

Answer: getImage(URL object, filename) is used for this purpose.

13

Collection Framework

1. **What are Collection related features in Java 8?**

   Answer: Java 8 has brought major changes in the Collection API. Some of the changes are:

   - Java Stream API for collection classes for supporting sequential as well as parallel processing
   - Iterable interface is extended with forEach() default method that we can use to iterate over a collection. It is very helpful when used with lambda expressions because it's argument Consumer is a function interface.
   - MiscellaneousCollectionAPIimprovementssuchasforEachRemaining(Consumer action) method inIterator interface, Map replaceAll(), compute(), merge() methods.

2. **What is Java Collections Framework? List out some benefits of Collections framework?**

   Answer: Collections are used in every programming language and initial java release contained few classes for collections: Vector, Stack, Hashtable, Array. But looking at the larger scope and usage, Java 1.2 came up with Collections Framework that group all the collections interfaces, implementations and algorithms.

   Java Collections have come through a long way with usage of Generics and Concurrent Collection classes for thread-safe operations. It also includes blocking interfaces and their implementations in java concurrent package.

   Some of the benefits of collections framework are;

   - Reduced development effort by using core collection classes rather than implementing our own collection classes.
   - Code quality is enhanced with the use of well tested collections framework classes.

- Reduced effort for code maintenance by using collection classes shipped with JDK.
- Reusability and Interoperability

3. What is the benefit of Generics in Collections Framework?

Answer: Java 1.5 came with Generics and all collection interfaces and implementations use it heavily. Generics allow us to provide the type of Object that a collection can contain, so if you try to add any element of other type it throws compile time error.

This avoids ClassCastException at Runtime because you will get the error at compilation. Also Generics make code clean since we don't need to use casting and instanceof operator. I would highly recommend to go through Java Generic Tutorial to understand generics in a better way.

4. What are the basic interfaces of Java Collections Framework?

Answer: Collection is the root of the collection hierarchy. A collection represents a group of objects known as its elements. The Java platform doesn't provide any direct implementations of this interface.

Set is a collection that cannot contain duplicate elements. This interface models the mathematical set abstraction and is used to represent sets, such as the deck of cards.

List is an ordered collection and can contain duplicate elements. You can access any element from it's index. List is more like array with dynamic length.

A Map is an object that maps keys to values. A map cannot contain duplicate keys: Each key can map to at most one value.

Some other interfaces are Queue, Dequeue, Iterator, SortedSet, SortedMap and ListIterator.

5. Why Collection doesn't extend Cloneable and Serializable interfaces?

Answer: Collection interface specifies group of Objects known as elements. How the elements are maintained is left up to the concrete implementations of Collection. For example, some Collection implementations like List allow duplicate elements whereas other implementations like Set don't.

A lot of the Collection implementations have a public clone method. However, it does't really make sense to include it in all implementations of Collection. This is because Collection is an abstract representation.

6. What matters is the implementation.

Answer: The semantics and the implications of either cloning or serializing come into play when dealing with the actual implementation; so concrete implementation should decide how it should be cloned or serialized, or even if it can be cloned or serialized.

So mandating cloning and serialization in all implementations is actually less flexible and more restrictive. The specific implementation should make the decision as to whether it can be cloned or serialized.

7. Why Map interface doesn't extend Collection interface?

Answer: Although Map interface and it's implementations are part of Collections Framework, Map are not collections and collections are not Map. Hence it doesn't make sense for Map to extend Collection or vice versa.

If Map extends Collection interface, then where are the elements? Map contains key-value pairs and it provides methods to retrieve list of Keys or values as Collection but it doesn't fit into the "group of elements" paradigm.

8. What is an Iterator?

Answer: Iterator interface provides methods to iterate over any Collection. We can get iterator instance from a Collection using iterator() method. Iterator takes the place of Enumeration in the Java Collections Framework. Iterators allow the caller to remove elements from the underlying collection during the iteration. Java Collection iterator provides a generic way for traversal through the elements of a collection and implements Iterator Design Pattern.

9. How do you traverse through a collection using its Iterator?

Answer: To use an iterator to traverse through the contents of a collection, follow these steps:

- Obtain an iterator to the start of the collection by calling the collections iterator() method.
- Set up a loop that makes a call to hasNext(). Have the loop iterate as long as hasNext() returns true.
- Within the loop, obtain each element by calling next().

10. How do you remove elements during Iteration?

Answer:

- Iterator also has a method remove() when remove is called, the current element in the iteration is deleted.

11. What is difference between Enumeration and Iterator interface?

Answer: Enumeration is twice as fast as Iterator and uses very less memory. Enumeration is very basic and fits to basic needs. But Iterator is much safer as compared to Enumeration because it always denies other threads to modify the collection object which is being iterated by it.

Iterator takes the place of Enumeration in the Java Collections Framework. Iterators allow the caller to remove elements from the underlying collection that is not possible with Enumeration. Iterator method names have been improved to make it's functionality clear.

12. Why there is not method like Iterator.add() to add elements to the collection?

Answer: The semantics are unclear, given that the contract for Iterator makes no guarantees about the order of iteration. Note, however, that ListIterator does provide an add operation, as it does guarantee the order of the iteration.

13. Why Iterator doesn't have a method to get next element directly without moving the cursor?

Answer: It can be implemented on top of current Iterator interface but since its use will be rare, it doesn't make sense to include it in the interface that everyone has to implement.

14. What is different between Iterator and ListIterator?

Answer:

- We can use Iterator to traverse Set and List collections whereas ListIterator can be used with Lists only.
- Iterator can traverse in forward direction only whereas ListIterator can be used to traverse in both the directions.
- ListIterator inherits from Iterator interface and comes with extra functionalities like adding an element, replacing an element, getting index position for previous and next elements.

15. What are different ways to iterate over a list?

Answer: We can iterate over a list in two different ways – using iterator and using for-each loop.

```
List&lt;String&gt; strList = new ArrayList&lt;&gt;();
//using for-each loop
for(String obj : strList){
System.out.println(obj);
}
//using iterator
Iterator&lt;String&gt; it = strList.iterator();
while(it.hasNext()){
    String obj = it.next();
    System.out.println(obj);
}
```

Using iterator is more thread-safe because it makes sure that if underlying list elements are modified, it will throw ConcurrentModificationException.

16. What do you understand by iterator fail-fast property?

Answer: Iterator fail-fast property checks for any modification in the structure of the underlying collection everytime we try to get the next element. If there are any modifications found, it throwsConcurrentModificationException. All the implementations of Iterator in Collection classes are fail-fast by design except the concurrent collection classes like ConcurrentHashMap and CopyOnWriteArrayList.

17. What is difference between fail-fast and fail-safe?

Answer: Iterator fail-safe property work with the clone of underlying collection, hence it's not affected by any modification in the collection. By design, all the collection classes in java.util package are fail-fast whereas collection classes in java.util.concurrent are fail-safe.

Fail-fast iterators throw ConcurrentModificationException whereas fail-safe iterator never throws ConcurrentModificationException.

18. How to avoid ConcurrentModificationException while iterating a collection?

Answer: We can use concurrent collection classes to avoid ConcurrentModificationException while iterating over a collection, for example CopyOnWriteArrayList instead of ArrayList.

19. Why there are no concrete implementations of Iterator interface?

Answer: Iterator interface declare methods for iterating a collection but it's implementation is responsibility of the Collection implementation classes. Every collection class that returns an iterator for traversing has it's own Iterator implementation nested class.

This allows collection classes to chose whether iterator is fail-fast or fail-safe. For example ArrayList iterator is fail-fast whereas CopyOnWriteArrayList iterator is fail-safe.

20. What is UnsupportedOperationException?

Answer: UnsupportedOperationException is the exception used to indicate that the operation is not supported. It's used extensively in JDK classes, in collections framework java.util.Collections.UnmodifiableCollectionthrows this exception for all add and remove operations.

21. How HashMap works in Java?

Answer: HashMap stores key-value pair in Map.Entry static nested class implementation. HashMap works on hashing algorithm and uses hashCode() and equals() method in put and get methods.

When we call put method by passing key-value pair, HashMap uses Key hashCode() with hashing to find out the index to store the key-value pair. The Entry is stored in the LinkedList, so if there are already existing entry, it uses equals() method to check if the passed key already exists, if yes it overwrites the value else it creates a new entry and store this key-value Entry.

When we call get method by passing Key, again it uses the hashCode() to find the index in the array and then use equals() method to find the correct Entry and return it's value. Below image will explain these details clearly.

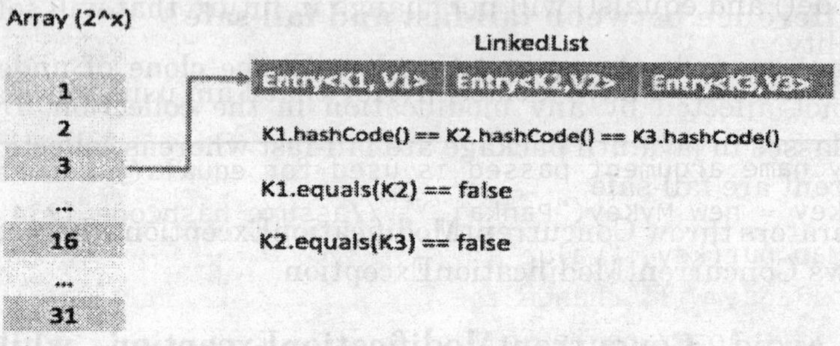

The other important things to know about HashMap are capacity, load factor, threshold resizing. HashMap initial default capacity is 32 and load factor is 0.75. Threshold is capacity multiplied by load factor and whenever we try to add an entry, if map size is greater than threshold, HashMap rehashes the contents of map into a new array with a larger capacity. The capacity is always power of 2, so if you know that you need to store a large number of key-value pairs, for example in caching data from database, it's good idea to initialize the HashMap with correct capacity and load factor.

22. What is the importance of hashCode() and equals() methods?

Answer: HashMap uses Key object hashCode() and equals() method to determine the index to put the key-value pair. These methods are also used when we try to get value from HashMap. If these methods are not implemented correctly, two different Key's might produce same hashCode() and equals() output and in that case rather than storing it at different location, HashMap will consider them same and overwrite them.

Similarly all the collection classes that doesn't store duplicate data use hashCode() and equals() to find duplicates, so it's very important to implement them correctly. The implementation of equals() and hashCode() should follow these rules.

- If o1.equals(o2), then o1.hashCode() == o2.hashCode()should always be true.
- If o1.hashCode() == o2.hashCode is true, it doesn't mean that o1.equals(o2) will be true.

23. Can we use any class as Map key?

Answer: We can use any class as Map Key, however following points should be considered before using them.

- If the class overrides equals() method, it should also override hashCode() method.
- The class should follow the rules associated with equals() and hashCode() for all instances. Please refer earlier question for these rules.
- If a class field is not used in equals(), you should not use it in hashCode() method.
- Best practice for user defined key class is to make it immutable, so that hashCode() value can be cached for fast performance. Also immutable classes make sure that hashCode() and equals() will not change in future that will solve any issue with mutability.

For example, let's say I have a class MyKey that I am using for HashMap key.

```
//MyKey name argument passed is used for equals() and hashCode()
MyKey key = new MyKey("Pankaj"); //assume hashCode=1234
myHashMap.put(key, "Value");
// Below code will change the key hashCode() and equals()
// but it's location is not changed.
key.setName("Amit"); //assume new hashCode=7890
//below will return null, because HashMap will try to look for key
//in the same index as it was stored but since key is mutated,
//there will be no match and it will return null.
myHashMap.get(new MyKey("Pankaj"));
```

- This is the reason why String and Integer are mostly used as HashMap keys.

24. What are different Collection views provided by Map interface?

Answer: Map interface provides three collection views:

- Set keySet(): Returns a Set view of the keys contained in this map. The set is backed by the map, so changes to the map are reflected in the set, and vice-versa. If the map is modified while an iteration over the set is in progress (except through the iterator's own remove operation), the results of the iteration are undefined. The set supports element removal, which removes the corresponding mapping from the map, via the Iterator.remove, Set.remove, removeAll, retainAll, and clear operations. It does not support the add or addAll operations.
- Collection values(): Returns a Collection view of the values contained in this map. The collection is backed by the map, so changes to the map are reflected in the collection, and vice-versa. If the map is modified while an iteration over the collection is in progress (except through the iterator's own remove operation), the results of the iteration are undefined. The collection supports element removal, which removes the corresponding mapping from the map, via the Iterator.remove, Collection.remove, removeAll, retainAll and clear operations. It does not support the add or addAll operations.

- Set<Map.Entry<K, V>> entrySet(): Returns a Set view of the mappings contained in this map. The set is backed by the map, so changes to the map are reflected in the set, and vice-versa. If the map is modified while an iteration over the set is in progress (except through the iterator's own remove operation, or through the setValue operation on a map entry returned by the iterator) the results of the iteration are undefined. The set supports element removal, which removes the corresponding mapping from the map, via the Iterator.remove, Set.remove, removeAll, retainAll and clear operations. It does not support the add or addAll operations.

25. What is the Dictionary class?

Answer: The Dictionary class is an abstract class. The class maps keys to values. The classes such as HashTable are the sub classes of the abstract class Dictionary. The key and values are objects. The key and value are non-null objects.

26. What is the ResourceBundle class?

Answer: A ResourceBundle is a group of related sub classes which are sharing the same base name. For example, ButtonLabel is the base name. All the characters following the base name indicates the following elements respectively.

27. What is the Vector class?

Answer: The Vector class implements an incremental array of objects.

The vector components can be accessed using an integer index.

The size of a Vector increases or decreases as needed to accommodate the items.

28. What is the SimpleTimeZone class?

Answer: SimpleTimeZone is a concrete subclass of TimeZone class. The TimeZone class represents a time zone that is to be used with Gregorian calendar.

29. What is Locale?

Answer: A Locale object represents a specific geographical, political, or cultural region.

30. How will you load a specific locale?

Answer: By ResourceBundle.getBundle(?) method.

31. What is the difference between Comparable and Comparator?

Answer:

No.	Comparable	Comparator
1)	Comparable provides only one sort of sequence.	Comparator provides multiple sorts of sequences.

2)	It provides one method named compareTo().	It provides one method named compare().
3)	It is found in java.lang package.	It is found in java.util package.
4)	If we implement Comparable interface, actual class is modified.	Actual class is not modified.

32. What is the advantage of Properties file?

Answer: If you change the value in properties file, you don't need to recompile the java class. So, it makes the application easy to manage.

33. What does the hashCode() method?

Answer: The hashCode() method returns a hash code value (an integer number). The hashCode() method returns the same integer number, if two keys (by calling equals() method) are same.

But, it is possible that two hash code numbers can have different or same keys.

34. Why we override equals() method?

Answer: The equals() method is used to check whether two objects are same or not. It needs to be overridden if we want to check the objects based on property.

For example, Employee is a class that has 3 data members: id, name and salary. But, we want to check the equality of employee object on the basis of salary. Then, we need to override the equals() method.

35. How to synchronize List, Set and Map elements?

Answer: Yes, Collections class provides methods to make List, Set or Map elements as synchronized:

public static List synchronizedList(List l){}
public static Set synchronizedSet(Set s){}
public static SortedSet synchronizedSortedSet(SortedSet s){}
public static Map synchronizedMap(Map m){}
public static SortedMap synchronizedSortedMap(SortedMap m){}

36. What is the advantage of generic collection?

Answer: If we use generic class, we don't need typecasting. It is typesafe and checked at compile time.

37. What is hash-collision in Hashtable and how it is handled in Java?

Answer: Two different keys with the same hash value is known as hash-collision. Two different entries will be kept in a single hash bucket to avoid the collision.

38. What is the Dictionary class?

Answer: The Dictionary class provides the capability to store key-value pairs.

39. What is the default size of load factor in hashing based collection?

Answer: The default size of load factor is 0.75. The default capacity is computed as initial capacity * load factor. **For example,** 16 * 0.75 = 12. So, 12 is the default capacity of Map.

40. Which package is used for pattern matching with regular expressions?

Answer: java.util.regex package is used for this purpose.

41. java.util.regex consists of which classes?

Answer: java.util.regex consists of three classes: Pattern class, Matcher class and PatternSyntaxException class.

42. What is the use of the 'SimpleDateFormat' and how can you use it to display the current system date in 'yyyy/MM/DD HH:mm:ss' format?

Answer: SimpleDateFormat is one such concrete class which is widely used by Java developers for parsing and formatting of dates. This is also used to convert Dates to String and vice-versa.

Literally every Enterprise level Java Application invariably uses the SimpleDateFormat for handling user dates. We of course aren't expecting Java interviewees to be absolutely spectacular with the syntaxes. But a basic know-how of this class is mandatory.

```
public class CurrentSystemDate {
public static void main(String[] args) {
      SimpleDateFormat sysForm = new SimpleDateFormat("yyyy/MM/DD
HH:mm:ss");
      Date curdate= new Date();
      System.out.println(sysForm.format(curdate));
}
}
```

43. What is difference between ArrayList and vector?

Answer:

1) **Synchronization:** ArrayList is not thread-safe whereas Vector is thread-safe. In Vector class each method like add(), get(int i) is surrounded with a synchronized block and thus making Vector class thread-safe.
2) **Data growth:** Internally, both the ArrayList and Vector hold onto their contents using an Array. When an element is inserted into an ArrayList or a

Vector, the object will need to expand its internal array if it runs out of room. A Vector defaults to doubling the size of its array, while the ArrayList increases its array size by 50 percent.

44. How can Arraylist be synchronized without using Vector?

Answer: Arraylist can be synchronized using:

Collection.synchronizedList(List list)

Other collections can be synchronized:

Collection.synchronizedMap(Map map)

Collection.synchronizedCollection(Collection c)

45. If an Employee class is present and its objects are added in an arrayList. Now I want the list to be sorted on the basis of the employeeID of Employee class. What are the steps?

Answer:

1) Implement Comparable interface for the Employee class and override the compareTo(Object obj) method in which compare the employeeID
2) Now call Collections.sort() method and pass list as an argument.

Now consider that Employee class is a jar file.

1) Since Comparable interface cannot be implemented, create Comparator and override the compare(Object obj, Object obj1) method .
2) Call Collections.sort() on the list and pass comparator as an argument.

46. What is difference between HashMap and HashTable?

Answer: Both collections implements Map. Both collections store value as key-value pairs. The key differences between the two are

1. Hashmap is not synchronized in nature but hshtable is.
2. Another difference is that iterator in the HashMap is fail-safe while the enumerator for the Hashtable isn't.

Fail-safe - if the Hashtable is structurally modified at any time after the iterator is created, in any way except through the iterator›s own remove method, the iterator will throw a ConcurrentModificationException?

3. HashMap permits null values and only one null key, while Hashtable doesn't allow key or value as null.

47. What are the classes implementing List interface?

Answer: There are three classes that implement List interface:

1) **ArrayList:** It is a resizable array implementation. The size of the ArrayList can be increased dynamically also operations like add,remove and get can be formed once the object is created. It also ensures that the data is retrieved in the manner it was stored. The ArrayList is not thread-safe.

2) **Vector:** It is thread-safe implementation of ArrayList. The methods are wrapped around a synchronized block.
3) **LinkedList:** The LinkedList also implements Queue interface and provide FIFO(First In First Out) operation for add operation. It is faster if than ArrayList if it performs insertion and deletion of elements from the middle of a list.

48. Which all classes implement Set interface?

Answer: A Set is a collection that contains no duplicate elements. More formally, sets contain no pair of elements e1 and e2 such that e1.equals(e2), and at most one null element. **HashSet, SortedSet and TreeSet** are the commonly used class which implements Set interface.

SortedSet - It is an interface which extends Set. A the name suggest , the interface allows the data to be iterated in the ascending order or sorted on the basis of Comparator or Comparable interface. All elements inserted into the interface must implement Comparable or Comparator interface.

TreeSet - It is the implementation of SortedSet interface. This implementation provides guaranteed log(n) time cost for the basic operations (add, remove and contains). The class is not synchronized.

HashSet: This class implements the Set interface, backed by a hash table (actually a HashMap instance). It makes no guarantees as to the iteration order of the set; in particular, it does not guarantee that the order will remain constant over time. This class permits the null element. This class offers constant time performance for the basic operations (add, remove, contains and size), assuming the hash function disperses the elements properly among the buckets

49. What is difference between List and a Set?

Answer:

1) List can contain duplicate values but Set doesn't allow. Set allows only to unique elements.
2) List allows retrieval of data to be in same order in the way it is inserted but Set doesn't ensures the sequence in which data can be retrieved.(Except HashSet)

50. What is difference between Arrays and ArrayList?

Answer: Arrays are created of fix size whereas ArrayList is of not fix size. It means that once array is declared as :

- int [] intArray= new int[6];
- intArray[7] // will give ArraysOutOfBoundException.
- Also the size of array cannot be incremented or decremented. But with arrayList the size is variable.

- Once the array is created elements cannot be added or deleted from it. But with ArrayList the elements can be added and deleted at runtime.

```
List list = new ArrayList();
list.add(1);
list.add(3);
list.remove(0) // will remove the element from the 1st location.
•    ArrayList is one dimensional but array can be multidimensional.
     int[][][] intArray= new int[3][2][1];  // 3 dimensional array
```

- To create an array the size should be known or initalized to some value. If not initialized carefully there could me memory wastage. But arrayList is all about dynamic creation and there is no wastage of memory.

51. When to use ArrayList or LinkedList?

Answer: Adding new elements is pretty fast for either type of list. For the ArrayList, doing random lookup using "get" is fast, but for LinkedList, it's slow. It's slow because there's no efficient way to index into the middle of a linked list. When removing elements, using ArrayList is slow. This is because all remaining elements in the underlying array of Object instances must be shifted down for each remove operation. But here LinkedList is fast, because deletion can be done simply by changing a couple of links. So an ArrayList works best for cases where you're doing random access on the list, and a LinkedList works better if you're doing a lot of editing in the middle of the list.

52. Consider a scenario. If an ArrayList has to be iterating to read data only, what are the possible ways and which is the fastest?

Answer: It can be done in two ways, using for loop or using iterator of ArrayList. The first option is faster than using iterator. Because value stored in arraylist is indexed access. So while accessing the value is accessed directly as per the index.

53. Now another question with respect to above question is if accessing through iterator is slow then why do we need it and when to use it.

Answer: For loop does not allow the updating in the array (add or remove operation) inside the loop whereas Iterator does. Also Iterator can be used where there is no clue what type of collections will be used because all collections have iterator.

54. Which design pattern Iterator follows?

Answer: It follows Iterator design pattern. Iterator Pattern is a type of behavioral pattern. The Iterator pattern is one, which allows you to navigate through a collection of data using a common interface without knowing about the underlying implementation. Iterator should be implemented as an interface. This allows the user to implement it anyway its easier for him/her to return data. The benefits of Iterator are about their strength to provide a common interface for iterating through collections without bothering about underlying implementation.

Example of Iteration design pattern - Enumeration The class java.util.Enumeration is an example of the Iterator pattern. It represents and abstract means of iterating over a collection of elements in some sequential order without the client having to know the representation of the collection being iterated over. It can be used to provide a uniform interface for traversing collections of all kinds.

55. Is it better to have a HashMap with large number of records or n number of small hashMaps?

Answer: It depends on the different scenario one is working on:

1) If the objects in the hashMap are same then there is no point in having different hashmap as the traverse time in a hashmap is invariant to the size of the Map.
2) If the objects are of different type like one of Person class, other of Animal class etc then also one can have single hashmap but different hashmap would score over it as it would have better readability.

56. Why is it preferred to declare: List<String> list = new ArrayList<String> (); instead of ArrayList<String> = new ArrayList<String>();

Answer: It is preferred because:

1. If later on code needs to be changed from ArrayList to Vector then only at the declaration place we can do that.
2. The most important one – If a function is declared such that it takes list. E.g. void showDetails(List list); When the parameter is declared as List to the function it can be called by passing any subclass of List like ArrayList,Vector,LinkedList making the function more flexible.

57. What is difference between iterator access and index access?

Answer: Index based access allow access of the element directly on the basis of index. The cursor of the datastructure can directly goto the 'n' location and get the element. It does not traverse through n-1 elements.

In Iterator based access, the cursor has to traverse through each element to get the desired element. So to reach the 'n'th element it needs to traverse through n-1 elements.

Insertion, updation or deletion will be faster for iterator based access if the operations are performed on elements present in between the datastructure.

Insertion,updation or deletion will be faster for index based access if the operations are performed on elements present at last of the datastructure.

Traversal or search in index based datastructure is faster.

ArrayList is index access and LinkedList is iterator access.

58. How to sort list in reverse order?

Answer: To sort the elements of the List in the reverse natural order of the strings, get a reverse Comparator from the Collections class with reverseOrder(). Then, pass the reverse Comparator to the sort() method.

```
List list = new ArrayList();
Comparator comp = Collections.reverseOrder();
Collections.sort(list, comp)
```

59. Can a null element added to a Treeset or HashSet?

Answer: A null element can be added only if the set contains one element because when a second element is added then as per set definition a check is made to check duplicate value and comparison with null element will throw NullPointerException. HashSet is based on hashMap and can contain null element.

60. How to sort list of strings - case insensitive?

Answer: Using Collections.sort(list, String.CASE_INSENSITIVE_ORDER);

61. How to make a List (ArrayList, Vector, LinkedList) read only?

Answer: A list implemenation can be made read only using **Collections. unmodifiableList(list)**. This method returns a new list. If a user tries to perform add operation on the new list; UnSupportedOperationException is thrown.

62. What is ConcurrentHashMap?

Answer: A concurrentHashMap is thread-safe implementation of Map interface. In this class put and remove method are synchronized but not get method. This class is different from Hashtable in terms of locking; it means that hashtable use object level lock but this class uses bucket level lock thus having better performance.

63. Which is faster to iterate LinkedHashSet or LinkedList?

Answer: LinkedList.

64. Which data structure HashSet implements

Answer: HashSet implements hashmap internally to store the data. The data passed to hashset is stored as key in hashmap with null as value.

65. Arrange in the order of speed - HashMap,HashTable, Collections. synchronizedMap, concurrentHashmap

Answer: HashMap is fastest, ConcurrentHashMap, Collections.synchronizedMap, HashTable.

66. What is identityHashMap?

Answer: The IdentityHashMap uses == for equality checking instead of equals(). This can be used for both performance reasons, if you know that two different elements will never be equals and for preventing spoofing, where an object tries to imitate another.

67. What is WeakHashMap?

Answer: A hashtable-based Map implementation with weak keys. An entry in a WeakHashMap will automatically be removed when its key is no longer in ordinary use. More precisely, the presence of a mapping for a given key will not prevent the key from being discarded by the garbage collector that is, made finalizable, finalized, and then reclaimed. When a key has been discarded its entry is effectively removed from the map, so this class behaves somewhat differently than other Map implementations.

68. Why Collection interface does not extend Cloneable and Serializable interface?

Answer: There is no need to do it because, extending an interface simply means that you are creating a subtype of interface, in other words a more specialized behavior and Collection interface is not expected to do what Cloneable and Serializable interfaces do.

Another reason is that not everybody will have a reason to have Cloneable collection because if it has very large data, then every **unnecessary clone operation will consume a big memory**. Beginners might use it without knowing the consequences.

Another reason is that **Cloneable and Serializable are very specialized behavior** and so should be implemented only when required. For example, many concrete classes in collection implement these interfaces. So if you want this feature. Use these collection classes otherwise use their alternative classes.

69. Why insertion and deletion in ArrayList is slow compared to LinkedList?

Answer:

- ArrayList internally uses and array to store the elements, when that array gets filled by inserting elements a new array of roughly 1.5 times the size of the original array is created and all the data of old array is copied to new array.
- During deletion, all elements present in the array after the deleted elements have to be moved one step back to fill the space created by deletion. In linked list data is stored in nodes that have reference to the previous node and the next node so adding element is simple as creating the node an updating the next pointer on the last node and the previous pointer on the new node. Deletion in linked list is fast because it involves only updating the next pointer in the node before the deleted node and updating the previous pointer in the node after the deleted node.

70. Difference between String, StringBuffer and StringBuilder?

Answer:

String	StringBuffer	StringBuilder
String is a immutable class	StringBuffer is a mutable class	StringBuilder is a mutable class
New object is created every time when modified	No new object is created, modification is done in existing one	No new object is created, modification is done in existing one
Syntax - String s1="hello";	Syntax - StringBuffer sf=new StringBuffer("hello");	Syntax - StringBuilder sb=new StringBuilder("hello");
-	StringBuffer methods are synchronized.	StringBuilder methods are non-synchronized and added in jdk 5.
Use String if you require immutability	use Stringbuffer in java if you need mutable + thread-safety.	use StringBuilder in Java if you require mutable + without thread-safety..

71. How will you sort a collection of String in case sensitive order?

Answer:

Use Collections.sort(list, String.CASE_INSENSITIVE_ORDER);

Example -

```
public class StringSortExample{
public static void main(String[] args){
            List list = new ArrayList();
            list.add("Shalabh");
            list.add("amit");
            list.add("Lalit");
            display(list);
            Collections.sort(list);
            display(lsit);
            Collections.sort(list, String.CASE_INSENSITIVE_ORDER);
            display(list);
      }
      Public static void display(List list)
      {
  for (String str : list){
                        System.out.print(str + " ");
            }
```

```
    }
  }
```

72. What is difference between poll() and remove() method of Queue interface?

Answer: Though both poll() and remove() method from Queue is used to remove object and returns head of the queue, there is subtle difference between them. If Queue is empty() then a call to remove() method will throw Exception, while a call to poll() method returns null. By the way, exactly which element is removed from the queue depends upon queue's ordering policy and varies between different implementation, for example PriorityQueue keeps lowest element as per Comparator or Comparable at head position.

73. How do you remove an entry from a Collection? and subsequently what is difference between remove() method of Collection and remove() method of Iterator, which one you will use, while removing elements during iteration?

Answer: Collection interface defines remove(Object obj) method to remove objects from Collection. List interface adds another method remove(int index), which is used to remove object at specific index. You can use any of these method to remove an entry from Collection, while not iterating. Things change, when you iterate. Suppose you are traversing a List and removing only certain elements based on logic, then you need to use Iterator's remove() method. This method removes current element from Iterator's perspective. If you use Collection's or List's remove() method during iteration then your code will throw ConcurrentModificationException. That's why it's advised to use Iterator remove() method to remove objects from Collection.

74. What is difference between Synchronized Collection and Concurrent Collection?

Answer: Java 5 has added several new Concurrent Collection classes e.g. ConcurrentHashMap, CopyOnWriteArrayList, BlockingQueue etc, which has made Interview questions on Java Collection even trickier. Java Also provided way to get Synchronized copy of collection e.g. ArrayList, HashMap by using Collections. synchronizedMap() Utility function.One Significant difference is that Concurrent Collections has better performance than synchronized Collection because they lock only a portion of Map to achieve concurrency and Synchronization.

75. What do you need to do to use a custom object as key in Collection classes like Map or Set?

Answer: If you are using any custom object in Map as key, you need to override equals() and hashCode() method, and make sure they follow their contract. On the other hand if you are storing a custom object in Sorted Collection e.g. SortedSet or SortedMap, you also need to make sure that your equals() method is consistent to compareTo() method, otherwise those collection will not follow their contacts e.g. Set may allow duplicates.

76. What is NavigableMap in Java ? What is benefit over Map?

Answer: NavigableMap Map was added in Java 1.6, it adds navigation capability to Map data structure. It provides methods like lowerKey() to get keys which is less than specified key, floorKey() to return keys which is less than or equal to specified key, ceilingKey() to get keys which is greater than or equal to specified key and higherKey() to return keys which is greater specified key from a Map. It also provide similar methods to get entries e.g. lowerEntry(), floorEntry(), ceilingEntry() and higherEntry(). Apart from navigation methods, it also provides utilities to create sub-Map e.g. creating a Map from entries of an exsiting Map like tailMap, headMap and subMap. headMap() method returns a NavigableMap whose keys are less than specified, tailMap() returns a NavigableMap whose keys are greater than the specified and subMap() gives a NavigableMap between a range, specified by toKey to fromKey.

77. Which one you will prefer between Array and ArrayList for storing object and why?

Answer: Though ArrayList is also backed up by array, it offers some usability advantage over array in Java. Array is fixed length data structure, once created you cannot change its length. On the other hand, ArrayList is dynamic, it automatically allocate a new array and copies content of old array, when it resize. Another reason of using ArrayList over Array is support of Generics. Array doesn't support Generics, and if you store an Integer object on a String array, you will only going to know about it at runtime, when it throws ArrayStoreException. On the other hand, if you use ArrayList, compiler and IDE will catch that error on the spot. So if you know size in advance and you don't need re-sizing than use array, otherwise use ArrayList.

78. Can we replace Hashtable with ConcurrentHashMap?

Answer: Yes we can replace Hashtable with ConcurrentHashMap and that's what suggested in Java documentation of ConcurrentHashMap. but you need to be careful with code which relies on locking behavior of Hashtable. Since Hashtable locks whole Map instead of portion of Map, compound operations like if(Hashtable.get(key) == null) put(key, value) works in Hashtable but not in concurrentHashMap. Instead of this use putIfAbsent() method of ConcurrentHashMap

79. What is CopyOnWriteArrayList, how it is different than ArrayList and Vector?

Answer: CopyOnWriteArrayList is new List implementation introduced in Java 1.5 which provides better concurrent access than Synchronized List. Better concurrency is achieved by Copying ArrayList over each write and replace with original instead of locking. Also CopyOnWriteArrayList doesn't throw any ConcurrentModification

Exception. Its different than ArrayList because its thread-safe and ArrayList is not thread safe and its different than Vector in terms of Concurrency. CopyOnWriteArrayList provides better Concurrency by reducing contention among readers and writers.

80. Why ListIterator has add() method but Iterator doesn't or Why add() method is declared in ListIterator and not on Iterator.

Answer: ListIterator has add() method because of its ability to traverse or iterate in both direction of collection. it maintains two pointers in terms of previous and next call and in position to add new element without affecting current iteration.

81. When does ConcurrentModificationException occur on iteration?

Answer: When you remove object using Collection's or List's remove method e.g. remove(Object element) or remove(int index), instead of Iterator's remove() method than ConcurrentModificationException occur. As per Iterator's contract, if it detect any structural change in Collection e.g. adding or removing of element, once Iterator begins, it can throw ConcurrentModificationException.

82. Difference between Set, List and Map Collection classes?

Answer: java.util.Set, java.util.List and java.util.Map define three of most popular data structure support in Java. Set provides uniqueness guarantee i.e.g you cannot store duplicate elements on it, but it's not ordered. On the other hand List is an ordered Collection and also allowes duplicates. Map is based on hashing and stores key and value in an Object called entry. It provides O(1) performance to get object, if you know keys, if there is no collision. Popular impelmentation of Set is HashSet, of List are ArrayList and LinkedList, and of Map are HashMap, Hashtable and ConcurrentHashMap. Another key difference between Set, List and Map are that Map doesn't implement Collection interface, while other two does. For a more detailed answer, see Set vs List vs Map in Java.

83. What is BlockingQueue, how it is different than other collection classes?

Answer: BlockingQueue is a Queue implementation available in java.util.concurrent package. It's one of the concurrent Collection class added on Java 1.5, main difference between BlockingQueue and other collection classes is that apart from storage, it also provides flow control. It can be used in inter thread communication and also provides built-in thread-safety by using happens-before guarantee. You can use BlockingQueue to solve Producer Consumer problem, which is what is needed in most of concurrent applications.

14

Java Database Connectivity (JDBC)

1. What is JDBC?

Answer: JDBC is a set of Java API for executing SQL statements. This API consists of a set of classes and interfaces to enable programs to write pure Java Database applications.

JDBC is a layer of abstraction that allows users to choose between databases. It allows you to change to a different database engine and to write to a single API. JDBC allows you to write database applications in Java without having to concern yourself with the underlying details of a particular database.

JDBC standards for Java Data Base Connectivity. It is a specification given by Sun Microsystems and standards followed by X/Open SAG (SQL Access Group) CLI (Call Level Interface) to interact with the DB.

Java programming language methods. The JDBC API provides database-independent connectivity between the JAVA Applications and a wide range of tabular data bases. JDBC technology allows an application component provider to:

- Perform connection and authentication to a database server
- Manage transactions
- Moves SQL statements to a database engine for preprocessing and execution
- Executes stored procedures
- Inspects and modifies the results from SELECT statements

2. What is JDBC? What are its advantages?

Answer: It is an API .The latest version of jdbc api is (3.0).

The JDBC 3.0 API is divided into two packages:

(1) java.sql and (2) javax.sql.

Both packages are included in the J2SE and J2EE platforms.

Advantages:

- The JDBC API can be used to interact with multiple data sources in a distributed, heterogeneous environment.
- It can connect to any of the database from java language.
- It can switch over to any backend database without changing java code or by minute changes.

3. What is JDBC API and when do we use it?

Answer: Java Data Base Connectivity API allows us to work with relational databases. JDBC API interfaces and classes are part of java.sql and javax.sql package. We can use JDBC API to get the database connection, run SQL queries and stored procedures in the database server and process the results.

JDBC API is written in a way to allow loose coupling between our Java program and actual JDBC drivers that makes our life easier in switching from one database to other database servers easily.

4. How many JDBC Drivers are there? What are they?

Answer: There are 4 types of JDBC drivers.

a. JDBC-ODBC Bridge Driver (Type-1 driver)
b. Native API Partly Java Driver (Type-2 driver)
c. Net protocol pure Java Driver (Type-3 driver)
d. Native protocol Pure Java Driver (Type-4 driver)

5. What is the difference between JDBC and ODBC?

Answer:

a) OBDC is for Microsoft and JDBC is for Java applications.
b) ODBC can't be directly used with Java because it uses a C interface.
c) ODBC makes use of pointers which have been removed totally from Java.
d) ODBC mixes simple and advanced features together and has complex options for simple queries. But JDBC is designed to keep things simple while allowing advanced capabilities when required.
e) ODBC requires manual installation of the ODBC driver manager and driver on all client machines. JDBC drivers are written in Java and JDBC code is automatically installable, secure, and portable on all platforms.
f) JDBC API is a natural Java interface and is built on ODBC. JDBC retains some of the basic features of ODBC.

6. What are the types of JDBC Driver Models and explain them?

Answer: There are two types of JDBC Driver Models and they are:

a) Two tier model and b) Three tier model

Two tier models: In this model, Java applications interact directly with the database. A JDBC driver is required to communicate with the particular database management system that is being accessed. SQL statements are sent to the database and the results are given to user. This model is referred to as client/server configuration where user is the client and the machine that has the database is called as the server.

Three tier model: A middle tier is introduced in this model. The functions of this model are:

a) Collection of SQL statements from the client and handing it over to the database,

b) Receiving results from database to the client and

c) Maintaining control over accessing and updating of the above.

7. What are the steps involved for making a connection with a database or how do you connect to a database?

Answer:

a) Loading the driver: To load the driver, Class.forName( ) method is used.

Class.forName("sun.jdbc.odbc.JdbcOdbcDriver");

When the driver is loaded, it registers itself with the java.sql.DriverManager class as an available database driver.

b) Making a connection with database: To open a connection to a given database, DriverManager.getConnection( ) method is used.

Connection con = DriverManager.getConnection ("jdbc:odbc:somedb", "user", "password");

c)Executing SQL statements: To execute a SQL query, java.sql.statements class is used.

createStatement( ) **method of Connection to obtain a new Statement object.**

Statement stmt = con.createStatement( );

A query that returns data can be executed using the executeQuery( ) method of Statement. This method xecutes the statement and returns a java.sql.ResultSet that encapsulates the retrieved data:

ResultSet rs = stmt.executeQuery("SELECT * FROM some table");

d) Process the results : ResultSet returns one row at a time. Next( ) method of ResultSet object can be called to move to the next row. The getString( ) and getObject( ) methods are used for retrieving column values:

```
while (rs.next( ) ) {
    String event = rs.getString("event");
    Object count = (Integer) rs.getObject("count");
}
```

8. What type of driver did you use in project?

Answer: JDBC-ODBC Bridge driver (is a driver that uses native(C language) libraries and makes calls to an existing ODBC driver to access a database engine).

9. What are the types of statements in JDBC?

Answer: **Statement** – To be used createStatement() method for executing single SQL statement.

PreparedStatement – To be used preparedStatement() method for executing same SQL statement over and over.

CallableStatement -- To be used prepareCall( ) method for multiple SQL statements over and over.

10. What is stored procedure?

Answer: Stored procedure is a group of SQL statements that forms a logical unit and performs a particular task.

Stored Procedures are used to encapsulate a set of operations or queries to execute on database. Stored procedures can be compiled and executed with different parameters and results and may have any combination of input/output parameters.

11. How to create and call stored procedures?

Answer: To create stored procedures:

```
Create procedure procedurename (specify in, out and in out parameters)
        BEGIN
        Any multiple SQL statement;
        END;

        To call stored procedures:
        CallableStatement  csmt  = con.prepareCall("{call procedure
name(?,?)}");
        csmt.registerOutParameter(column no., data type);
        csmt.setInt(column no., column name)
csmt.execute( );
```

12. What is connection pooling? Is it advantageous?

Answer: A connection pooling is a methodology of reusing open connections. After finishing of a transaction the connection is not closed, but is put to the pool, and when a user requests a database connection the next time, he gets a pooled connection instead of a newly opened one. This greatly reduces the time to perform single database operations, because of avoiding heavyweight open/close operations. It's recommended to use database connection pooling as widely as possible.

13. What is Connection Pooling?

Answer: Connection pooling is a cache of data base connections that is maintained in memory, so that the connections may be reuse.

Connection pooling is a place where a set of connections are kept and are used by the different programmers without creating connections to the database (it means there is a readymade connection available for the programmers where he can use). After using the connection he can send back that connection to the connection pool. Number of connections in connection pool may vary.

14. How do you implement Connection Pooling?

Answer: Connection Pooling can be implemented by the following way.

- A javax.sql.ConnectionPoolDataSource interface that serves as a resource manager connection factory for pooled java.sql.Connection objects. Each database vendors provide the implementation for that interface.

For example, the oracle vendor's implementation is as follows:

oracle.jdbc.pool.oracleConnectionPoolDataSource Class.

- A javax.sql.PooledConnection interface encapsulates the physical connection for the database. Again, the vendor provides the implementation.

15. What Class.forName( ) method will do?

Answer: Class.forName() is used to load the Driver class which is used to connect the application with Database. Here Driver class is a Java class provided by Database vendor.

16. What is the difference between JDBC 1.0 and JDBC 2.0?

Answer: The JDBC 2.0 API includes many new features in the java.sql package as well as the new Standard Extension package, javax.sql. This new JDBC API moves Java applications into the world of heavy-duty database computing. New features in the java.sql package include support for SQL3 data types, scrollable result sets, programmatic updates, and batch updates. The new JDBC Standard Extension API, an integral part of Enterprise JavaBeans (EJB) technology, allows you to write distributed transactions that use connection pooling, and it also makes it possible to connect to virtually any tabular data source, including files and spread sheets.

The JDBC 2.0 API includes many new features like

1. Scrollable result sets
2. Batch updates
3. Connection Pooling
4. Distributed transactions
5. set autocomit ( )

17. Which methods and classes are used for connection pooling?

Answer: JDBC provides an interface, which must be implemented by a JDBC driver supporting connection pooling. This interface is called ConnectionPoolDataSource. Most existing JDBC drivers (DataSource instances) implement this interface. It provides the following methods for obtaining PooledConnections:

PooledConnection getPooledConnection () throws SQLException;

PooledConnection getPooledConnection (String user, String password) throws SQLException;

Such connections can be closed by issuing connection.close(), but it's only a logical closing, not physical. Physically, no connection is closed, it's just returned to the pool.

18. What are the two major components of JDBC?

Answer: One implementation interface for database manufacturers, the other implementation interface for application and applet writers.

19. What is JDBC Driver interface?

Answer: The JDBC Driver interface provides vendor-specific implementations of the abstract classes provided by the JDBC API. Each vendor's driver must provide implementations of the java.sql.Connection, Statement, PreparedStatement, CallableStatement, ResultSet and Driver.

20. What are the common tasks of JDBC?

Answer:

- Create an instance of a JDBC driver or load JDBC drivers through jdbc.drivers
- Register a driver
- Specify a database
- Open a database connection
- Submit a query
- Receive results

21. What packages are used by JDBC?

Answer: There are 8 packages: java.sql.Driver, Connection,Statement, PreparedStatement, CallableStatement, ResultSet, ResultSetMetaData, DatabaseMetaData.

22. What are the flow statements of JDBC?

Answer: A URL string -->getConnection-->DriverManager-->Driver-->Connection-->Statement-->executeQuery-->ResultSet.

23. What are the steps involved in establishing a connection?

Answer: This involves two steps: (1) loading the driver and (2) making the connection.

24. How can you load the drivers?

Answer: Loading the driver or drivers you want to use is very simple and involves just one line of code. If, for example, you want to use the JDBC-ODBC Bridge driver, the following code will load it:

E.g.

Class.forName("sun.jdbc.odbc.JdbcOdbcDriver");

Your driver documentation will give you the class name to use. For instance, if the class name is jdbc.DriverXYZ, you would load the driver with the following line of code: E.g.

Class.forName("jdbc.DriverXYZ");

25. What Class.forName will do while loading drivers?

Answer: It is used to create an instance of a driver and register it with the DriverManager. When you have loaded a driver, it is available for making a connection with a DBMS.

26. How can you make the connection?

Answer: In establishing a connection is to have the appropriate driver connect to the DBMS. The following line of code illustrates the general idea:

E.g.

String url = "jdbc:odbc:Fred";

Connection con = DriverManager.getConnection(url, "Fernanda", "J8");

27. How can you create JDBC statements?

Answer: A Statement object is what sends your SQL statement to the DBMS. You simply create a Statement object and then execute it, supplying the appropriate execute method with the SQL statement you want to send. For a SELECT statement, the method to use is executeQuery. For statements that create or modify tables, the method to use is executeUpdate. E.g. It takes an instance of an active connection to create a Statement object. In the following example, we use our Connection object con to create the Statement object stmt:

Statement stmt = con.createStatement();

28. How can you retrieve data from the ResultSet?

Answer: **First:**

JDBC returns results in a ResultSet object, so we need to declare an instance of the class ResultSet to hold our results. The following code demonstrates declaring the ResultSet object rs.

E.g.

ResultSet rs = stmt.executeQuery("SELECT COF_NAME, PRICE FROM COFFEES");

Second:

String s = rs.getString("COF_NAME");

The method getString is invoked on the ResultSet object rs, so getString() will retrieve (get) the value stored in the column COF_NAME in the current row of rs.

29. What are the different types of Statements?

Answer: 1. Statement (use createStatement method) 2. PreparedStatement (Use prepareStatement method) and 3. CallableStatement (Use prepareCall)

30. How can you use PreparedStatement?

Answer: This special type of statement is derived from the more general class, Statement. If you want to execute a Statement object many times, it will normally reduce execution time to use a PreparedStatement object instead. The advantage to this is that in most cases, this SQL statement will be sent to the DBMS right away, where it will be compiled. As a result, the PreparedStatement object contains not just an SQL statement, but an SQL statement that has been precompiled. This means that when the PreparedStatement is executed, the DBMS can just run the PreparedStatement's SQL statement without having to compile it first.

E.g.

PreparedStatement updateSales = con.prepareStatement("UPDATE COFFEES SET SALES = ? WHERE COF_NAME LIKE?");

31. How to call a Stored Procedure from JDBC?

Answer: The first step is to create a CallableStatement object. As with Statement an and PreparedStatement objects, this is done with an open Connection object. A CallableStatement object contains a call to a stored procedure;

E.g.

CallableStatement cs = con.prepareCall("{call SHOW_SUPPLIERS}");

ResultSet rs = cs.executeQuery();

32. How to Retrieve Warnings?

Answer: SQLWarning objects are a subclass of SQLException that deal with database access warnings. Warnings do not stop the execution of an application, as exceptions do; they simply alert the user that something did not happen as planned. A warning can be reported on a Connection object, a Statement object (including PreparedStatement and CallableStatement objects), or a ResultSet object. Each of these classes has a getWarnings method, which you must invoke in order to see the first warning reported on the calling object

E.g.

```
SQLWarning warning = stmt.getWarnings();
if (warning != null) {
```

```
while (warning != null) {
System.out.println("Message: " + warning.getMessage());
System.out.println("SQLState: " + warning.getSQLState());
System.out.print("Vendor error code: ");
System.out.println(warning.getErrorCode());
warning = warning.getNextWarning();
}
}
```

33. How to Make Updates to Updatable Result Sets?

Answer: Another new feature in the JDBC 2.0 API is the ability to update rows in a result set using methods in the Java programming language rather than having to send an SQL command. But before you can take advantage of this capability, you need to create a ResultSet object that is updatable. In order to do this, you supply the ResultSet constant CONCUR_UPDATABLE to the createStatement method. E.g.

*Connect*ion con = DriverManager.getConnection("jdbc:mySubprotocol:mySubName");

Statement stmt = con.createStatement(ResultSet.TYPE_SCROLL_SENSITIVE, ResultSet.CONCUR_UPDATABLE);

ResultSet uprs = ("SELECT COF_NAME, PRICE FROM COFFEES");

34. How to Interact with DB?

Answer: Generally every DB vendor provides a User Interface through which we can easily execute SQL queries and gets the result (For example Oracle Query Manager for Oracle, and TOAD (www.quest.com) tool common to all the databases). And these tools will help DB developers to create database. But as a programmer we want to interact with the DB dynamically to execute some SQL queries from our application (Any application like C, C++, JAVA etc), and for this requirement DB vendors provide some Native Libraries (Vendor Specific) using this we can interact with the DB i.e. If you want to execute some queries on Oracle DB, oracle vendor provides an OCI (Oracle Call Interface) Libraries to perform the same.

35. What for JDBC?

Answer: As we have studied about ODBC and is advantages and came to know that it provides a common API to interact with any DB which has an ODBC Service Provider's Implementation written in Native API that can be used in your applications.

If an application wants to interact with the DB then the options which have been explained up to now in this book are:

1. Using Native Libraries given by the DB vendor
2. Using ODBC API

And we have listed their Advantages and Disadvantages.

But if the application is a JAVA application then the above given options are not recommended to be used due to the following reasons

1. Native Libraries given by DB vendor
   a. Application becomes vendor dependent and
   b. The application has to use JNI to interact with Native Lib which may cause serious problem for Platform Independency in our applications.
2. And the second option given was using ODBC API which can solve the 1.a problem but again this ODBC API is also a Native API, so we have to use JNI in our Java applications which lead to the 1.b described problem.

And the answer for these problems is JDBC (Java Data Base Connectivity) which provides a common Java API to interact with any DB.

36. What is a transaction?

Answer: Transaction is collection of logical operation that performs a task.

Transaction should ACID properties.

A for Atomicity

C for Consistency

I for Isolation

D for Durability.

A transaction can be termed as any operation such as storing, retrieving, updating or deleting records in the table that hits the database.

37. What is the purpose of setAutoCommit( )

Answer: It is set as

ConnectionObject.setAutoComit();

After any updates through the program cannot be affected to the database. We have committed the transactions. For this purpose we can set AutoCommit flag to Connection Object.

38. What is stored procedure? How do you create stored procedure?

Answer: Stored procedures are a group of SQL statements that performs a logical unit and performs a particular task.

Stored procedures are used to encapsulate a set of operations or queries to execute on data.

Stored Procedure is a stored program in database, PL/SQL program is a Stored Procedure. Stored Procedures can be called from java by CallableStatement

A precompiled collection of SQL statements stored under a name and processed as a unit.

Stored procedures can:

1. Accept input parameters and return multiple values in the form of output parameters to the calling procedure or batch.
2. Contain programming statements that perform operations in the database, including calling other procedures.
3. Return a status value to a calling procedure or batch to indicate success or failure (and the reason for failure).

39. What are batch updates?

Answer: Batch Update facility allows multiple update operations to be submitted to a database for processing at once. Using batch updates will improve the performance.

40. What is the difference between Resultset and Rowset

Answer: A RowSet is a disconnected, serializable version of a JDBC ResultSet.

The RowSet is different than other JDBC interfaces in that you can write a RowSet to be vendor neutral. A third party could write a RowSet implementation that could be used with any JDBC-compliant database. The standard implementation supplied by Sun uses a ResultSet to read the rows from a database and then stores those rows as Row objects in a Vector inside the RowSet. In fact, a RowSet implementation could be written to get its data from any source. The only requirement is that the RowSet acts as if it was a ResultSet. Of course, there is no reason that a vendor couldn't write a RowSet implementation that is vendor specific.

The standard implementations have been designed to provide a fairly good range of functionality. The **implementations provided** are:

CachedRowSetImpl - This is the implementation of the RowSet that is closest to the definition of RowSet functionality that we discussed earlier. There are two ways to load this RowSet. The execute ( ) method will load the RowSet using a Connection object. The populate( ) method will load the RowSet from a previously loaded ResultSet.

WebRowSetImpl - This is very similar to the CachedRowSetImpl (it is a child class) but it also includes methods for converting the rows into an XML document and loading the RowSet with an XML document. The XML document can come from any Stream or Reader/Writer object. This could be especially useful for Web Services.

JdbcRowSetImpl - This is a different style of implementation that is probably less useful in normal circumstances. The purpose of this RowSet is to make a ResultSet look like a JavaBean. It is not serializable and it must maintain a connection to the database.

The remaining two implementations are used with the first three implementations:

FilteredRowSetImpl - This is used to filter data from an existing RowSet. The filter will skip records that don't match the criteria specified in the filter when a next() is used on the RowSet.

JoinRowSetImpl - This is used to simulate a SQL join command between two or more RowSet objects.

41. What are the steps for connecting to the database using JDBC

Answer: **Using DriverManager:**

1. Load the driver class using class.forName(driverclass) and Class.forName() loads the driver class and passes the control to DriverManager class
2. DriverManager.getConnection() creates the connection to the database

Using DataSource:

DataSource is used instead of DriverManager in Distributed Environment with the help of JNDI.

1. Use JNDI to lookup the DataSource from Naming service server.

- DataSource.getConnection method will return Connection object to the database.

42. What are the two major components of JDBC?

Answer: One implementation interface for database manufacturers, the other implementation interface for application and applet writers.

43. What is JDBC Driver interface?

Answer: The JDBC Driver interface provides vendor-specific implementations of the abstract classes provided by the JDBC API. Each vendors driver must provide implementations of the java.sql.Connection,Statement,PreparedStatement, CallableStatement, ResultSet and Driver.

44. What are the common tasks of JDBC?

Answer: Create an instance of a JDBC driver or load JDBC drivers through jdbc. drivers

Register a driver

Specify a database

Open a database connection

Submit a query

Receive results

45. What are the steps involved in establishing a connection?

Answer: This involves two steps:

1) loading the driver and

2) making the connection.

46. What Class.forName will do while loading drivers?

Answer: It is used to create an instance of a driver and register it with the DriverManager. When you have loaded a driver, it is available for making a connection with a DBMS.

47. What are the different types of Statements?

Answer:

1. Create Statement: For Simple statement used for static query.
2. Prepared Statement: For a runtime / dynamic query .Where String is a dynamic query you want to execute
3. Callable Statement (Use prepareCall): //For Stored procedure Callable statement, where sql is stored procedure.

```
try {
Connection conn = DriverManager.getConnection("URL",'USER"."PWD");
Statement stmt = conn.createStatement();
PreparedStatement pstmt = conn.prepareStatement(String sql);
CallableStatement cstmt = conn.prepareCall(String sql);
}
catch (SQLException ee)
{
ee.printStackTrace();
}
```

Don't forget all the above statements will throw the SQLException, so we need to use try catch for the same to handle the exception.

48. How can you use PreparedStatement?

Answer: This special type of statement is derived from the more general class, Statement. If you want to execute a Statement object many times, it will normally reduce execution time to use a PreparedStatement object instead. The advantage to this is that in most cases, this SQL statement will be sent to the DBMS right away, where it will be compiled. As a result, the PreparedStatement object contains not just an SQL statement, but an SQL statement that has been precompiled. This means that when the PreparedStatement is executed, the DBMS can just run the PreparedStatement's SQL statement without having to compile it first.

E.g. PreparedStatement updateSales = con.prepareStatement("UPDATE COFFEES SET SALES = ? WHERE COF_NAME LIKE ?");

49. How to call a Stored Procedure from JDBC?

Answer: The first step is to create a CallableStatement object. As with Statement an and PreparedStatement objects, this is done with an open Connection object. A

CallableStatement object contains a call to a stored procedure;

E.g.

CallableStatement cs = con.prepareCall("{call SHOW_SUPPLIERS}");

ResultSet rs = cs.executeQuery();

50. Explain about JDBC-ODBC driver (Type-1)? When this type of driver is used?

Answer: In this mechanism the flow of execution will be

Java code(JDBC API)<------>JDBC-ODBC bridge driver<------->ODBC API<------->ODBC Layer<-------->DataBase

This type of JDBC Drivers provides a bridge between JDBC API and ODBC API.

Type-1: JDBC-ODBC Bridge Driver:

Since ODBC is written in C-language using pointers, so JAVA doesn't support pointers, a java program can't communicate directly with the Database. The JDBC-ODBC bridge driver translates JDBC API calls to ODBC API calls.

Architecture

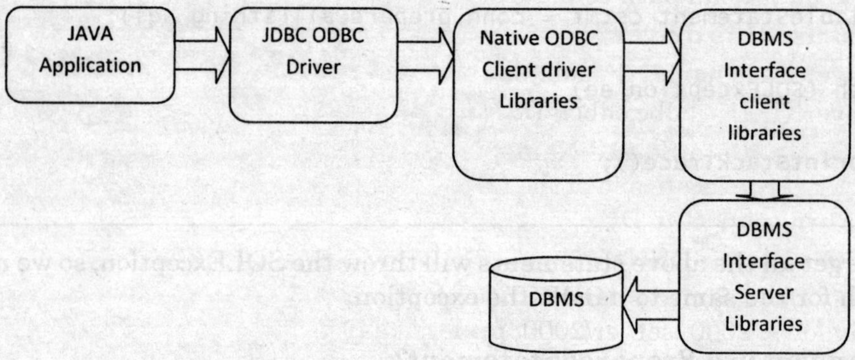

This type of Driver is designed to convert the JDBC request call to ODBC call and ODBC response call to JDBC call.

The JDBC uses this interface in order to communicate with the database, so neither the database nor the middle tier need to be Java compliant. However ODBC binary code must be installed on each client machine that uses this driver. This bridge driver uses a configured data source.

Advantages

- Simple to use because ODBC drivers comes with DB installation/Microsoft front/ back office product installation
- JDBC ODBC Drivers comes with JDK software

Disadvantages

- More number of layers between the application and DB. And more number of API conversions leads to the downfall of the performance.

- Slower than type-2 driver

Where to use?

This type of drivers is generally used at the development time to test your applications. Because of the disadvantages listed above it is not used at production time. But if we are not available with any other type of driver implementations for a DB then we are forced to use this type of driver (for example **Microsoft Access**).

Examples of this type of drivers

JdbcOdbcDriver from sun

Sun's JdbcOdbcDriver is one of type-1 drivers and comes along with sun j2sdk (JDK).

Setting environment to use this driver

1. Software
   ODBC libraries has to be installed.
2. classpath
   No additional classpath settings are required apart from the runtime jar (c:\j2sdk1.4\jre\lib\rt.jar) which is defaultly configured.
3. Path
   No additional path configuration is required.

How to use this driver

- Driver class name □ sun.jdbc.odbc.JdbcOdbcDriver
- Driver URL □ dbc:odbc:<DSN>

here <DSN> (Data Source Name) is an ODBC data source name which is used by ODBC driver to locate one of the ODBC Service Provider implementation API which can in-turn connect to DB.

Steps to create <DSN>

- Run 'Data Sources (ODBC)' from Control Panel\Administrative Tools\ (for Windows 2000 server/2000 professional/XP) run 'ODBC Data Sources' from Control Panel\
- Click on Add button available on the above displayed screen. This opens a new window titled 'Create New Data Source' which displays all the available DB's label DB's ODBC drivers currently installed on your system.
- Select the suitable driver and click on Finish
- Give the required info to the driver (like username, service id etc)

51. Explain about Type-2 driver? When this type of driver is used?

Answer: The Drivers which are written in Native code will come into this category

In this mechanism the flow of Execution will be

Java code (JDBC API) <------>Type-2 driver (JDBC driver) <------->Native API (vendor specific) <------->Database

When database call is made using JDBC, the driver translates the request into vendor-specific API calls.

The database will process the request and sends the results back through the Native API, which will forward them back to the JDBC driver. The JDBC driver will format the results to conform to the JDBC standard and return them to the application.

Type-2 : Native API Partly JAVA Driver (Thick Driver) :

JDBC Database calls are translated into Vendor-specific API calls. The database will process the request and send the results back through API to JDBC Driver – this will translate the results to the JDBC standard and return them to the Java application.

The Vendor specific language API must be installed on every client that runs the JAVA application.

Architecture:

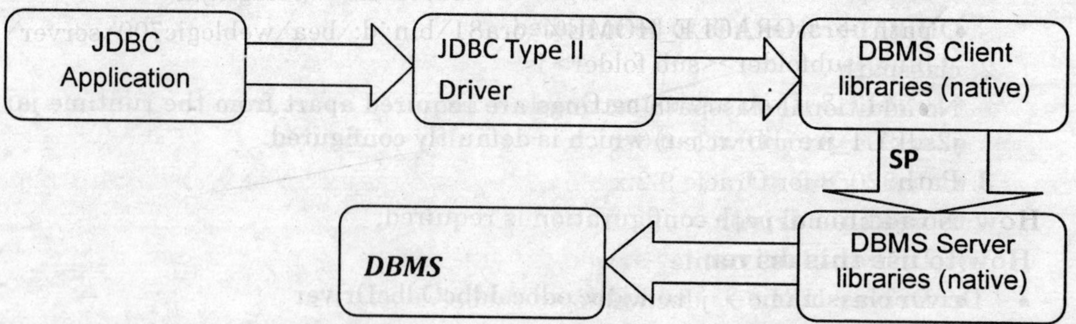

This driver converts the JDBC call given by the Java application to a DB specific native call (i.e. to C or C++) using JNI (Java Native Interface).

Advantages: Faster than the other types of drivers due to native library participation in socket programming.

Disadvantage: DB specific native client library has to be installed in the client machine.

- Preferably work in local network environment because network service name must be configured in client system

Where to use?

This type of drivers is suitable to be used in server side applications.

Not recommended to use with the applications using two tire model (i.e. client and database layer's) because in this type of model client used to interact with DB using the driver and in such a situation the client system should have the DB native library.

Examples of this type of drivers

1. OCI 8 (Oracle Call Interface) for Oracle implemented by Oracle Corporation.

   Setting environment to use this driver

   - Software: Oracle client software has to be installed in client machine
   - classpath → %ORACLE_HOME%\ora81\jdbc\lib\classes111.zip

- path → %ORACLE_HOME%\ora81\bin

How to use this driver?

- Driver class name → oracle.jdbc.driver.OracleDriver
- Driver URL → jdbc:oracle:oci8:@TNSName

Note: TNS Names of Oracle is available in Oracle installed folder %ORACLE_HOME%\Ora81\network\admin\tnsnames.ora

2. Weblogic Jdriver for Oracle implemented by BEA Weblogic:

   Setting environment to use this driver

   - Oracle client software has to be installed in client machine
   - weblogic dll's has to be set in the path
   - classpath → d:\bea\weblogic700\server\lib\weblogic.jar
   - path → %ORACLE_HOME%\ora81\bin; d:\bea\weblogic700\server\bin\<subfolder><sub folder> is
   - oci817_8 if you are using Oracle 8.1.x
   - oci901_8 for Oracle 9.0.x
   - oci920_8 for Oracle 9.2.x

How to use this driver

- **Driver class name** → weblogic.jdbc.oci.Driver
- **Driver URL** → jdbc:weblogic:oracle:HostName

52. Explain about Type-3 driver? When this type of driver is used?

Answer: In this mechanism the flow of Execution will be

Java code (JDBC API) <------> JDBC driver <-------> JDBC driver server <--------> Native driver <-------> Database

The Java Client Application sends the calls to the Intermediate data access server(JDBC driver server)

The middle tier then handles the request using other driver (Type-II or Type-IV drivers) to complete the request.

Type-3 Intermediate Database Access Server:

Type-3 Driver uses an Intermediate (middleware) database driver that has the ability to connect multiple JAVA clients to multiple database servers.

Client connects to the Database server via an Intermediate server component (such as listener) that acts as a gateway for multiple database servers.

Bea weblogic includes Type-3 Driver.

Architecture:

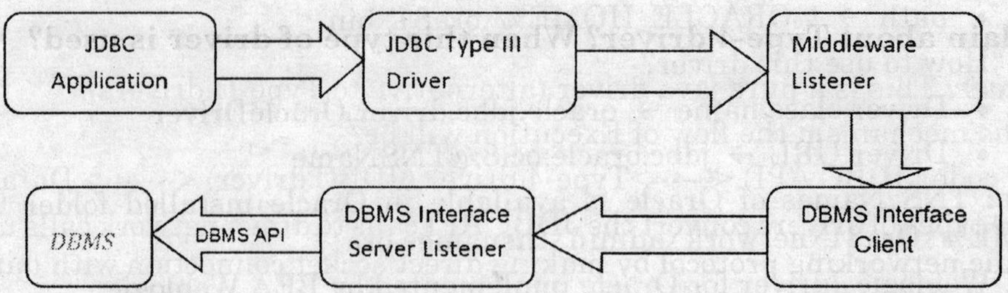

This type of driver's responsibility is to convert JDBC call to Net protocol (Middleware listener dependent) format and redirect the client request to Middleware Listener and middleware listener inturn uses type-1, type-2 or type-4 driver to interact with DB.

Advantages:

- It allows the flexibility on the architecture of the application.
- In absence of DB vendor supplied driver we can use this driver
- Suitable for Applet clients to connect DB, because it uses Java libraries for communication between client and server.

Disadvantages:

- From client to server communication this driver uses Java libraries, but from server to DB connectivity this driver uses native libraries, hence number of API conversion and layer of interactions increases to perform operations that leads to performance deficit.
- Third party vendor dependent and this driver may not provide suitable driver for all DBs

Where to use?

- Suitable for Applets when connecting to databases

Examples of this type of drivers:

1. **IDS Server (Intersolv)** driver available for most of the Databases

Setting environment to use this driver

- Software: IDS software required to be downloaded from the following URL

[http://www.idssoftware.com/idsserver.html -> Export Evaluation]

- classpath → C:\IDSServer\classes\jdk14drv.jar
- path →

How to use this driver?

- Driver class name → ids.sql.IDSDriver
- Driver URL → jdbc:ids://localhost:12/conn?dsn='IDSExamples'

Note: DSN Name must be created in ServerDSN

53. **Explain about Type-4 driver? When this type of driver is used?**

Answer: This is a pure java driver (alternative to Type-II drivers).

In this mechanism the flow of Execution will be

Java code (JDBC API) <------>Type-4 driver (JDBC driver) <-------> Database

These types of drivers convert the JDBC API calls to direct network calls using vendor specific networking protocol by making direct socket connection with database.

Examples of this type of drivers are

1. Tabular Data Stream for Sybase
2. Oracle Thin JDBC driver for Oracle

Type-4 Pure JAVA Driver (Thin driver):

Type-4 Driver translates JDBC-API calls to direct network calls using vendor specific networking protocols by making direct server connections with the database.

Architecture

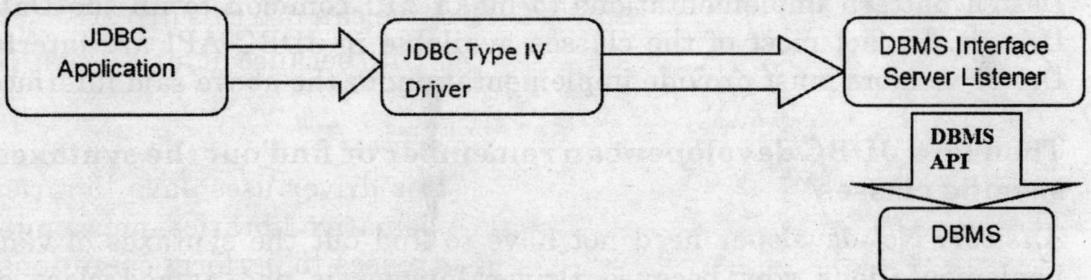

This type of driver converts the JDBC call to a DB defined native protocol.

Advantage

- Type-4 driver are simple to deploy since there is No client native libraries required to be installed in client machine
- Comes with most of the Databases

Disadvantages:

- Slower in execution compared with other JDBC Driver due to Java libraries are used in socket communication with the DB

Where to use?

- This type of drivers is suitable to be used with server side applications, client side application and Java Applets also.

Examples of this type of drivers

1) Thin driver for Oracle implemented by Oracle Corporation

Setting environment to use this driver

♦ classpath → %ORACLE_HOME%\ora81\jdbc\lib\classes111.zip

How to use this driver

♦ Driver class name → oracle.jdbc.driver.OracleDriver

- Driver URL → jdbc:oracle:thin:@HostName:<port no>:<SID>
  <port no> → 1521
  <SID> -> ORCL

2) MySQL Jconnector for MySQL database

Setting environment to use this driver

- classpath → C:\mysql\mysql-connector-java-3.0.8-stable\mysql-connector-java-3.0.8-stable-bin.jar

How to use this driver

- Driver class name → com.mysql.jdbc.Driver
- Driver URL → jdbc:mysql:///test

54. How JDBC API is common to all the Databases and also to all drivers?

Answer: Fine! The answer is JDBC API uses Factory Method and Abstract Factory Design pattern implementations to make API common to all the Databases and Drivers. In fact most of the classes available in JDBC API are interfaces, where Driver vendors must provide implementation for the above said interfaces.

55. Then how JDBC developer can remember or find out the syntaxes of vendor specific classes?

Answer: No! developer need not have to find out the syntaxes of vendor specific implementations why because DriverManager is one named class available in JDBC API into which if you register Driver class name, URL, user and password, DriverManager class in-turn brings us one Connection object.

56. Why most of the classes given in JDBC API are interfaces?

Answer: Abstract class forces all sub classes to implement common methods whichever are required implementations. Only abstract method and class can do this job. That's' why most part of the JDBC API is a formation of interfaces.

57. Which Driver is preferable for using JDBC API in Applets?

Answer: Type-4 Drivers.

58. Write the Syntax of URL to get connection? Explain?

Answer: **Syntax:** jdbc:<subprotocal>:<subname>

jdbc: is a protocal .This is only allowed protocol in JDBC.

<subprotocal>: The subprotocal is used to identify a database driver, or the name of the database connectivity mechanism, chosen by the database driver providers.

<subname>: The syntax of the subname is driver specific. The driver may choose any syntax appropriate for its implementation

Ex: jdbc:odbc:dsn

jdbc:oracle:oci8:@ database name.

jdbc:orale:thin:@ database name:port number:SID

59. How do u Load a driver?

Answer: Using Driver Class.forName(java.lang.String driverclass) or registerDriver(Driver driver) .

60. What are the types of resultsets in JDBC3.0? How you can retrieve information of resultset?

Answer: ScrollableResultSet and ResultSet. We can retrieve information of resultset by using java.sql.ResultSetMetaData interface. You can get the instance by calling the method getMetaData() on ResulSet object.

61. Can java objects be stored in database? How?

Answer: Yes. We can store java objects, BY using setObject(),setBlob() and setClob() methods in PreparedStatement

62. What do u mean by isolation level?

Answer: Isolation means that the business logic can proceed without consideration for the other activities of the system.

63. How do u set the isolation level?

Answer: By using setTransactionIsolation(int level) in java.sql.Connection interface.

level MEAnswer:-

static final int TRANSACTION_READ_UNCOMMITTED //cannot prevent any reads.

static final int TRANSACTION_READ_COMMITTED //prevents dirty reads

static final int TRANSACTION_REPEATABLE_READ //prevents dirty reads & non-repeatable read.

static final int TRANSACTION_SERIALIZABLE //prevents dirty reads , non-repeatable read & phantom read.

These are the static final fields in java.sql.Connection interface.

64. What is a dirty read?

Answer: A Dirty read allows a row changed by one transaction to be read by another transaction before any change in the row have been committed. This problem can be solved by setting the transaction isolation level to TRANSACTION_READ_COMMITTED

65. What is a non-repeatable read?

Answer: A non-repeatable read is where one transaction reads a row, a second transaction alters or deletes the row, and the first transaction re-reads the row,getting different values the second time. This problem can be solved by setting the transaction isolation level to TRANSACTION_REPEATABLE_READ

66. What is phantom read?

Answer: A phantom read is where one transaction reads all rows that satisfy a WHERE condition, a second transaction inserts a row that satisfies that WHERE condition, and the first transaction re-reads for the same condition, retrieving the additional 'phantom' row in the second read This problem can be solved by setting the transaction isolation level to TRANSACTION_SERIALIZABLE

67. What is the difference between java.sql.Statement & java.sql. PreparedStatement ?

Answer: write the appropriate situations to use these statements?

68. How to retrieve the information about the database?

Answer: We can retrieve the info about the database by using inerface java.sql. DatabaseMetaData we can get this object by using getMetaData() method in Connection interface.

69. What are the Different types of exceptions in jdbc?

Answer: BatchUpdateException
DataTruncation
SQLException
SQLWarning

70. How to execute no of queries at one go?

Answer: By using a batchUpdate's (ie throw addBAtch() and executeBatch()) in java.sql.Statement interface,or by using procedures.

71. What are the advantages of connection pool.

Answer: Performance

72. In which interface the methods commit() & rollback() are defined ?

Answer: java.sql.Connection interface

73. How to store images in database?

Answer: Using binary streams (i.e. getBinaryStream(), setBinaryStream()). But it is not visible in database; it is stored in form of bytes, to make it visible we have to use any one frontend tool.

74. How to check null value in JDBC?

Answer: By using the method wasNull() in ResultSet ,it returns boolean value. Returns whether the last column read had a value of SQL NULL.

Note that you must first call one of the getXXX() methods on a column to try to read its value and then call the method wasNull to see if the value read was SQL NULL.

75. Give one Example of static Synchronized method in JDBC API?

Answer: getConnection() method in DriverManager class. Which is used to get object of Connection interface.

76. What is a Connection?

Answer: Connection is an interface which is used to make a connection between client and Database (i.e. opening a session with a particular database).

77. What is the difference between execute(), executeUpdate() and executeQuery() ? Where we will use them?

Answer: execute() method returns a boolean value (ie if the given query returns a resutset then it returns true else false),so depending upon the return value we can get the ResultSet object (getResultset())or we can know how many rows have been affected by our query (getUpdateCount()).That is we can use this method for Fetching queries and Non-Fetching queries. Fetching queries are the queries which are used to fetch the records from database (i.e. which returns resutset) ex: Select * from emp.

Non-Fetching queries are the queries which are used to update,insert,create or delete the records from database

Ex: update emp set sal=10000 where empno=7809.

executeUpdate() method is used for non-fetching queries, which returns int value.

executeQuery() method is used for fetching queries which returns ResulSet object ,Which contains methods to fetch the values.

78. What is the difference between JDBC and ODBC?

Answer:

a) OBDC is for Microsoft and JDBC is for Java applications.
b) ODBC can't be directly used with Java because it uses a C interface.
c) ODBC makes use of pointers which have been removed totally from Java.
d) ODBC mixes simple and advanced features together and has complex options for simple queries. But JDBC is designed to keep things simple while allowing advanced capabilities when required.
e) ODBC requires manual installation of the ODBC driver manager and driver on all client machines. JDBC drivers are written in Java and JDBC code is automatically installable, secure, and portable on all platforms.

f) JDBC API is a natural Java interface and is built on ODBC. JDBC retains some of the basic features of ODBC.

79. What are the steps involved for making a connection with a database or how do you connect to a database?

Answer:

a) Loading the driver: To load the driver, Class.forName( ) method is used.

Class.forName("sun.jdbc.odbc.JdbcOdbcDriver");

When the driver is loaded, it registers itself with the java.sql.DriverManager class as an available database driver.

b) Making a connection with database: To open a connection to a given database, DriverManager.getConnection( ) method is used.

Connection con = DriverManager.getConnection ("jdbc:odbc:somedb", "user", "password");

c) Executing SQL statements: To execute a SQL query, java.sql.Statement class is used.

createStatement( ) method of Connection to obtain a new Statement object.

Statement stmt = con.createStatement( );

d) A query that returns data can be executed using the executeQuery( ) method of Statement. This method executes the statement and returns a java.sql. ResultSet that encapsulates the retrieved data:

ResultSet rs = stmt.executeQuery("SELECT * FROM some table");

e) Process the results: ResultSet returns one row at a time. next( ) method of ResultSet object can be called to move to the next row. The getString( ) and getObject( ) methods are used for retrieving column values:

```
while(rs.next( ) ) {
String event = rs.getString("event");
Object count = (Integer) rs.getObject("count");
}
```

80. What type of driver did you use in project?

Answer: JDBC-ODBC Bridge driver (is a driver that uses native(C language) libraries and makes calls to an existing ODBC driver to access a database engine).

81. What are the types of statements in JDBC?

Answer: **Statement:** To be used createStatement() method for executing single SQL statement

PreparedStatement: To be used preparedStatement() method for executing same SQL statement over and over

CallableStatement: To be used prepareCall( ) method for multiple SQL statements over and over

82. What is stored procedure?

Answer: Stored procedure is a group of SQL statements that forms a logical unit and performs a particular task. Stored Procedures are used to encapsulate a set of operations or queries to execute on database. Stored procedures can be compiled and executed with different parameters and results and may have any combination of input/output parameters.

83. What's the JDBC 2.0 API?

Answer: The JDBC 2.0 API is the latest update of the JDBC API. It contains many new features, including scrollable result sets and the new SQL: 1999 (formerly SQL 3) data types. There are two parts to the JDBC 2.0 API: the JDBC 2.0 core API (the java.sql package), which is included in the Java TM 2 SDK, Standard Edition the JDBC 2.0 Optional Package API (the javax.sql package), which is available separately or as part of the Java 2 SDK, Enterprise Edition.

84. Does the JDBC-ODBC Bridge support the new features in the JDBC 2.0 API?

Answer: No, the JDBC-ODBC Bridge that is included in the Java 2 Platform initial release does not support the new features in the JDBC 2.0 API. However, Sun and Merant are working to produce a new version of the Bridge that does support the new features. Note that we do not recommend using the Bridge except for experimental purposes or when you have no other driver available.

85. Can the JDBC-ODBC Bridge be used with applets?

Answer: Use of the JDBC-ODBC bridge from an untrusted applet running in a browser, such as Netscape Navigator, isn't allowed. The JDBC-ODBC bridge doesn't allow untrusted code to call it for security reasons. This is good because it means that an untrusted applet that is downloaded by the browser can't circumvent Java security by calling ODBC. Remember that ODBC is native code, so once ODBC is called, the Java programming language can't guarantee that a security violation won't occur. On the other hand, Pure Java JDBC drivers work well with applets. They are fully downloadable and do not require any client-side configuration.

Finally, we would like to note that it is possible to use the JDBC-ODBC bridge with applets that will be run in appletviewer since appletviewer assumes that applets are trusted. It is also possible to use the JDBC-ODBC bridge with applets that are run in the HotJavaTM browser (available from Java Software), since Hot Java provides an option to turn off applet security. In general, it is dangerous to turn applet security off, but it may be appropriate in certain controlled situations, such as for applets that will only be used in a secure intranet environment. Remember to exercise caution if you choose this option, and use an all-Java JDBC driver whenever possible to avoid security problems.

86. How do I start debugging problems related to the JDBC API?

Answer: A good way to find out what JDBC calls are doing is to enable JDBC tracing. The JDBC trace contains a detailed listing of the activity occurring in the system that is related to JDBC operations.

If you use the DriverManager facility to establish your database connection, you use the DriverManager.setLogWriter method to enable tracing of JDBC operations. If you use a DataSource object to get a connection, you use the DataSource. setLogWriter method to enable tracing. (For pooled connections, you use the ConnectionPoolDataSource.setLogWriter method, and for connections that can participate in distributed transactions, you use the XADataSource.setLogWriter method.)

87. How can I use the JDBC API to access a desktop database like Microsoft Access over the network?

Answer: Most desktop databases currently require a JDBC solution that uses ODBC underneath. This is because the vendors of these database products haven't implemented all-Java JDBC drivers.

The best approach is to use a commercial JDBC driver that supports ODBC and the database you want to use. See the JDBC driver's page for a list of available JDBC drivers.

The JDBC-ODBC bridge from Sun's Java Software does not provide network access to desktop databases by itself. The JDBC-ODBC bridge loads ODBC as a local DLL, and typical ODBC drivers for desktop databases like Access aren't networked. The JDBC-ODBC bridge can be used together with the RMI-JDBC bridge, however, to access a desktop database like Access over the net. This RMI-JDBC-ODBC solution is free.

88. Does the JDK include the JDBC API and the JDBC-ODBC Bridge?

Answer: Yes, the JDK 1.1 and the Java 2 SDK, Standard Edition (formerly known as the JDK 1.2), contain both the JDBC API and the JDBC-ODBC Bridge. The Java 2 SDK, Standard Edition, contains the JDBC 2.0 core API, which is the latest version. It does not include the JDBC 2.0 Optional Package, which is part of the Java 2 SDK, Enterprise Edition, or which you can download separately.

Note that the version of the JDBC API and the JDBC-ODBC Bridge provided for separate download on the JDBC download page are only for use with the JDK 1.0.2.

89. Are there any ODBC drivers that do not work with the JDBC-ODBC Bridge?

Answer: Most ODBC 2.0 drivers should work with the Bridge. Since there is some variation in functionality between ODBC drivers, the functionality of the bridge may be affected. The bridge works with popular PC databases, such as Microsoft Access and FoxPro.

90. Does the JDBC-ODBC Bridge work with Microsoft J++?

Answer: No, J++ does not support the JDBC-ODBC bridge since it doesn't implement the Java Native Interface (JNI). Any all-Java JDBC driver should work with J++, however.

91. What causes the "No suitable driver" error?

Answer: "No suitable driver" is an error that usually occurs during a call to the DriverManager.getConnection method. The cause can be failing to load the appropriate JDBC drivers before calling the getConnection method, or it can be specifying an invalid JDBC URL—one that isn't recognized by your JDBC driver. Your best bet is to check the documentation for your JDBC driver or contact your JDBC driver vendor if you suspect that the URL you are specifying is not being recognized by your JDBC driver.

In addition, when you are using the JDBC-ODBC Bridge, this error can occur if one or more the shared libraries needed by the Bridge cannot be loaded. If you think this is the cause, check your configuration to be sure that the shared libraries are accessible to the Bridge.

92. Why isn't the java.sql.DriverManager class being found?

Answer: This problem can be caused by running a JDBC applet in a browser that supports the JDK 1.0.2, such as Netscape Navigator 3.0. The JDK 1.0.2 does not contain the JDBC API, so the DriverManager class typically isn't found by the Java virtual machine running in the browser.

Here's a solution that doesn't require any additional configuration of your web clients. Remember that classes in the java.* packages cannot be downloaded by most browsers for security reasons. Because of this, many vendors of all-Java JDBC drivers supply versions of the java.sql.* classes that have been renamed to jdbc.sql.*, along with a version of their driver that uses these modified classes. If you import jdbc.sql.* in your applet code instead of java.sql.*, and add the jdbc.sql.* classes provided by your JDBC driver vendor to your applet's codebase, then all of the JDBC classes needed by the applet can be downloaded by the browser at run time, including the DriverManager class.

This solution will allow your applet to work in any client browser that supports the JDK 1.0.2. Your applet will also work in browsers that support the JDK 1.1, although you may want to switch to the JDK 1.1 classes for performance reasons. Also, keep in mind that the solution outlined here is just an example and that other solutions are possible.

93. Why doesn't calling the method Class.forName load my JDBC driver?

Answer: There is a bug in the JDK 1.1.x that can cause the method Class.forName to fail. A workaround is to explicitly call the method DriverManager.registerDriver(new YourDriverClass()). The exact problem in the JDK is a race condition in the class loader that prevents the static section of code in the driver class from executing and registering the driver with the DriverManager.

94. Why do the java.sql and java.math packages fail to download java.* packages? Is there a workaround?

Answer: For security reasons, browsers will not download java.* packages. In order to use the JDBC API with browsers that have not been upgraded to JDK1.1 or beyond, we recommend that the java.sql and java.math packages be renamed jdbc. sql and jdbc.math. Most vendors supplying JDBC technology-enabled drivers that are written purely in the Java programming language already provide versions of these renamed packages. When JDK 1.1 support has been added to your browser, you should convert your applets back to the java.* package names.

95. Why is the precision of java.math.BigDecimal limited to 18 digits in the JDK 1.0.2 add-on version of the JDBC API?

Answer: In JDK 1.1, java.math.BigInteger is implemented in C. It supports a precision of thousands of digits. The same is true for BigDecigmal.

The version of BigInteger provided with the JDK 1.0.2 add-on version of the JDBC API is a simplified version written in the Java programming language, and it is limited to 18 digits. Because the implementation of BigDecimal is based on BigInteger, it also is limited to this precision.

In the JDBC 2.0 API, you can use a new version of the method ResultSet.getBigDecimal that does not take a scale parameter and returns a BigDecimal with full precision.

96. Can the JDBC API be added to JDK 1.0.2?

Answer: Yes. Download the JDBC 1.22 API from the JDBC download page and follow the installation instructions in the release notes.

If you are using any version of the JDK from 1.1 on, the JDBC API is already included, and you should not download the JDBC 1.22 API.

97. How do I retrieve a whole row of data at once, instead of calling an individual ResultSet.getXXX method for each column?

Answer: The ResultSet.getXXX methods are the only way to retrieve data from a ResultSet object, which means that you have to make a method call for each column of a row. It is unlikely that this is the cause of a performance problem, however, because it is difficult to see how a column could be fetched without at least the cost of a function call in any scenario. We welcome input from developers on this issue.

98. Why does the ODBC driver manager return 'Data source name not found and no default driver specified Vendor: 0'

Answer: This type of error occurs during an attempt to connect to a database with the bridge. First, note that the error is coming from the ODBC driver manager.

This indicates that the bridge-which is a normal ODBC client-has successfully called ODBC, so the problem isn't due to native libraries not being present. In this case, it appears that the error is due to the fact that an ODBC DSN (data source name) needs to be configured on the client machine. Developers often forget to do this, thinking that the bridge will magically find the DSN they configured on their remote server machine.

99. Are all the required JDBC drivers to establish connectivity to my database part of the JDK?

Answer: No. There aren't any JDBC technology-enabled drivers bundled with the JDK 1.1.x or Java 2 Platform releases other than the JDBC-ODBC Bridge. So, developers need to get a driver and install it before they can connect to a database. We are considering bundling JDBC technology- enabled drivers in the future.

100. Is the JDBC-ODBC Bridge multi-threaded?

Answer: No. The JDBC-ODBC Bridge does not support concurrent access from different threads. The JDBC-ODBC Bridge uses synchronized methods to serialize all of the calls that it makes to ODBC. Multi-threaded Java programs may use the Bridge, but they won't get the advantages of multi-threading. In addition, deadlocks can occur between locks held in the database and the semaphore used by the Bridge. We are thinking about removing the synchronized methods in the future. They were added originally to make things simple for folks writing Java programs that use a single-threaded ODBC driver.

101. Does the JDBC-ODBC Bridge support multiple concurrent open statements per connection?

Answer: No. You can open only one Statement object per connection when you are using the JDBC-ODBC Bridge.

102. Does the JDBC-ODBC Bridge developed by Merant and Sun support result sets that contain Japanese Characters (DBCS)?

Answer: Yes, but we haven't tested this ourselves. The version of the Bridge in the Java 2 SDK, Standard Edition, and Java 2 SDK, Enterprise Edition, also supports a new charSet Connection property for specifying the character encoding used by the underlying DBMS.

103. Why can't I invoke the ResultSet methods afterLast and beforeFirst when the method next works?

Answer: You are probably using a driver implemented for the JDBC 1.0 API. You need to upgrade to a JDBC 2.0 driver that implements scrollable result sets. Also be sure that your code has created scrollable result sets and that the DBMS you are using supports them.

104. How can I retrieve a String or other object type without creating a new object each time?

Answer: Creating and garbage collecting potentially large numbers of objects (millions) unnecessarily can really hurt performance. It may be better to provide a way to retrieve data like strings using the JDBC API without always allocating a new object.

We are studying this issue to see if it is an area in which the JDBC API should be improved. Stay tuned, and please send us any comments you have on this question.

105. There is a method getColumnCount in the JDBC API. Is there a similar method to find the number of rows in a result set?

Answer: No, but it is easy to find the number of rows. If you are using a scrollable result set, rs, you can call the methods rs.last and then rs.getRow to find out how many rows rs has. If the result is not scrollable, you can either count the rows by iterating through the result set or get the number of rows by submitting a query with a COUNT column in the SELECT clause.

106. I would like to download the JDBC-ODBC Bridge for the Java 2 SDK, Standard Edition (formerly JDK 1.2). I'm a beginner with the JDBC API, and I would like to start with the Bridge. How do I do it?

Answer: The JDBC-ODBC Bridge is bundled with the Java 2 SDK, Standard Edition, so there is no need to download it separately.

107. If I use the JDBC API, do I have to use ODBC underneath?

Answer: No, this is just one of many possible solutions. We recommend using a pure Java JDBC technology-enabled driver, type 3 or 4, in order to get all of the benefits of the Java programming language and the JDBC API.

108. Once I have the Java 2 SDK, Standard Edition, from Sun, what else do I need to connect to a database?

Answer: You still need to get and install a JDBC technology-enabled driver that supports the database that you are using. There are many drivers available from a variety of sources. You can also try using the JDBC-ODBC Bridge if you have ODBC connectivity set up already. The Bridge comes with the Java 2 SDK, Standard Edition, and Enterprise Edition, and it doesn't require any extra setup itself. The Bridge is a normal ODBC client. Note, however, that you should use the JDBC-ODBC Bridge only for experimental prototyping or when you have no other driver available.

109. What is a JDBC Driver?

Answer: A JDBC driver is the set of classes that implement the JDBC interfaces for a particular database.

There are four different types of JDBC driver:

A Type 1 driver is a JDBC-ODBC bridge driver; this type of driver enables a client to connect to an ODBC database via Java calls and JDBC—neither the database nor middle tier need to be Java compliant.However, ODBC binary code must be installed on each client machine that uses this driver.

A Type 2 driver converts JDBC calls into calls for a specific database. This driver is referred to as a native-API, partly Java driver. As with the Type 1 driver, some binary code may be required on the client machine, which means this type of driver is not suitable for downloading over a network to a client.

A Type 3 driver is a JDBC-Net pure Java driver, which translates JDBC calls into a database -independent net protocol. Vendors of database middleware products can implement this type of driver into their products to provide interoperability with the greatest number of database servers.

Finally, a Type 4 driver, or, native protocol, pure Java driver converts JDBC calls into the network protocol used by the database directly. A Type 4 driver requires no client software, so it's ideal for deployment to browsers at runtime. Each of these driver types has its own optimal usage scenarios, and will affect the way you deploy a given Java application.

For example, because Type 4 drivers are 100% Java, use Java sockets to connect to the database, and require no client-side data access code, they are ideal for applets or other download situations inside a firewall.

110. What are the Oracle's JDBC Drivers?

Answer: Oracle provides both Type 2 and Type 4 drivers. All Oracle JDBC drivers support the full JDBC specification, but in addition, they support the extended capabilities of the Oracle database. For example, the JDBC specification doesn't support LOB data, but the Oracle OCI8 JDBC driver does. Oracle's implementation of the Type 2 JDBC driver is referred to as the Oracle "OCI driver," and the version of this driver that supports an Oracle 7 database is the OCI7 driver and the OCI8 supports Oracle 8. These drivers are platform specific; for example, the Windows NT and Windows 95 version of the driver (oci805jdbc.dll.) is implemented as a dynamic link library (DLL) in C. As mentioned previously, Type 2 drivers may require client code. In the case of the OCI8 driver, the clients must have Oracle's Net*8 and all other dependent files loaded.

A common way to implement Oracle OCI drivers is to use Oracle Application Server with the JWeb cartridge on the middle tier and deploy the client presentation logic as an applet; the interaction with the Oracle database is conducted from the middle tier only, with just the results sent to the client applet as pure HTML or Java and HTML. All Oracle drivers are compliant with the Java Development Kit JDK 1.0 and 1.1.x and support the JDBC 1.22 standard. In addition, all Oracle JDBC drivers support data types such as RAW and LONG RAW, ROWID, and RECURSOR, which are supported in Oracle databases but not part of the JDBC standard. Oracle's drivers also support execution of PL/SQL stored procedures and anonymous blocks (for dynamic execution), and include capabilities such as row pre-fetching, execution batching, and defining query columns to reduce the network round trips to Oracle database. In addition, the OCI driver for Oracle8 supports oracle data types CLOB, BLOB, NCLOB, and BFILE. The screenshot shows an example of one of the classes in the Oracle JDBC, as part of the class hierarchy from which it descends, as displayed in Oracle's JDeveloper integrated development environment. As you can see, the OraclePreparedStatement class inherits from the java.sql.PreparedStatement class, which in turn inherits from the java.sql.Statement.

Oracle also provides a Type 4 JDBC driver, referred to as the Oracle "thin" driver. This driver includes its own implementation of a TCP/IP version of Oracle's Net8 written entirely in Java, so it is platform independent, can be downloaded to a browser at runtime, and does not require any Oracle software on the client side. This driver requires a TCP/IP listener on the server side, and the client connection string uses the TCP/IP port address, not the TNSNAMES entry for the database name.

1. Add JDBC classes to your Java application or applet class by adding the following statement to your Java source code:

   import java.sql.*;

   To use the extended capabilities of the Oracle database, you must also import the Oracle JDBC driver. The statement in Java source looks like this:

   import oracle.JDBC.driver.*

2. Load the JDBC driver by including the following statement in your class.

   Class.forName("oracle.JDBC.driver.OracleDriver");

   You can load the driver from your class-initialization routine.

3. Obtain a connection to an Oracle database by calling the getConnection() method of the JDBC DriverManager class. When you call this method you need to specify the connection information for the database in the form of a URL. The form the URL will take depends on the driver used. For example, to use the pure Java Type 4 Oracle driver (the thin driver) to connect to an Oracle7 database, the URL would read:

   jdbc:oracle:thin@database_name:port_no:SID

   To connect to an Oracle8 database using the OCI driver, the URL would be more like:

   jdbc:oracle:oci8@database_name

   To specify the database for use with an OCI driver, you can use either a SQL*Net name- value pair, or, if you're using an Oracle Name server, you can use the name from the tnsname.ora file. (Both of these strings would conclude with the logon information as well—specifically the user name and password—but we've eliminated that from this example.)

   The preliminary driver and database-connection issues now taken care of, there are still several other things your Java source code must include in order for the compiled code to submit queries to the database and process results.

4. Create a Statement object by calling the createStatement() method of the Connection object you created in the previous step. The following statement creates a Statement object stmt:

   Statement stmt = conn.createStatement ();

5. Once the Statement object exists (in code), the application can then include code to execute a SQL query by calling the executeQuery() method of the Statement object.The executeQuery() method returns the result of the query in the ResultSet object. The following statement executes a query:

   ResultSet rset = stmt.executeQuery (SELECT ename from emp where empno = 7900);

6. Finally, call the next() method of a ResultObject to retrieve a row and display it. Use a loop if the query returns more then one row from the database. For example, the following statements get the name of an employee from the ResultSet object and display it in the java.awt text control placed on the GUI.

   rset.next();

   enameTxtb.setText = ((String)rset.getString(1));

111. What is Annotation in Java?

Answer: An annotation, in the java programming language is a special form of syntactic metadata that can be added to Java Source Code.

Classes, methods, variables parameters and packages may be annotated.

Unlike Java doc tags, Java annotation are reflective, in that they are embedded in class files generated by the compiler and may be retained by the java VM to make retrievable at run-time. Annotation is basically to attach metadata to method, class or package. Metadata is used by the compiler to perform some basic compile-time checking.

112. What is the difference between PreparedStatement and Statement in java?

Answer:

- A statement is parsed and executed each time its call sent to database.
- A prepared statement may be parsed once and executed repeatedly with different parameters.

There are four steps for the execution of query:

1. Query is parsed
2. Query is compiled.
3. Query is optimized.
4. Query is executed.

- In case of statement, the above four steps are performed every time. And in case of prepared statement the above three steps are performed once.

113. What is CallableStatement? How you can call stored procedure to pass IN parameter?

Answer: CallableStatement in java is used for calling database stored procedures.

Example: Adding Employee details in DB whenever new Employee is joining.

Employee Information: Employee Id, Name and joining Date.

Code:

```
package com.mytest.jdbc;
import java.sql.CallableStatement;
import java.sql.DriverManager; import java.sql.Connection;
import java.sql.SQLException;
public class AddEmployeeExample {
private static final String DB_DRIVER = "oracle.jdbc.driver.
OracleDriver";
private static final String DB_CONNECTION = "jdbc:oracle:thin:@
localhost:1521:MYTEST";
private static final String DB_USER = "my_user";
private static final String DB_PASSWORD = "my_password";
public static void main(String[] argv) {
try
{
    addEmployeeInfo();
}catch (SQLException e) {
System.out.println(e.getMessage());
}
}
private static void addEmployeeInfo() throws SQLException {
Connection dbConnection = null;
CallableStatement callableStatement = null;
String insertEmployeeStoreProc = "{call insertEmployee(?,?,?)}";
try {
dbConnection = getDBConnection();
callableStatement = dbConnection.prepareCall(insertEmployeeStoreProc);
callableStatement.setInt(1, 377602);
callableStatement.setString(2, "Nishant Singh");
callableStatement.setDate(3, getCurrentDate());
// execute insert store procedure
callableStatement.executeUpdate();
} catch (SQLException exp) {
System.out.println(exp.getMessage());
} finally {
```

```
if (callableStatement != null) {
callableStatement.close();
}
if (dbConnection != null) {
dbConnection.close();
}
}
}
private static Connection getDBConnection() {
Connection dbConnection = null;
try {
Class.forName(DB_DRIVER);
} catch (ClassNotFoundException e) {
System.out.println(e.getMessage());
}
try {
dbConnection = DriverManager.getConnection( DB_CONNECTION, DB_USER,DB_
PASSWORD);
return dbConnection;
} catch (SQLException e) {
System.out.println(e.getMessage());
}
return dbConnection;
}
private static java.sql.Date getCurrentDate() {
java.util.Date today = new java.util.Date();
return new java.sql.Date(today.getTime());
}
}
```

114. Using Callable Statement how can you pass OUT Parameters, explain with example?

Answer: Take the example of Employee, where you want the details of Employee by Id.

Code: Use the same code structure get DB Connection etc.

```
//getDBUSERByUserId is a stored procedure
String getEmpInfoByEmpIdSql = "{call getEmpInfoByEmpId(?,?,?,?)}";
callableStatement = dbConnection.prepareCall(getEmpInfoByEmpIdSql);
callableStatement.setInt(1, 377602);
```

```
callableStatement.registerOutParameter(2, java.sql.Types.VARCHAR);
callableStatement.registerOutParameter(3, java.sql.Types.DATE);
execute getEmpInfoByEmpId store procedure
callableStatement.executeUpdate();
String empName = callableStatement.getString(2);
String joiningDate = callableStatement.getDate(3);
```

115. How can you determine SGA site?

Answer: Database - JDBC (java.sql)

Connecting to a Database

This example uses the JDBC-ODBC bridge to connect to a database called "mydatabase".

```
try {
Class.forName("sun.jdbc.odbc.JdbcOdbcDriver");
String url = "jdbc:odbc:mydatabase";
Connection con = DriverManager.getConnection(url, "login", "password");
} catch (ClassNotFoundException e) {
} catch (SQLException e) {
}
```

Creating a Table

This example creates a table called "mytable" with three columns: COL_A which holds strings, COL_B which holds integers, and COL_C which holds floating point numbers.

```
try {
Statement stmt = con.createStatement();
stmt.executeUpdate("CREATE TABLE mytable (COL_A VARCHAR(100), COL_B
INTEGER, COL_C FLOAT)");
} catch (SQLException e) {
}
```

Entering a New Row into a Table

This example enters a row containing a string, an integer, and a floating point number into the table called "mytable".

```
try {
Statement stmt = connection.createStatement();
stmt.executeUpdate("INSERT INTO mytable VALUES ('Patrick Chan', 123,
1.23)");
```

```
connection.close();
} catch (SQLException e) {
}
```

Getting All Rows from a Table

This example retrieves all the rows from a table called "mytable". A row in "mytable" consists of a string, integer, and floating point number.

```
try {
Statement stmt = connection.createStatement();
// Get data using colunm names.
ResultSet rs = stmt.executeQuery("SELECT * FROM mytable");
while (rs.next()) {
String s = rs.getString("COL_A");
int i = rs.getInt("COL_B");
float f = rs.getFloat("COL_C");
process(s, i, f);
}
```

Get data using colunm numbers.

```
\rs = stmt.executeQuery("SELECT * FROM mytable");
while (rs.next()) {
String s = rs.getString(1);
int i = rs.getInt(2);
float f = rs.getFloat(3);
process(s, i, f);
}
```

Getting Particular Rows from a Table

This example retrieves all rows from a table called "mytable" whose column COL_A equals "Patrick Chan". A row in "mytable" consists of a string, integer, and floating point number.

```
try {
Statement stmt = connection.createStatement();
ResultSet rs = stmt.executeQuery("SELECT * FROM mytable WHERE COL_A =
'Patrick Chan'");
rs.next();
String s = rs.getString("COL_A");
int i = rs.getInt("COL_B");
```

```
float f = rs.getFloat("COL_C");
process(s, i, f);
} catch (SQLException e) {
}
```

Updating a Row of Data in a Table

This example updates a row in a table called "mytable". In particular, for all rows whose column COL_B equals 123, column COL_A is set to "John Doe".

```
try {
Statement stmt = connection.createStatement();
int numUpdated = stmt.executeUpdate("UPDATE mytable SET COL_A = 'John
Doe' WHERE COL_B = 123");
connection.close();
} catch (SQLException e) {
}
```

Using a Prepared Statement

A prepared statement should be used in cases where a particular SQL statement is used frequently. The prepared statement is more expensive to set up but executes faster than a statement. This example demonstrates a prepared statement for getting all rows from a table called "mytable" whose column COL_A equals "Patrick Chan". This example also demonstrates a prepared statement for updating data in the table. In particular, for all rows whose column COL_B equals 123, column COL_A is set to "John Doe".

```
try {
// Retrieving rows from the database.
PreparedStatement stmt = connection.prepareStatement("SELECT * FROM
mytable WHERE COL_A = ?");
int colunm = 1;
stmt.setString(colunm, "Patrick Chan");
ResultSet rs = stmt.executeQuery();
// Updating the database.
stmt = connection.prepareStatement("UPDATE mytable SET COL_A = ? WHERE
COL_B = ?");
colunm = 1;
stmt.setString(colunm, "John Doe");
colunm = 2;
stmt.setInt(colunm, 123);
int numUpdated = stmt.executeUpdate();
} catch (SQLException e) {
}
```

116. How to Interact with DB?

Answer: Generally every DB vendor provides a User Interface through which we can easily execute SQL queries and gets the result (For example Oracle Query Manager for Oracle, and TOAD (www.quest.com) tool common to all the databases). And these tools will help DB developers to create database. But as a programmer we want to interact with the DB dynamically to execute some SQL queries from our application (Any application like C, C++, JAVA etc), and for this requirement DB vendors provide some Native Libraries (Vendor Specific) using this we can interact with the DB i.e. If you want to execute some queries on Oracle DB, oracle vendor provides an OCI (Oracle Call Interface) Libraries to perform the same.

117. What is ODBC?

Answer: ODBC (Open Database Connectivity) is an ISV (Independent software vendor product) composes of native API to connect to different databases through via a single API called ODBC.

Open Database Connectivity (ODBC) is an SQL oriented application programming interface developed by in collaboration with IBM and some other database vendors.

ODBC comes with Microsoft products and with all databases on Windows OS.

ODBC Architecture

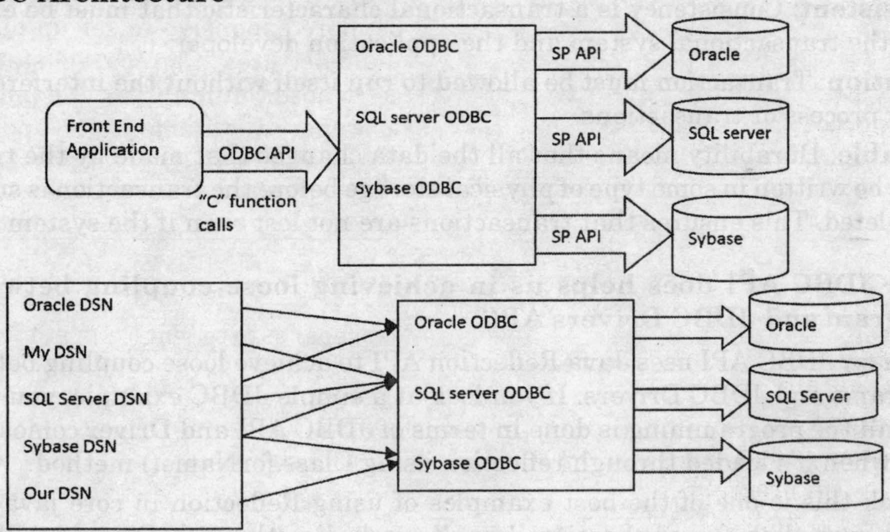

Advantages

- Single API (Protocol) is used to interact with any DB
- Switching from one DB to another is easy
- Doesn't require any modifications in the Application when you want to shift from one DB to other

118. How to Make Updates to Updatable Result Sets?

Answer: Another new feature in the JDBC 2.0 API is the ability to update rows in a result set using methods in the Java programming language rather than having to send an SQL command. But before you can take advantage of this capability, you need to create a ResultSet object that is updatable. In order to do this, you supply the ResultSet constant CONCUR_UPDATABLE to the createStatement method.

E.g.

Connection con = DriverManager.getConnection("jdbc:mySubprotocol:mySubName");

Statement stmt = con.createStatement(ResultSet.TYPE_SCROLL_SENSITIVE, ResultSet.CONCUR_UPDATABLE);

ResultSet uprs = ("SELECT COF_NAME, PRICE FROM COFFEES");

119. What is ACID?

Answer: **ACID** is related to transactions. It is an acronym of Atomic, Consistent, Isolation and Durable. Transaction must following the above four properties to be a better one.

Atomic: It means a transaction must execute all or nothing at all.

Consistent: Consistency is a transactional characteristic that must be enforced by both the transactional system and the application developer

Isolation: Transaction must be allowed to run itself without the interference of the other process or transactions.

Durable: Durability means that all the data changes that made by the transaction must be written in some type of physical storage before the transaction is successfully completed. This ensures that transactions are not lost even if the system crashes.

120. How JDBC API does helps us in achieving loose coupling between Java Program and JDBC Drivers API?

Answer: JDBC API uses Java Reflection API to achieve loose coupling between java programs and JDBC Drivers. If you look at a simple JDBC example, you will notice that all the programming is done in terms of JDBC API and Driver comes in picture only when it's loaded through reflection using Class.forName() method.

I think this is one of the best examples of using Reflection in core java classes to make sure that our application doesn't work directly with Drivers API and that makes it very easy to move from one database to another. Please read more at JDBC Example.

121. What is JDBC Connection? Explain steps to get Database connection in a simple java program.

Answer: JDBC Connection is like a Session created with the database server. You can also think Connection is like a Socket connection from the database server.

Creating a JDBC Connection is very easy and requires two steps:

A. Register and Load the Driver: Using Class.forName(), Driver class is registered to the DriverManager and loaded in the memory.

B. Use DriverManager to get the Connection object: We get connection object fromDriverManager.getConnection() by passing Database URL String, username and password as argument.

```
Connection con = null;
try{
    // load the Driver Class
    Class.forName("com.mysql.jdbc.Driver");
// create the connection now
con = DriverManager.getConnection("jdbc:mysql://localhost:3306/
UserDB","pankaj", "pankaj123");
}catch (SQLException e) {
System.out.println("Check database is UP and configs are correct");
e.printStackTrace();
}catch (ClassNotFoundException e) {
System.out.println("Please include JDBC MySQL jar in classpath");
    e.printStackTrace();
}
```

122. What is the use of JDBC DriverManager class?

Answer: JDBC DriverManager is the factory class through which we get the Database Connection object. When we load the JDBC Driver class, it registers itself to the DriverManager, you can look up the JDBC Driver classes source code to check this.

Then when we call DriverManager.getConnection() method by passing the database configuration details, DriverManager uses the registered drivers to get the Connection and return it to the caller program.

123. How to get the Database server details in java program?

Answer: We can use DatabaseMetaData object to get the database server details. When the database connection is created successfully, we can get the meta data object by calling getMetaData() method. There are so many methods in DatabaseMetaData that we can use to get the database product name, its version and configuration details.

DatabaseMetaData metaData = con.getMetaData();

String dbProduct = metaData.getDatabaseProductName();

124. What is JDBC Statement?

Answer: JDBC API Statement is used to execute SQL queries in the database. We can create the Statement object by calling Connection getStatement() method. We can use Statement to execute static SQL queries by passing query through different execute methods such as execute(), executeQuery(), executeUpdate() etc.

Since the query is generated in the java program, if the user input is not properly validated it can lead to SQL injection issue, more details can be found at SQL Injection Example.

By default, only one ResultSet object per Statement object can be open at the same time. Therefore, if we want to work with multiple ResultSet objects, then each must have been generated by different Statement objects. All execute() methods in the Statement interface implicitly close a statment's current ResultSet object if an open one exists.

125. What is the difference between execute, executeQuery, executeUpdate?

Answer: Statement execute(String query) is used to execute any SQL query and it returns TRUE if the result is an ResultSet such as running Select queries. The output is FALSE when there is no ResultSet object such as running Insert or Update queries. We can use getResultSet() to get the ResultSet and getUpdateCount() method to retrieve the update count.

Statement executeQuery(String query) is used to execute Select queries and returns the ResultSet. ResultSet returned is never null even if there are no records matching the query. When executing select queries we should use executeQuery method so that if someone tries to execute insert/update statement it will throw java.sql. SQLException with message "executeQuery method can not be used for update".

Statement executeUpdate(String query) is used to execute Insert/Update/Delete (DML) statements or DDL statements that returns nothing. The output is int and equals to the row count for SQL Data Manipulation Language (DML) statements. For DDL statements, the output is 0.

You should use execute() method only when you are not sure about the type of statement else use executeQuery or executeUpdate method.

126. What is JDBC PreparedStatement?

Answer: JDBC PreparedStatement object represents a precompiled SQL statement. We can use it's setter method to set the variables for the query.

Since PreparedStatement is precompiled, it can then be used to efficiently execute this statement multiple times. PreparedStatement is better choice that Statement because it automatically escapes the special characters and avoid SQL injection attacks.

127. How to set NULL values in JDBC PreparedStatement?

Answer: We can use PreparedStatement setNull() method to bind the null variable to a parameter. The setNull method takes index and SQL Types as argument, for example

ps.setNull(10, java.sql.Types.INTEGER);.

128. What is the use of getGeneratedKeys() method in Statement?

Answer: Sometimes a table can have auto generated keys used to insert the unique column value for primary key. We can use Statement getGeneratedKeys() method to get the value of this auto generated key.

129. What causes No suitable driver error?

Answer: "No suitable driver" is occurs during a call to the DriverManager. getConnection method, may be of any of the following reason:

- Due to failing to load the appropriate JDBC drivers before calling the getConnection method.
- It can be specifying an invalid JDBC URL, one that is not recognized by JDBC driver.
- This error can occur if one or more the shared libraries needed by the bridge cannot be loaded

130. What does setAutoCommit do?

Answer: setAutoCommit() invoke the commit state query to the database. To perform batch updation we use the setAutoCommit() which enable us to execute more than one statement together, which in result minimize the database call and send all statement in one batch.

setAutoCommit() allowed us to commit the transaction commit state manually the default values of the setAutoCommit() is true.

131. Why Prepared Statements are faster?

Answer: Prepared execution is faster than direct execution for statements executed more than three or four times because the statement is compiled only once. Prepared statements and JDBC driver are linked with each other. We can bind drivers with columns by triggering the query into the database. When we execute Connection. prepareStatement(), all the columns bindings take place, in oder to reduce the time.

132. How can we store and retrieve images from the database?

Answer: By using PreparedStaement interface, we can store and retrieve images.

Example to store image in Oracle database:

You can store images in the database in java by the help of PreparedStatement interface.

The **setBinaryStream() method** of PreparedStatement is used to set Binary information into the parameterIndex.

Signature of setBinaryStream method

The syntax of setBinaryStream() method is given below:

1. public void setBinaryStream(int paramIndex,InputStream stream) throws SQLException
2. Public void set Binary Stream (int paramIndex,InputStream stream,long length)throws SQL Exception

For storing image into the database, BLOB (Binary Large Object) datatype is used in the table. For example:

1. CREATE TABLE "IMGTABLE"
2. («NAME» VARCHAR2(4000),
3. «PHOTO»BLOB
4.)
5. /

Let's write the jdbc code to store the image in the database. Here we are using d:\\d.jpg for the location of image. You can change it according to the image location.

```
import java.sql.*;
import java.io.*;
public class InsertImage {
public static void main(String[] args) {
try{
Class.forName("oracle.jdbc.driver.OracleDriver");
Connection con=DriverManager.getConnection( "jdbc:oracle:thin:@localhos
t:1521:xe","system","oracle");

PreparedStatement ps=con.prepareStatement("insert into imgtable
values(?,?)");
ps.setString(1,"sonoo");
FileInputStream fin=new FileInputStream(«d:\\g.jpg»);
ps.setBinaryStream(2,fin,fin.available());
int i=ps.executeUpdate();
System.out.println(i+" records affected");
con.clo     se();
}catch (Exception e) {e.printStackTrace();}
}
}
```

If you see the table, record is stored in the database but image will not be shown. To do so, you need to retrieve the image from the database which we are covering in the next page.

133. Differentiate between TYPE_SCROLL_INSENSITIVE and TYPE_SCROLL_SENSITIVE.

Answer:

- We will get a scrollable ResultSet object if we specify either one of the ResultSet constants.
- The difference between the two depends on, whether a resultset is showing fv changes or not.
- This difference depends on certain methods which are called to detect changes or not.
- The resultset TYPE_SCROLL_INSENSITIVE does not show the change to it but the ResultSet srs = TYPE_SCROLL_SENSITIVE will show the change.

The following code explains the difference:

```
Statement stmt = con.createStatement (ResultSet.TYPE_SCROLL_
INSENSITIVE, ResultSet.CONCUR_READ_ONLY);
ResultSet srs = stmt.executeQuery ("SELECT COF_NAME, PRICE FROM
COFFEES");
srs.afterLast();
while (srs.previous())
{
String name = srs.getString("COF_NAME");
float price 1= srs.getFloat("PRICE");
System.out.println(name + " " + price1);
}
```

134. Name the new features added in JDBC 4.0.

Answer: The major features introduced in JDBC 4.0 are:

- Auto-loading by JDBC driver class.
- Enhanced Connection management
- RowId SQL enabled.
- DataSet implemented by SQL by using Annotations
- Enhancements of SQL exception handling
- Supporting SQL XML files.

135. Briefly tell about the JDBC Architecture.

Answer: The JDBC Architecture consists of two layers:

1. The JDBC API
2. The JDBC Driver API
   - The JDBC API provides the application-JDBC Manager connection.
   - The JDBC Driver API supports the JDBC Manager-to-Driver Connection.
   - The JDBC API interacts with a driver manager, database-specific driver for providing transparent connectivity for the heterogeneous databases.
   - The JDBC driver manager authenticates that the correct driver has been used to access each data source.
   - The driver manager supports multiple concurrent drivers connected to the multiple heterogeneous databases.

136. Describe how the JDBC application works.

Answer: A JDBC application may be divided into two layers:

- Driver layer
- Application layer
- The Driver layer consists of DriverManager class & the JDBC drivers.
- The Application layer begins after putting a request to the DriverManager for the connection.
- An appropriate driver is chosen and used for establishing the connection.
- This connection is linked to the application layer.
- The application needs the connection for creating the Statement kind of objects by which the results are obtained.

137. Explain how to Make Updates to the Updatable ResultSets.

Answer:

- The JDBC 2.0 API can update rows in a ResultSet using the methods in the Java rather than using a SQL command.
- But before doing that, we create a ResultSet object which is updatable.
- For doing this, we give the ResultSet CONCUR_UPDATABLE in the createStatement method.

Code:

```
Connection con = DriverManager.getConnection("jdbc:mySubprotocol:mySubN
ame");
Statement stmt = con.createStatement(ResultSet.TYPE_SCROLL_SENSITIVE,
ResultSet.CONCUR_UPDATABLE);
ResultSet uprs = stmt.executeQuery("SELECT COF_NAME, PRICE ");
```

15

Java Networking

1. What are Datagrams and Sockets?

Answer: A socket represents a connection point into a TCP/IP network between two computers; one of which is the server and the other is the client. Sockets are used to access the Web server. These sockets are available in the Java Socket class. Sockets act as virtual passageways for communication through which the data travels from one host to another. Sockets are of two types, connection-oriented or connectionless. The connection-oriented socket operates similarly to a telephone where the connection is established prior to the transmission of data. The second type of socket is the connectionless socket. This type of socket is called a Datagram. This socket operates similarly to the mail. A characteristic of the Datagram is that it allows only one message to be sent at a time. The delivery of data is not guaranteed because Datagrams use the UDP protocol.

2. What's the Factory Method?

Answer: Factory methods are merely a convention whereby static methods in a class return an instance of that class. The InetAddress class has no visible constructors. To create an InetAddress object, you have to use one of the available factory methods. In InetAddress the three methods getLocalHost, getByName, getByAllName can be used to create instances of InetAddress.

3. What's the difference between TCP and UDP?

Answer: These two protocols differ in the way they carry out the action of communicating. A TCP protocol establishes a two way connection between a pair of computers, while the UDP protocol is a one-way message sender. The common analogy is that TCP is like making a phone call and carrying on a two-way communication, while UDP is like mailing a letter.

4. What is the Proxy Server?

Answer: A proxy server speaks the client side of a protocol to another server. This is often required when clients have certain restrictions on which servers they can connect to. And when several users are hitting a popular web site, a proxy server can get the contents of the web server's popular pages once, saving expensive internetwork transfers while providing faster access to those pages to the clients.

Also, we can get multiple connections for a single server.

5. What are the seven layers of OSI model?

Answer:

Application
Presentation
Session
Transport
Network
DataLink
Physical Layer.

6. What Transport Layer does?

Answer: It ensures that the mail gets to its destination. If a packet fails to get its destination, it handles the process of notifying the sender and requesting that another packet be sent.

7. What is DHCP?

Answer: Dynamic Host Configuration Protocol, a piece of the TCP/IP protocol suite that handles the automatic assignment of IP addresses to clients.

8. What is SMTP?

Answer: Simple Mail Transmission Protocol, the TCP/IP Standard for Internet mails. SMTP exchanges mail between servers; contrast this with POP, which transmits mail between a server and a client.

9. In OSI N/W architecture, the dialogue control and token management are responsibilities of which layer?

Answer: b) Session Layer.

10. In OSI N/W Architecture, the routing is performed by which layer?

Answer: Network Layer.

11. What is the difference between URL instance and URLConnection instance?

Answer: A URL instance represents the location of a resource, and a URLConnection instance represents a link for accessing or communicating with the resource at the location.

12. How do I make a connection to URL?

Answer: You obtain a URL instance and then invoke openConnection on it.

URLConnection is an abstract class, which means you can't directly create instances of it using a constructor. We have to invoke openConnection method on a URL instance, to get the right kind of connection for your URL.

13. What Is a Socket?

Answer: A socket is one end-point of a two-way communication link between two programs running on the network. A socket is bound to a port number so that the TCP layer can identify the application that data is destined to be sent.Socket classes are used to represent the connection between a client program and a server program. The java.net package provides two classes--Socket and ServerSocket--which implement the client side of the connection and the server side of the connection, respectively.

14. What information is needed to create a TCP Socket?

Answer: The Local System's IP Address and Port Number. And the Remote System's IPAddress and Port Number.

15. What are the two important TCP Socket classes?

Answer: Socket and ServerSocket.

ServerSocket is used for normal two-way socket communication. Socket class allows us to read and write through the sockets.

getInputStream() and getOutputStream() are the two methods available in Socket class.

16. When MalformedURLException and UnknownHostException throws?

Answer: When the specified URL is not connected then the URL throw MalformedURLException and If InetAddress' methods getByName and getLocalHost are unabletoresolve the host name they throwan UnknownHostException.

17. Define Network Programming?

Answer: It refers to writing programs that execute across multiple devices (computers), in which the devices are all connected to each other using a network.

18. What is a Socket?

Answer: Sockets provide the communication mechanism between two computers using TCP. A client program creates a socket on its end of the communication and attempts to connect that socket to a server.

19. Advantages of Java Sockets?

Answer: Sockets are flexible and sufficient. Efficient socket based programming can be easily implemented for general communications. It cause low network traffic.

20. Disadvantages of Java Sockets?

Answer: Socket based communications allows only to send packets of raw data between applications. Both the client-side and server-side have to provide mechanisms to make the data useful in any way.

21. Which class is used by server applications to obtain a port and listen for client requests?

Answer: java.net.ServerSocket class is used by server applications to obtain a port and listen for client requests.

22. Which class represents the socket that both the client and server use to communicate with each other?

Answer: java.net.Socket class represents the socket that both the client and server use to communicate with each other.

23. How do I convert a numeric IP address like 192.18.97.39 into a hostname like java.sun.com?

Answer: By InetAddress.getByName("192.18.97.39").getHostName() where 192.18.97.39 is the IP address.

24. How do I get the IP address of a machine from its hostname?

The InetAddress class is able to resolve IP addresses for you. Obtain an instance of InetAddress for the machine, and call the getHostAddress() method, which returns a string in the xxx.xxx.xxx.xxx address form.

```
InetAddress inet = InetAddress.getByName("www.davidreilly.com");
System.out.println ("IP: " + inet.getHostAddress());
```

25. How do I perform a hostname lookup for an IP address?

The InetAddress class contains a method that can return the domain name of an IP address. You need to obtain an InetAddress class, and then call its getHostName() method. This will return the hostname for that IP address. Depending on the platform, a partial or a fully qualified hostname may be returned.

```
InetAddress inet = InetAddress.getByName("209.204.220.121");
System.out.println ("Host: " + inet.getHostName());
```

26. How can I find out who is accessing my server?

If you're using a DatagramSocket, every packet that you receive will contain the address and port from which it was sent.

```
DatagramPacket packet = null;
// Receive next packet
myDatagramSocket.receive (packet);
// Print address + port
System.out.println ("Packet From: " + packet.getAddress().
getHostAddress() + ':' + packet.getPort());
```

If you're using a ServerSocket, then every socket connection you accept will contain similar information. The Socket class has a getInetAddress() and getPort() method which will allow you to find the same information.

```
Socket mySock = myServerSocket.accept();
// Print address + port
System.out.println ("Connection From: " + mySock.getInetAddress().
getHostAddress() + ':' + mySock.getPort());
```

27. How can I find out the current IP address for my machine?

The InetAddress has a static method called getLocalHost() which will return the current address of the local machine. You can then use the getHostAddress() method to get the IP address.

```
InetAddress local = InetAddress.getLocalHost();
// Print address
System.out.println ("Local IP: " + local.getHostAddress());
```

28. Why can't my applet connect via sockets, or bind to a local port?

Applets are subject to heavy security constraints when executing under the control of a browser. Applets are unable to access the local file-system, to bind to local ports, or to connect to a computer via sockets other than the computer from which the applet is loaded. While it may seem to be an annoyance for developers, there are many good reasons why such tight constraints are placed on applets. Applets could bind to well known ports, and service network clients without authorization or consent. Applets executing within firewalls could obtain privileged information, and then send it across the network. Applets could even be infected by viruses, such as the Java StrangeBrew strain. Applets might become infected without an applet author's knowledge and then send information back that might leave hosts vulnerable to attack.

Signed applets may be allowed greater freedom by browsers than unsigned applets, which could be an option. In cases where an applet must be capable of network communication, HTTP can be used as a communication mechanism. An applet could communicate via java.net.URLConnection with a CGI script, or a Java servlet. This has an added advantage - applets that use the URLConnection will be able to communicate through a firewall.

29. What are socket options, and why should I use them?

Socket options give developers greater control over how sockets behave. Most socket behavior is controlled by the operating system, not Java itself, but as of JDK1.1, you can control several socket options, including SO_TIMEOUT, SO_LINGER, TCP_NODELAY, SO_RCVBUF and SO_SNDBUF.

These are advanced options, and many programmers may want to ignore them. That's OK, but be aware of their existence for the future. You might like to specify a timeout for read operations, to control the amount of time a connection will linger for before a reset is sent, whether Nagle's algorithm is enabled/disabled, or the send and receive buffers for datagram sockets.

30. How do I display more than one page from an applet?

The showDocument method of the AppletContext interface is overloaded - meaning that it can accept more than one parameter. It can accept a second parameter, which represents the name of the browser window that should display a page.

For example,

myAppletContext.showDocument (myurl, "frame1") will display the document in frame1. If there exists no window named frame1, then a brand new window will be created.

31. How do I use a proxy server for HTTP requests?

When a Java applet under the control of a browser (such as Netscape or Internet Explorer) fetches content via an URLConnection, it will automatically and transparently use the proxy settings of the browser.

If you're writing an application, however, you'll have to manually specify the proxy server settings. You can do this when running a Java application or you can write code that will specify proxy settings automatically for the user (providing you allow the users to customize the settings to suit their proxy servers).

To specify proxy settings when running an application, use the -D parameter:

```
jre -DproxySet=true -DproxyHost=myhost -DproxyPort=myport MyApp
```

Alternately, your application can maintain a configuration file, and specify proxy settings before using an URLConnection:

```
// Modify system properties
Properties sysProperties = System.getProperties();
// Specify proxy settings
sysProperties.put("proxyHost", "myhost");
sysProperties.put("proxyPort", "myport");
sysProperties.put("proxySet", "true");
```

32. What is a malformed url, and why is it exceptional?

When you create an instance of the java.net.URL class, its constructor can throw a MalformedURLException. This occurs when the URL is invalid. When it is thrown, it isn't because the host machine is down, or the URL path points to a missing file; a malformed URL exception is thrown when the URL cannot be correctly parsed. Common mistakes include:-

- leaving out a protocol (eg "www.microsoft.com" instead of "http://www.microsoft.com/")
- specifying an invalid protocol (eg "www://netscape.com")
- leaving out the ':' character (eg http//www.micrsoft.com/)

MalformedURLException will not be thrown if:-

- the host name is invalid (eg "www.microsoft-rules-the-world.com")
- the path is invalid (eg "http://www.microsoft.com/company_secrets.htm")

33. Why is a security exception thrown when using java.net.URL or java.net.URLConnection from an applet?

Web browsers impose security restrictions on applets, which prevent applets from establishing network connections to servers other than that from which they were loaded. Like socket connections, HTTP connections will cause security exceptions to be thrown. If you absolutely, positively, have to access other hosts (and replacing your applet with a Java servlet is impractical), consider using a digitally signed applet.

34. How do I prevent caching of HTTP requests?

By default, caching will be enabled. You must use a URLConnection, rather than the URL.openStream() method, and explicitly specify that you do not want to cache the requests. This is achieved by calling the URLConnection.setUseCaches (boolean) method with a value of false.

35. What's the Factory Method?

Answer: Factory methods are merely a convention whereby static methods in a class return an instance of that class. The InetAddress class has no visible constructors. To create an InetAddress object, you have to use one of the available factory methods. In InetAddress the three methods getLocalHost, getByName, getByAllName can be used to create instances of InetAddress.

36. What's the difference between TCP and UDP?

Answer: These two protocols differ in the way they carry out the action of communicating. A TCP protocol establishes a two way connection between a pair of computers, while the UDP protocol is a one-way message sender. The common analogy is that TCP is like making a phone call and carrying on a two-way communication, while UDP is like mailing a letter.

37. What is the Proxy Server?

Answer: A proxy server speaks the client side of a protocol to another server. This is often required when clients have certain restrictions on which servers they can connect to. And when several users are hitting a popular web site, a proxy server can get the contents of the web server's popular pages once, saving expensive internetwork transfers while providing faster access to those pages to the clients. Also, we can get multiple connections for a single server.

38. How do I make a connection to URL?

Answer: You obtain a URL instance and then invoke open Connection on it. URLConnection is an abstract class, which means you can't directly create instances of it using a constructor. We have to invoke openConnection method on a URL instance, to get the right kind of connection for your URL.

E.g.

```
URL url;
URLConnection connection;
try{ url = new URL("…");
conection = url.openConnection();
} catch (MalFormedURLException e) { }
```

39. When MalformedURLException and UnknownHostException throw?

Answer: When the specified URL is not connected then the URL throw MalformedURLException and If InetAddress' methods getByName() and getLocalHost() are unabletoresolve the host name they throwan UnknownHostException.

40. What are the two important TCP Socket classes?

Answer: Socket and ServerSocket.

ServerSocket is used for normal two-way socket communication. Socket class allows us to read and write through the sockets.

getInputStream() and getOutputStream() are the two methods available in Socket class.

16

Remote Method Invocation (RMI)

1. What is RMI and steps involved in developing an RMI object?

Answer: Remote Method Invocation (RMI) allows java object that executes on one machine and to invoke the method of a Java object to execute on another machine. The steps involved in developing an RMI object are:

a) Define the interfaces
b) Implementing these interfaces
c) Compile the interfaces and their implementations with the java compiler
d) Compile the server implementation with RMI compiler
e) Run the RMI registry
f) Run the application

2. What is RMI architecture?

Answer: - RMI architecture consists of four layers and each layer performs specific functions:

a) Application layer ---- contains the actual object definition
b) Proxy layer ---- consists of stub and skeleton
c) Remote Reference layer ---- gets the stream of bytes from the transport layer and sends it to the proxy layer
d) Transportation layer ---- responsible for handling the actual machine-to-machine communication

3. What is UnicastRemoteObject?

Answer: All remote objects must extend UnicastRemoteObject, which provides functionality that is needed to make objects available from remote machines.

4. **Explain the methods, rebind( ) and lookup() in Naming class?**

   Answer: rebind( ) of the Naming class(found in java.rmi) is used to update the RMI registry on the server machine.

   Naming. rebind("AddSever", AddServerImpl);

   lookup( ) of the Naming class accepts one argument, the rmi URL and returns a reference to an object of type AddServerImpl.

17

Unified Modelling Language (UML)

1. What is UML and how is it useful in designing large systems?

Answer: Unified Modeling Language (UML) is a notational language which comprises of several tools and techniques to support object oriented development. UML captures scenarios (use case diagram), object interactions (sequence diagram), class interactions (class diagrams) and object states (state diagrams). UML helps in designing large and complex systems. It starts with analysis of business requirement and coming up with basic business flow chart and static diagrams i.e. use case diagrams which gives pictorial view of business requirements and captures scenarios. The next step is Interaction diagrams, which mainly consists of Sequence diagrams. A Sequence diagram tells how objects interact with each other through message passing in most importantly in what sequence. Then classes are identified of the system with various class identification approaches like 'Noun Phrase Approach', 'CRC Approach', this exercise results in UML class diagrams.

A modular approach helps in breaking down the complex system where each module can further be divided into components like classes and objects. Once the whole system is refined in terms of reusability of objects, omitting unnecessary objects and classes. The building of skeleton code on best practices of coding, like pattern based approach, helps in foundation of efficient code.

2. Is UML useful for procedural programming?

Answer: Procedural programming is an unstructured way of programming which consists of set of procedures/method calls/instructions to be executed sequentially in such a way to attain the objective of a program.UML can help here in a very basic way in laying out the sequence of executions of instructions.

3. What are different notations used in UML?

Answer: UML predominantly includes static and dynamic model diagrams and each diagram has their own set of notations. In brief, the classification of these diagrams is given as below: #

Structure Diagrams includes the Class Diagram, Object Diagram, Component Diagram, Composite Structure Diagram, Package Diagram, and Deployment Diagram.

Behavior Diagrams include the Use Case Diagram (used by some methodologies during requirements gathering); Activity Diagram, and State Machine Diagram.

Interaction Diagrams, all derived from the more general Behavior Diagram, include the Sequence Diagram, Communication Diagram, Timing Diagram, and Interaction Overview Diagram.

4. What is a Use case and an Actor?

Answer: A Use case represents a particular scenario which corresponds to functional requirement (s) of a system to be designed and developed. An Actor is a user/external program or a system (anyone or anything), which interacts with a system. An Actor may input/receive or both (input and receive) information from the system.

In the diagram shown below, a scenario of buying bus/train/tram ticket from a vending machine is captured through a use case diagram. Here actor is a 'Customer' as shown by a stickman and in ovals all use cases have been documented.

5. How to identify an Actor?

Answer: An Actor can be identified by finding an answer for following points: Who is:

- interacting
- benefited
- maintaining
- supplying information
- using information
- removing information does system use an external resource?

A good/refined set of actors of system will be arrived iteratively.

6. What is Generalization?

Answer: In UML, a generalization relationship is a relationship in which one model element (the child) is based on another model element (the parent). Generalization relationships are used in class, component, deployment, and use case diagrams. Generalization corresponds to inheritance implementation amongst classes.

7. What is Association and how it maps into a Java class?

Answer: An Association specifies how objects are related to one another. To identify associations, look for verb and prepositional phrases like 'part of', 'next to', 'works for' or 'contained in'. While identifying implicit associations, a lot common sense and general knowledge is required. It is very important to eliminate redundant associations while designing a system. The most important aspects of associations are: Cardinality - a cardinality of one on a given relationship end generates a Java reference, for example

public class Customer

```
{
    Purchase purchase; ...
}
```

A cardinality of many (depicted as a number or *) generates a Java container:

```
public class Customer
{
    List purchases; ...
}
```

Navigability - For given an instance of an object on one side of a association you can access an instance on the other side. If a association can only be traversed in one direction then this will be indicated with arrows. If there are no arrows then the association is bi-directional.

Association end - A given class only sees the association through the attributes set on the association end. In other words that simple line actually represents two independent sets of data, one for each of the two classes involved. Besides the cardinality and navigability the most important attribute is the association end name. This name is used to generate the getter and setter methods and in persistent classes database column names.

The different types of associations can be Aggregation and Composition. I will describe them in more details in next blogs to come.

8. **What is Aggregation and how it maps into a Java class?**

Answer: An Aggregation is an Association which denotes an "is part of" relationship. Take a 'Car', for example, it is consisted of an engine, a steering wheel, four tires, seats, gear box, fuel tank, engine oil tank, air filters etc. So all constituents of car are parts of it.

If a car is destroyed/smashed, its parts can still be used separately as spares in other cars, so these parts have individual use even when their container entity is destroyed.

In a Java class, an aggregation can be represented from above example as:

class Car

```
{
List getTires();
```

```
List getSeats();
List getAllParts();
}
```

9. What is Composition and how it maps into a Java class?

Answer: A Composition is a tight Association and denotes "whole-part" relationship. So when an object is destroyed then all its constituents are also destroyed, these 'parts' have no meaning/sense in their lone existence from their 'whole'.

The best example of Composition is a 'Human body' which is composed of two legs, two hands, two eyes, two ears and so on. During the lifetime of a human being, all organs make sense being part of whole, but once a human being is dead most of these parts are also dead, unless some of his body parts are not medically reused.

Now come to map composition to Java world, the best example is garbage collection feature of the language. While garbage collecting objects, whole has the responsibility of preventing all its parts being garbage collected by holding some references to them.

It is the responsibility of whole to protect references to its parts not being exposed to outside world. The only way to have true composition in Java is to never let references to internal objects escape their parent's scope.

An example of Inner class as shown in the following code snippet may give you an idea how to implement Composition in Java.

```
public class Human
{
public Human()
{
Brain brain = new Brain();
}
private class Brain
{
....
....
}
}
```

10. What is Dependency and how it maps into a Java class

Answer: A Dependency relationship means when a class consumes/uses methods or variables from other class (supplier).So a change to supplier class affects the consumer class as well. Here supplier is independent of any changes being made to consumer class.

In UML class diagrams, a dependency relationship connector appears as a dashed line with an open arrow that points from the consumer class to the supplier class. A dependency relationship means an "import" statement.

11. What is the purpose of State machine diagrams?

Answer: Objects have both attributes and behaviors. Attribute is also known as state. When objects are incredibly complicated then to have better understanding during different state changes one should develop one or more state machine diagrams, formerly called state chart diagrams in UML 1.x, describing how their instances work.

12. What are different kinds of Structure diagrams?

Answer: Structure Diagrams as part of UML2.1:

- Class diagrams
- Object diagrams
- Composite structure diagrams
- Component diagrams
- Deployment diagrams
- Package diagrams

13. What are different kinds of Interaction diagrams?

Answer: The Interaction diagrams represent how objects interact with one another through message passing.

There are two kinds of Interaction Diagrams:

1. Sequence Diagram
2. Collaboration Diagram

14. What are different kinds of Behavior diagrams?

Answer: Behavior Diagrams include:

- Use Case Diagram (used by some methodologies during requirements gathering)
- Activity Diagram
- State Machine Diagram.

18

J2EE & XML

1. **What is J2EE?**

   Answer: J2EE is a standard for building enterprise applications. It includes technologies for implementing business logic, database access, message exchange, transaction management, web requests processing and many other features. The main approach of J2EE is separating presentation level from business logic (lightweight client applications) and business logic from data storage (application level of n-tier architecture).

   J2EE is an environment for developing and deploying enterprise applications. The J2EE platform consists of a set of services, application programming interfaces (APIs), and protocols that provide the functionality for developing multitiered, web-based applications.

2. **Are J2EE applications portable and scalable?**

   Answer: Nowadays industry requires portable and scalable information systems to stay in touch with rapidly changing world. J2EE applications proved the right to be called portable, because of the platform-independence of Java. J2EE applications can be developed at home and deployed to a multiprocessor server cluster. Object-oriented approach for application design makes applications scalable and easy maintaining.

3. **What makes J2EE suitable for distributed multitiered Applications?**

   Answer: The J2EE platform uses a multitiered distributed application model. Application logic is divided into components according to function, and the various application components that make up a J2EE application are installed on different machines depending on the tier in the multitiered J2EE environment to which the application component belongs. The J2EE application parts are:

   - Client-tier components run on the client machine.
   - Web-tier components run on the J2EE server.

- Business-tier components run on the J2EE server.
- Enterprise information system (EIS)-tier software runs on the EIS server.

4. What are the components of J2EE application?

Answer: A J2EE component is a self-contained functional software unit that is assembled into a J2EE application with its related classes and files and communicates with other components. The J2EE specification defines the following J2EE components:

1. Application clients and applets are client components.
2. Java Servlet and JavaServer Pages technology components are web components.
3. Enterprise JavaBeans components (enterprise beans) are business components.
4. Resource adapter components provided by EIS and tool vendors.

5. What do Enterprise JavaBeans components contain?

Answer: Enterprise JavaBeans components contains Business code, which is logic that solves or meets the needs of a particular business domain such as banking, retail, or finance, is handled by enterprise beans running in the business tier. All the business code is contained inside an Enterprise Bean which receives data from client programs, processes it (if necessary), and sends it to the enterprise information system tier for storage. An enterprise bean also retrieves data from storage, processes it (if necessary), and sends it back to the client program.

6. Is J2EE application only a web-based?

Answer: No, It depends on type of application that client wants. A J2EE application can be web-based or non-web-based. if an application client executes on the client machine, it is a non-web-based J2EE application. The J2EE application can provide a way for users to handle tasks such as J2EE system or application administration. It typically has a graphical user interface created from Swing or AWT APIs, or a command-line interface. When user request, it can open an HTTP connection to establish communication with a servlet running in the web tier.

7. Are JavaBeans J2EE components?

Answer: No. JavaBeans components are not considered J2EE components by the J2EE specification. They are written to manage the data flow between an application client or applet and components running on the J2EE server or between server components and a database. JavaBeans components written for the J2EE platform have instance variables and get and set methods for accessing the data in the instance variables. JavaBeans components used in this way are typically simple in design and implementation, but should conform to the naming and design conventions outlined in the JavaBeans component architecture.

8. **Is HTML page a web component?**

   Answer: No. Static HTML pages and applets are bundled with web components during application assembly, but are not considered web components by the J2EE specification. Even the server-side utility classes are not considered web components, either.

9. **What can be considered as a web component?**

   Answer: J2EE Web components can be either servlets or JSP pages. Servlets are Java programming language classes that dynamically process requests and construct responses. JSP pages are text-based documents that execute as servlets but allow a more natural approach to creating static content.

10. **What is the container?**

    Answer: Containers are the interface between a component and the low-level platform specific functionality that supports the component. Before a Web, enterprise bean, or application client component can be executed, it must be assembled into a J2EE application and deployed into its container.

11. **What are container services?**

    Answer: A container is a runtime support of a system-level entity. Containers provide components with services such as lifecycle management, security, deployment, and threading.

12. **What is the web container?**

    Answer: Servlet and JSP containers are collectively referred to as Web containers. It manages the execution of JSP page and servlet components for J2EE applications. Web components and their container run on the J2EE server.

13. **What is Enterprise JavaBeans (EJB) container?**

    Answer: It manages the execution of enterprise beans for J2EE applications. Enterprise beans and their container run on the J2EE server.

14. **What is Applet container?**

    Answer: IManages the execution of applets. Consists of a Web browser and Java Plugin running on the client together.

15. **How do we package J2EE components?**

    Answer: J2EE components are packaged separately and bundled into a J2EE application for deployment. Each component, its related files such as GIF and HTML files or server-side utility classes, and a deployment descriptor are assembled into a module and added to the J2EE application. A J2EE application is composed of one or more enterprise bean,Web, or application client component modules. The final enterprise solution can use one J2EE application or be made up of two or more J2EE applications, depending on design requirements. A J2EE application and each of its modules has its own deployment descriptor. A deployment descriptor is an XML document with an .xml extension that describes a component's deployment settings.

16. What is life cycle (J2EE component)?

Answer: The framework events of a J2EE component's existence. Each type of component has defining events that mark its transition into states in which it has varying availability for use. For example, a servlet is created and has its init method called by its container before invocation of its service method by clients or other servlets that require its functionality. After the call of its init method, it has the data and readiness for its intended use. The servlet's destroy method is called by its container before the ending of its existence so that processing associated with winding up can be done and resources can be released. The init and destroy methods in this example are callback methods. Similar considerations apply to the life cycle of all J2EE component types: enterprise beans, Web components (servlets or JSP pages), applets, and application clients.

17. What is a thin client?

Answer: A thin client is a lightweight interface to the application that does not have such operations like query databases, execute complex business rules, or connect to legacy applications.

18. What are types of J2EE clients?

Answer: Following are the types of J2EE clients:

- Applets
- Application clients
- Java Web Start-enabled rich clients, powered by Java Web Start technology.
- Wireless clients, based on Mobile Information Device Profile (MIDP) technology.

19. What is deployment descriptor?

Answer: A deployment descriptor is an Extensible Markup Language (XML) text-based file with an .xml extension that describes a component's deployment settings. A J2EE application and each of its modules has its own deployment descriptor. For example, an enterprise bean module deployment descriptor declares transaction attributes and security authorizations for an enterprise bean. Because deployment descriptor information is declarative, it can be changed without modifying the bean source code. At run time, the J2EE server reads the deployment descriptor and acts upon the component accordingly.

20. What is the EAR file?

Answer: An EAR file is a standard JAR file with an .ear extension, named from Enterprise ARchive file. A J2EE application with all of its modules is delivered in EAR file.

21. What is JTA and JTS?

Answer: JTA is the abbreviation for the Java Transaction API. JTS is the abbreviation for the Jave Transaction Service. JTA provides a standard interface and allows you to demarcate transactions in a manner that is independent of the transaction manager implementation. The J2EE SDK implements the transaction manager with JTS. But your code doesn't call the JTS methods directly. Instead, it invokes the JTA methods, which then call the lower-level JTS routines. Therefore, JTA is a high level transaction interface that your application uses to control transaction. and JTS is a low level transaction interface and ejb uses behind the scenes (client code doesn't directly interact with JTS. It is based on object transaction service(OTS) which is part of CORBA.

22. What is JAXP?

Answer: JAXP stands for Java API for XML. XML is a language for representing and describing text-based data which can be read and handled by any program or tool that uses XML APIs. It provides standard services to determine the type of an arbitrary piece of data, encapsulate access to it, discover the operations available on it, and create the appropriate JavaBeans component to perform those operations.

23. What is J2EE Connector?

Answer: The J2EE Connector API is used by J2EE tools vendors and system integrators to create resource adapters that support access to enterprise information systems that can be plugged into any J2EE product. Each type of database or EIS has a different resource adapter. Note: A resource adapter is a software component that allows J2EE application components to access and interact with the underlying resource manager. Because a resource adapter is specific to its resource manager, there is typically a different resource adapter for each type of database or enterprise information system.

24. What is JAAP?

Answer: The Java Authentication and Authorization Service (JAAS) provide a way for a J2EE application to authenticate and authorize a specific user or group of users to run it. It is a standard Pluggable Authentication Module (PAM) framework that extends the Java 2 platform security architecture to support user-based authorization.

25. What is Java Naming and Directory Service?

Answer: The JNDI provides naming and directory functionality. It provides applications with methods for performing standard directory operations, such as associating attributes with objects and searching for objects using their attributes. Using JNDI, a J2EE application can store and retrieve any type of named Java object. Because JNDI is independent of any specific implementations, applications can use JNDI to access multiple naming and directory services, including existing naming and directory services such as LDAP, NDS, DNS, and NIS.

26. What is J2EE application?

Answer: Any deployable unit of J2EE functionality. This can be a single J2EE module or a group of modules packaged into an EAR file along with a J2EE application deployment descriptor. J2EE applications are typically engineered to be distributed across multiple computing tiers.

27. What is J2EE component?

Answer: A self-contained functional software unit supported by a container and configurable at deployment time. The J2EE specification defines the following J2EE components: Application clients and applets are components that run on the client. Java servlet and JavaServer Pages (JSP) technology components are Web components that run on the server.

Enterprise JavaBeans (EJB) components (enterprise beans) are business components that run on the server.

J2EE components are written in the Java programming language and are compiled in the same way as any program in the language. The difference between J2EE components and "standard" Java classes is that J2EE components are assembled into a J2EE application, verified to be well formed and in compliance with the J2EE specification, and deployed to production, where they are run and managed by the J2EE server or client container.

28. What is J2EE module?

Answer: A software unit that consists of one or more J2EE components of the same container type and one deployment descriptor of that type. There are four types of modules: EJB, Web, application client, and resource adapter. Modules can be deployed as stand-alone units or can be assembled into a J2EE application.

29. What is J2EE product?

Answer: An implementation that conforms to the J2EE platform specification.

30. What is J2EE product provider?

Answer: A vendor that supplies a J2EE product.

31. What is J2EE server?

Answer: The runtime portion of a J2EE product. A J2EE server provides EJB or Web containers or both.

32. Explain J2EE architecture.

Answer: The JEE platform provides the environment to develop enterprise applications / services using multitier architecture. The highly intensified technology made the need for scalable, efficient, faster solutions for information management. The JEE technology is rightly apt for meeting these requirements. JEE provides a programming development environment which improves the productivity of development, standards for hosting / deploying enterprise applications.

The following are the tiers in JEE application

Client Tier: The client tier includes the web components such as Servlets, JSP or standalone Java Desktop applications. This tier provides dynamic interfaces to the middle tier.

- Middle Tier: This also called as the server tier. In the middle tier enterprise beans and web services encapsulate distributable business logic for the applications which are reusable. The JEE application server contains the server-tier components which provides the platform for these web components for actions to be performed and data to be stored / persisted.
- Enterprise data tier: The enterprise level data is stored / persisted preferably or typically in a relational database, in this tier.

The JEE applications comprises of components, containers and services. All the web components (Servlets, JSP) provide dynamic requests and responses from a web page. The EJB components contain the server-side business logic for enterprise applications.

33. J2EE is a container centric architecture. Explain.

Answer: A container acts as an interface between a platform-specific functionality and a component. The component must be assembled before a web or enterprise bean or application client component execution, into a JEE application and deployed into its container.

The settings of a container can be customized for underlying support provided by the JEE server. These include security, transaction management, and Java Naming and Directory Interface lookups.

The management of non configurable services such as servlet life cycle, enterprise bean life cycle, database connection, data persistence, database connection pooling also can be done by the container.

34. Explain the four types of container that the J2EE specification defines.

Answer: A container is a runtime support of a system level entity [Applet, Servlet/ JSP, EJB]

The four types of container that the J2EE specification defines are applet container, application-client container, web container and EJB container.

Applet Container: An applet is a java program that can be embedded into a web page. Most of the web pages are authored in HTML. To use an applet in HTML document, the tags <APPLET> and </APPLET> are used. They are used to indicate to the browser that a java applet should be loaded. "These tags act as a container for the java applet definition. " Applet container manages the execution of applet, and contains the web browser.

Application-client Container: The Application Client Container (ACC) is a combination of Java classes, libraries, and other files. They are used to distribute along with Java client programs that execute on their own JVM. The execution of the application client components is managed by the application-client container. The ACC can take the responsibility to collect user name and password which is treated as authentication data.

Web Container: A web container is a part of web server. It provides the run time environment to execute a web application such as a servlet, JSP. A servlet container translates the URL requests into servlet requests. The JSP implicit objects such as request, response, out, page, pageContext etc., are exposed by JSP container.

EJB Container: The EJB container, like other containers provides run-time environment to execute EJB components such as enterprise beans. An EJB Container manages transactions, state management details, multi threading, connection pooling. The applications are provided with security using EJB container. All database access required by the entity bean will be handled by the EJB container.

35. Explain the J2EE container architecture.

Answer: J2EE Container Architecture:

The J2EE application components need support at runtime. This support is provided by J2EE containers. They use protocols, methods of the containers to access other application components. The containers of J2EE are 1) Web container 2) EJB container.

1) The web container is used to host web applications. It provides the run time environment to execute Servlet and JSP component types.
2) The business logic is dealt by the server components called EJB components. The access to local and remote enterprise beans is provided by the EJB container. The operations of the three beans namely Entity Bean, Session Bean and Message-driven bean are handled by the EJB Container.

36. Explain the technologies that J2EE platform provides for developing components.

Answer:

1) **Servlet Technology:** It is considered as the foundation of web technologies. It overcomes the limitations of CGI technology. It is a server side component

to serve the clients and to generate dynamic content. Servlets interacts with web clients using the paradigm 'request-response'. All client requests are sent through web servers to the servlet container. The servelt then process the request and sends the response back to the client. Servlets are reliable, scalable, efficient and reusable server side components.

2) **JSP Technology:** It is the extension of servlet technology. It is easy to author JSP without much knowledge of the supporting API. JSP can be used to work with HTTP requests and HTTP responses, session management and so on. It is easy to combine both static and dynamic content with JSP. The factor to develop JSP technology is to use regular HTML tags. The JSP author can place servlet or simple java code in the page by using special designated tags. The entire JSP will be translated into Servlet and the servlet related code is communicated to container to run.

3) **EJB Technology:** EJB is a server-side web component. It depends on other Java technologies for proper functionality such as Remote Method Invocation. RMI is used as a protocol between 2 enterprise beans and between an enterprise bean and its client. EJB encapsulates the business logic. All EJBs are developed, deployed and run only in an EJB container. This is similar to servlets and JSP run in a web container.

EJB applications are easy to develop because the applications developer can concentrate on business logic. The developer can utilize the services provided by the EJB container, like connection pooling and transactions.

37. Explain the J2EE APIs, i.e. RMI/IIOP, JNDI, JDBC, Java Mail and JMS.

Answer: **RMI/IIOP:** RMI stands for Remote Method Invocation. IIOP stands for Inter Internet-ORB Protocol. ORB

RMI/IIOP API is used to write distributed objects using Java technology, which enables communication between objects in the memory, across JVM and also physical devices.

RMI/IIOP yields the benefits of OOP such as inheritance, polymorphism and encapsulation and is platform independent. In RMI/IIOP, the code related to network is written by applying the interface but not the implementations. The operation can solely on the interface that object's class.

RMI-IIOP relies on object serialization for passing parameters via remote method invocations.

JNDI (Java Naming and Directory Interface) API: To enable java programs to access the naming and directory services, the JNDI API is utilized. Naming services emphasizes on the services that are to associate names with objects.

We are familiar with naming systems such as the file system which has a directory or path associated it. Surfing web is associated a name that is the URL called Domain Naming System. EJB components of a J2EE application server, user profiles are associated in LDAP (Lightweight Directory Access Protocol) directory.

For example, JNDI is the best API to write a java application that is used for search utility over network-enabled desktop, class-browser or an address book search utility.

JDBC (Java Database Connectivity) API: Many java applications use a database and database accessing and programming is a significant role in web application development. JDBC is an API that enables the accessibility to a database in order to manipulate the database.

The JDBC API supports both two-tier and three-tier models for database access.

Two-tier model -- a Java application interacts directly with the database. Three-tier model -- introduces a middle-level server for execution of business logic: the middle tier to maintain control over data access.

The application that uses the JDBC implements the following sequence.

1. Importing Packages
2. Registering the JDBC Drivers
3. Opening a Connection to a Database
4. Creating a Statement Object
5. Executing a query and Returning a Result Set Object
6. Processing the Result Set
7. Closing the Result Set and Statement Objects
8. Closing the Connection

Java Mail API: Mailing and Messaging applications can be modeled or developed using Java Mail. The e-mail messaging applications can be developed for both high-level implementation and low-level implementation. That is, a small company which is heading towards growth can develop solutions which ensure the accessing to their mail server in an efficient manner. A blue-chip company can focus on providing the access to industry-level access which is a wider reach and provides vast support.

JMS: Java Message Services is an API that enables the components of an application, could it be JSE or JEE component to provide messaging services such as create, send, receive and read messages. Using the loosely coupled, reliable and asynchronous communications are enabled by JMS.

The JMS application contains the following parts:

1. JMS Provider: It implements the JMS interface and provides the administration and control services for the messages. J2EE 1.3 includes the JMS Provider service.
2. JMS Clients: These are the java applications that produce or consume the messages.
3. Messages: These are the objects that communicate the messages between clients.
4. Administered Objects: They are the JMS objects created by the administrator that can be used by the clients. They are namely destinations and connection factories.

5. Native Clients: These are the applications that use message client's native client API instead of JMS API.

38. What are the 3 different Java platform editions? Explain them.

Answer: Java 2 Platform, Standard Edition (J2SE)

Java 2 Platform, Enterprise Edition (J2EE)

Java 2 Platform, Micro Edition (J2ME)

Java 2 Platform, Standard Edition (JSE): J2SE is used to develop stand alone / desktop portable java applications. J2SE consists of two components. Core component and desktop component. Core component provides back end functionality. Desktop component provides GUI functionality. J2SE consists of Java Development Kit and Java Runtime Environment. JDK consists of java compiler and other related tools to enable the users to create Java Applications. Java Runtime Environment consists of java virtual machine, libraries and all other components that are necessary to run a java application.

Java 2 Platform, Enterprise Edition (JEE): J2EE is a platform to develop multi-tier enterprise applications. JEE includes Servlets API, Java Server Pages and Enterprise Java Beans. It was built on J2SE technology.

Java 2 Platform, Micro Edition (JME): JME is the technology for microelectronic devices like PDAs, Mobile phones etc. JME supports the flexibility for user interfaces, provides the security and uses the built-in network protocols for networked applications.JME applications can be ported across different devices.

39. What are the components of J2EE application?

Answer: A J2EE component is a self-contained functional software unit that is assembled into a J2EE application with its related classes and files and communicates with other components. The J2EE specification defines the following J2EE components:

Application clients and applets are client components.

Java Servlet and JavaServer PagesTM (JSPTM) technology components are web components.

Enterprise JavaBeansTM (EJBTM) components (enterprise beans) are business components.

Resource adapter components provided by EIS and tool vendors.

40. What are the four types of J2EE modules?

Answer:

1. Application client module
2. Web module
3. Enterprise JavaBeans module
4. Resource adapter module

41. What does application client module contain?

Answer: The application client module contains:

- class files,
- an application client deployment descriptor.

Application client modules are packaged as JAR files with a .jar extension.

42. What does web module contain?

Answer: The web module contains:

- JSP files,
- class files for servlets,
- GIF and HTML files, and
- a Web deployment descriptor.

Web modules are packaged as JAR files with a .war (Web ARchive) extension.

43. What are the differences between Ear, Jar and War files? Under what circumstances should we use each one?

Answer: There are no structural differences between the files; they are all archived using zip-jar compression. However, they are intended for different purposes.

- Jar files (files with a .jar extension) are intended to hold generic libraries of Java classes, resources, auxiliary files, etc.
- War files (files with a .war extension) are intended to contain complete Web applications. In this context, a Web application is defined as a single group of files, classes, resources, .jar files that can be packaged and accessed as one servlet context.
- Ear files (files with a .ear extension) are intended to contain complete enterprise applications. In this context, an enterprise application is defined as a collection of .jar files, resources, classes, and multiple Web applications.

Each type of file (.jar, .war, .ear) is processed uniquely by application servers, servlet containers, EJB containers, etc.

44. What is "application client"?

Answer: A first-tier J2EE client component that executes in its own Java virtual machine. Application clients have access to some J2EE platform APIs.

45. What is "application client container"?

Answer: A container that supports application client components.

46. What is "application client module"?

Answer: A software unit that consists of one or more classes and an application client deployment descriptor.

47. What is "application component provider"?

Answer: A vendor that provides the Java classes that implement components' methods, JSP page definitions, and any required deployment descriptors.

48. What is "application configuration resource file"?

An XML file used to configure resources for a Java Server Faces application, to define navigation rules for the application, and to register converters, Validator, listeners, renders, and components with the application.

49. What is "archiving"?

Answer: The process of saving the state of an object and restoring it.

50. What is "asant"?

Answer: A Java-based build tool that can be extended using Java classes. The configuration files are XML-based, calling out a target tree where various tasks get executed.

51. What is URI?

Answer: Uniform resource identifier. A globally unique identifier for an abstract or physical resource. A URL is a kind of URI that specifies the retrieval protocol (http or https for Web applications) and physical location of a resource (host name and host-relative path). A URN is another type of URI.

52. What is URL?

Answer: Uniform resource locator. A standard for writing a textual reference to an arbitrary piece of data in the World Wide Web. A URL looks like this: protocol://host/local info where protocol specifies a protocol for fetching the object (such as http or ftp), host specifies the Internet name of the targeted host, and local info is a string (often a file name) passed to the protocol handler on the remote host.

53. What is URL path?

Answer: The part of a URL passed by an HTTP request to invoke a servlet. A URL path consists of the context path + servlet path + path info, where Context path is the path prefix associated with a servlet context of which the servlet is a part. If this context is the default context rooted at the base of the Web server's URL namespace, the path prefix will be an empty string. Otherwise, the path prefix starts with a / character but does not end with a / character. Servlet path is the path section that directly corresponds to the mapping that activated this request. This path starts with a / character. Path info is the part of the request path that is not part of the context path or the servlet path

54. What is URN?

Answer: Uniform resource name. A unique identifier that identifies an entity but doesn't tell where it is located. A system can use a URN to look up an entity locally before trying to find it on the Web. It also allows the Web location to change, while still allowing the entity to be found.

55. What is Web application?

Answer: An application written for the Internet, including those built with Java technologies such as JavaServer Pages and servlets, as well as those built with non-Java technologies such as CGI and Perl.

56. What is Web application, distributable?

Answer: A Web application that uses J2EE technology written so that it can be deployed in a Web container distributed across multiple Java virtual machines running on the same host or different hosts. The deployment descriptor for such an application uses the distributable element.

57. What is Web component?

Answer: A component that provides services in response to requests; either a servlet or a JSP page.

58. What is Web container?

Answer: A container that implements the Web component contract of the J2EE architecture. This contract specifies a runtime environment for Web components that includes security, concurrency, life-cycle management, transaction, deployment, and other services. A Web container provides the same services as a JSP container as well as a federated view of the J2EE platform APIs. A Web container is provided by a Web or J2EE server.

59. What is Web container, distributed?

Answer: A Web container that can run a Web application that is tagged as distributable and that executes across multiple Java virtual machines running on the same host or on different hosts.

60. What is Web container provider?

Answer: A vendor that supplies a Web container.

61. What is Web module?

Answer: A deployable unit that consists of one or more Web components, other resources, and a Web application deployment descriptor contained in a hierarchy of directories and files in a standard Web application format.

62. What is Web resource?

Answer: A static or dynamic object contained in a Web application that can be referenced by a URL.

63. What is Web resource collection?

Answer: A list of URL patterns and HTTP methods that describe a set of Web resources to be protected.

64. What is Web server?

Answer: Software that provides services to access the Internet, an intranet, or an extranet. A Web server hosts Web sites, provides support for HTTP and other protocols, and executes server-side programs (such as CGI scripts or servlets) that perform certain functions. In the J2EE architecture, a Web server provides services to a Web container. For example, a Web container typically relies on a Web server to provide HTTP message handling. The J2EE architecture assumes that a Web container is hosted by a Web server from the same vendor, so it does not specify the contract between these two entities. A Web server can host one or more Web containers.

65. What is Web server provider?

Answer: A vendor that supplies a Web server.

66. What is life cycle (J2EE component)?

Answer: The framework events of a J2EE component's existence. Each type of component has defining events that mark its transition into states in which it has varying availability for use. For example, a servlet is created and has its init method called by its container before invocation of its service method by clients or other servlets that require its functionality. After the call of its init method, it has the data and readiness for its intended use. The servlet's destroy method is called by its container before the ending of its existence so that processing associated with winding up can be done and resources can be released. The init and destroy methods in this example are callback methods. Similar considerations apply to the life cycle of all J2EE component types: enterprise beans, Web components (servlets or JSP pages), applets, and application clients.

67. What is life cycle (JavaServer Faces)?

Answer: A set of phases during which a request for a page is received, a UI component tree representing the page is processed, and a response is produced. During the phases of the life cycle:

The local data of the components is updated with the values contained in the request parameters.

Events generated by the components are processed.

Validators and converters registered on the components are processed.

The components' local data is updated to back-end objects.

The response is rendered to the client while the component state of the response is saved on the server for future requests.

68. What is Entity Bean and Session Bean?

Answer: A session bean is a non-persistent object that implements some business logic running on the server. One way to think of a session object is as a logical extension of the client program that runs on the server. An entity bean is a component that represents an object-oriented view of some entities stored in a persistent storage, such as a database, or entities that are implemented by an existing enterprise application.

69. What are the methods of Entity Bean?

Answer: Here we will talk about the implementation of an Entity Bean, not about a home interface. An entity bean consists of 4 groups of methods:

1. create methods. They look like this: EntityBeanClass ejbCreateXXX(parameters), where EntityBeanClass is an Entity Bean you are trying to instantiate, ejbCreateXXX(parameters) methods are used for creating Entity Bean instances according to the parameters specified and to some programmer-defined conditions. Implementation of create() methods of home interface is necessary only in Entity Beans with Bean-Managed Persistence.
2. finder methods. Each finder method is used for finding Entity Beans (single objects or a collection of objects) within the home. There is a method used for finding objects by the unique identifier (a Primary Key) - findByPrimaryKey(PrimaryKeyClass). This method returns a single Entity Bean, whereas most other finder methods return a Collection of remote interfaces.
3. remove methods. These methods (you may have up to 2 remove methods, or don't have them at all) allow the client to physically remove Entity Beans. You can remove these beans by specifying either Handle or a Primary Key for the Entity Bean.
4. home methods. These methods are designed and implemented by a developer, and EJB specification doesn't have any requirements for them except the need to throw a RemoteException is each home method.

70. How does Stateful Session bean store its state?

Answer: First of all, a Stateful Session bean is a Session Bean instance containing some conversational state (a result of data interchange or processing), which needs to be retained across methods and transactions.

A Stateful Session bean stores its state in the instance's fields and objects referred to from these fields. These fields may contain some up-to-time information as open sockets or database connections.

71. Why does Stateless Session bean not store its state even though it has ejbActivate() and ejbPassivate()?

Answer: To answer this question you need to remember what a Stateless Session bean is. It's a Session Bean instance NOT containing any conversational state. Such beans are used mostly for performing some atomic operations, because NO data is saved in the instance's variables. The other point is that you never know which instance serves your application request at a given time. If your application requests a Stateless Session bean once and another Stateless Session bean in some time, you can never be sure that a Container gives you the same reference. As a conclusion, the Stateless Session beans have the ejbActivate() and ejbPassivate() methods, but there is no sense to rely on their persistence, because of the implementation of such beans.

72. What are the services provided by the container?

Answer: A container provides a set of services listed below:

1. Enterprise Java Beans support. The support for EJBs is mandatory for each container. It must support all types of beans specified by SUN. (The latest specification is 2.0, though it's final version is not yet released, but most EJB containers already support it.)
2. JTS (Java Transaction Service). This service is intended to control transactions within an enterprise system.
3. JNDI (Java Naming and Directory Interface). Every EJB Container MUST provide a name space for accessing resources (including EJB instances), as well as a way to access them using JNDI.
4. JDBC (Java DataBase Connection). A Container must be able to provide EJBs with ability to access existing database(s). In most cases the XA and connection pooling are also supported, but it's also a headache of a JDBC driver vendor.
5. JMS (Java Messaging Service). This service is new to EJB, and it was introduced in EJB 2.0. This service allows interchange of asynchronous messages. EJB 2.0 also introduced the new type of beans - Message-driven Beans invoked by a Container only.

73. Types of transaction?

Answer: EJBs may participate (and often do it) in database transactions. Just remember some database fundamentals:

1. Simple transactions. Transactions performing simple operations. This type of transactions is the most often used.
2. Nested transactions. Transactions can be nested, i.e. some method, which opens a transaction, may call another method, also opening a transaction. In such case a nested transaction appears. There is no need to make such transactions explicitly, because most systems don't require such complicated logic. Nevertheless, modern database servers support nested transactions.

Note that if an inner transaction rolls back, the outer transaction automatically rolls back, and if an inner transaction fails, the outer transaction also fails.

3. Distributed transactions. This kind of transaction is used for performing operations on data located in different databases. If more than one database is involved in a transaction, such transaction is called a distributed transaction.

74. What is bean-managed transaction?

Answer: If a developer doesn't want a Container to manage transactions, it's possible to implement all database operations manually by writing the appropriate JDBC code. This often leads to productivity increase, but it makes an Entity Bean incompatible with some databases and it enlarges the amount of code to be written. A developer explicitly performs all transaction management.

75. Why does EJB need two interfaces (Home and Remote Interface)?

Answer: A client searches for a home interface to instantiate a remote interface. A remote interface is a client-side mapping to a server object performing business methods. Such schema was introduced purposely to demarcate the difference between server and client interfaces.

76. What are transaction attributes?

Answer: The transaction attribute specifies how the Container must manage transactions for a method when a client invokes the method via the enterprise bean's home or component interface or when the method is invoked as the result of the arrival of a JMS message. (Sun's EJB Specification) Below is a list of transactional attributes:

1. NotSupported - transaction context is unspecified.
2. Required - bean's method invocation is made within a transactional context. If a client is not associated with a transaction, a new transaction is invoked automatically.
3. Supports - if a transactional context exists, a Container acts like the transaction attribute is Required, else - like NotSupported.
4. RequiresNew - a method is invoked in a new transaction context.
5. Mandatory - if a transactional context exists, a Container acts like the transaction attribute is required, else it throws a javax.ejb.TransactionRequiredException.
6. Never - a method executes only if no transaction context is specified.

77. What is the difference between Container-Managed Persistent (CMP) bean and Bean-Managed (BMP) persistent entity bean?

Answer: A CMP bean developer doesn't need to worry about JDBC code and transactions, because the Container performs database calls and transaction management instead of the programmer. All table mapping is specified in the deployment descriptor. Otherwise, a BMP bean developer takes the load of linking an application and a database on his shoulders. BMP beans are not 100% database-independent, because they may contain database-specific code, but CMP beans are unable to perform complicated DML (data manipulation language) statements. EJB 2.0 specification introduced some new ways of querying database (by using the EJB QL - query language).

78. How entity bean is created using CMP entity bean?

Answer: The container creates an entity bean automatically. Here, "automatically" means that a developer doesn't need to write any SQL code for it. Certainly, this doesn't exempt a programmer from implementing business methods.

79. What is software architecture of EJB?

Answer: Session and Entity EJBs consist of 4 or 5 parts: a remote interface (a client interacts with it), a home interface (used for creating objects and for declaring business methods) a bean object (an object, which actually performs business logic and EJB-specific operations). The fourth part is a deployment descriptor (an XML file containing all information required for maintaining the EJB) or a set of deployment descriptors (if you are using some container-specific features). The fifth part - a Primary Key class - is only Entity bean specific.

80. Can Entity Beans have no create() methods?

Answer: Certainly. In some cases the data is inserted NOT using Java application, so you may only need to retrieve the information, perform its processing, but not create your own information of this kind.

81. In which case ejbLoad() doesn't read data from the database?

Answer: ejbLoad() reads data from the database in all cases except one: when the information stored in an Entity Bean has not been changed after creation or retrieving. In this case ejbLoad() becomes a redundant operation.

82. What is an "eager loading of state"?

Answer: An EJB container usually reads all data to construct the Entity Bean. This is opposite to "lazy loading" when data is read as pieces, not as a whole block. This increases speed in most cases but makes the application more complicated.

83. How would you implement a case when Entity Bean 1 calls Entity Bean 2, which calls Entity Bean 1?

Answer: You need to mark Entity Bean 1 as re-entrant.

84. How would you implement EJB subclassing?

Answer: The following guidelines assume that we have EJB2, which subclasses EJB1. (Both EJBs are session ones.)

The Remote interface of EJB2 implements the Remote interface of EJB1
The Bean class of EJB2 extends the Bean class of EJB1

85. What is difference between StateFul and Stateless Session Bean?

Answer: A Stateful Session Bean is a bean that is designed to service business processes that span multiple method requests or transactions. Stateful Session beans retain state on behalf of an individual client. Stateless Session Beans do not maintain state.

EJB containers pools stateless session beans and reuses them to service many clients. Stateful session beans can be passivated and reused for other clients. But this involves I/O bottlenecks. Because a stateful session bean caches client conversation in memory, a bean failure may result in loosing the entire client conversation. Therefore, while writing a stateful session bean the bean developer has to keep the bean failure and client conversation loss in mind.

In case of stateless session beans, client specific data has to be pushed to the bean for each method invocation, which will result in increase in the network traffic. This can be avoided in a number of ways like persisting the client specific data in database or in JNDI. But this also results in I/O performance bottlenecks.

If the business process spans multiple invocations thereby requiring a conversation then stateful session bean will be the ideal choice. On the other hand, if business process lasts only for a single method call, stateless session bean model suits.

Stateful session beans remembers the previous request and responses. But stateless beans do not. stateful does not have pooling concept, whereas the stateless bean instances are pooled

86. Difference between forward(request,response) and SendRedirect(url) in Servlet?

Answer: With Forward, request & response would be passed to the destination URL which should be relative (means that the destination URL should be within a servlet context). Also, after executing forward method, the control will return back to the same method from where the forward method was called. All the opposite to the above points apply to sendRedirect.

(OR)The forward will redirect in the application server itself. It does not come to the client. Whereas Response.sendredirect() will come to the client and go back ...i.e. URL appending will happen.

87. What is enterprise bean?

Answer:

- Server side reusable java component
- Offers services that are hard to implement by the programmer
- Sun: Enterprise Bean architecture is a component architecture for the deployment and development of component-based distributed business applications.

Applications written using enterprise java beans are scalable, transactional and multi-user secure. These applications may be written once and then deployed on any server platform that supports enterprise java beans specification.

- Enterprise beans are executed by the J2EE server.

First version 1.0 contained session beans, entity beans were not included.

Entity beans were added to version 1.1 which came out during year 1999.

Current release is EJB version 1.2

88. Services of EJB?

Answer: Database management

- Database connection pooling
- DataSource, offered by the J2EE server. Needed to access connection pool of the server.
- Database access is configured to the J2EE server -> easy to change database / database driver
- Transaction management
- Distributed transactions
- J2EE server offers transaction monitor which can be accessed by the client.
- Security management
- Authetication
- Authorization
- encryption

Enterprise java beans can be distributed /replicated into separate machines lDistribution/replication offers

- Load balancing, load can be divided into separate servers.
- Failover, if one server fails, others can keep on processing normally.
- Performance, one server is not so heavy loaded. Also, for example Weblogic has thread pools for improving performance in one server.

89. When to choose EJB?

Answer: Server will be heavy loaded

- Distribution of servers helps to achieve better performance.
- Server should have replica for the case of failure of one server.
- Replication is invisible to the programmer
- Distributed transactions are needed
- J2EE server offers transaction monitor that takes care of transaction management.
- Distributed transactions are invisible to the programmerl Other services vs. money

Weblogic J2EE server ~ 80 000 mk and Jbuilder X Professional Edition ~ 5 000mk

90. Why not to use free J2EE servers?

Answer:

- no tecnical support
- harder to use (no graphical user interface ...)
- no integration to development tools (for example, Jbuilder)
- Bugs? Other problems during project?

91. What J2EE server offers?

Answer: DataSource.

- Object that can be used to achieve database connection from the connection pool.
- Can be accessed by the interface DataSource
- Transaction monitor
- Can be accessed by the interface UserTransaction.

Java Naming and the Directory Service

92. Java Naming and the Directory Service

Answer: Naming service is needed to locate beans home interfaces or other objects (DataSource, UserTransaction)

- For example, jndi name of the DataSource

Directory service is needed to store and retrieve properties by their name.

- jndi name: java:comp/env/propertyName

93. XML – deployment descriptor

Answer: ejb-jar.xml + server-specific xml- file Which is then Packed in a jar – file together with bean classes.

Beans are packaged into EJB JAR file , Manifest file is used to list EJB's and jar file holding Deployment descriptor.

94. Session Bean

Answer: Developer programs three classes:

- Home interface, contains methods for creating (and locating for entity beans) bean instances.
- Remote interface contains business methods the bean offers.
- Bean class contains the business logic of the enterprise bean.

95. Entity Beans

Answer: Represents one row in the database.

- Easy way to access database
- Business logic concept to manipulate data.

- Container managed persistence vs. bean managed persistence.

Programmer creates three or four classes:

- Home interface for locating beans
- Remote interface that contains business methods for clients.
- Bean class that implements bean's behavior.
- Primary key class – that represents primary key in the database. Used to locate beans.

Primary key class is not needed if primary key is a single field that could be j

When to use which bean?

Entity beans are effective when application wants to access one row at a time. If many rows need to be fetched, using session beans can be better alternativeava class (for example, Integer).

Entity beans are efficient when working with one row at a time

Cause a lot of network traffic.

Session Beans are efficient when client wants to access database directly.

- fetching/updating multiple rows from the database

96. Explain J2EE Architecture?

Answer: Normally, thin-client multitiered applications are hard to write because they involve many lines of intricate code to handle transaction and state management, multithreading, resource pooling, and other complex low-level details.

The component-based and platform-independent J2EE architecture makes J2EE applications easy to write because business logic is organized into reusable components and the J2EE server provides underlying services in the form of a container for every component type. Because you do not have to develop these services yourself, you are free to concentrate on solving the business problem at hand.

Containers and Services

Components are installed in their containers during deployment and are the interface between a component and the low-level platform-specific functionality that supports the component. Before a web, enterprise bean, or application client component can be executed, it must be assembled into a J2EE application and deployed into its container.

The assembly process involves specifying container settings for each component in the J2EE application and for the J2EE application itself. Container settings customize the underlying support provided by the J2EE Server, which include services such as security, transaction management, Java Naming and Directory Interface TM (JNDI) lookups, and remote connectivity.

Figure: J2EE Server and Containers

Container Types

The deployment process installs J2EE application components in the following types of J2EE containers. The J2EE components and container addressed in this tutorial are shown in Figure 5.

- An Enterprise JavaBeans (EJB) container manages the execution of all enterprise beans for one J2EE application. Enterprise beans and their container run on the J2EE server.
- A web container manages the execution of all JSP page and servlet components for one J2EE application. Web components and their container run on the J2EE server.
- An application client container manages the execution of all application client components for one J2EE application. Application clients and their container run on the client machine.
- An applet container is the web browser and Java Plug-in combination running on the client machine.

97. Explain DOM and SAX Parser?

Answer: DOM parser is one which makes the entire XML passed as a tree Structure and will have it in memory. Any modification can be done to the XML.

SAX parser is one which triggers predefined events when the parser encounters the tags in XML. Event-driven parser. Entire XML will not be stored in memory. Bit faster than DOM. NO modifications can be done to the XML.

98. What is difference between StateFul and Stateless Session Bean?

Answer: A Stateful Session Bean is a bean that is designed to service business processes that span multiple method requests or transactions. Stateful Session beans retain state on behalf of an individual client. Stateless Session Beans do not maintain state.

EJB containers pools stateless session beans and reuses them to service many clients. Stateful session beans can be passivated and reused for other clients. But this involves I/O bottlenecks. Because a stateful session bean caches client conversation in memory, a bean failure may result in loosing the entire client conversation. Therefore, while writing a stateful session bean the bean developer has to keep the bean failure and client conversation loss in mind.

In case of stateless session beans, client specific data has to be pushed to the bean for each method invocation, which will result in increase in the network traffic. This can be avoided in a number of ways like persisting the client specific data in database or in JNDI. But this also results in I/O performance bottlenecks.

If the business process spans multiple invocations thereby requiring a conversation then stateful session bean will be the ideal choice. On the other hand, if business process lasts only for a single method call, stateless session bean model suits.

Stateful session beans remembers the previous request and responses. But stateless beans do not. stateful does not have pooling concept, whereas the stateless bean instances are pooled.

99. What is difference between BeanMangedPersistance and Container-MangedPersistance?

Answer: CMP: Tx behaviour in beans are defined in transaction attributes of the methods

BMP: Programmers has to write a code that implements Tx behaviour to the bean class.

Tuned CMP entity beans offer better performance than BMP entity beans. Moving towards the CMP based approach provides database independence since it does not contain any database storage APIs within it. Since the container performs database operations on behalf of the CMP entity bean, they are harder to debug. BMP beans offers more control and flexibility that CMP beans.

Diff 1) In BMP you will take care of all the connection and you write the SQL code inside the bean whereas in CMP the container will take care of it

Diff 2) The BMP is not portable across all DB's.whereas the CMP is

100. How Servlet Maintain Session and EJB Maintain Session?

Answer: Servlets maintain session in ServleContext and EJB's in EJBContext.

101. What is "attribute"?

Answer: A qualifier on an XML tag that provides additional information.

102. What is authentication?

Answer: The process that verifies the identity of a user, device, or other entity in a computer system, usually as a prerequisite to allowing access to resources in a system. The Java servlet specification requires three types of authentication-basic, form-based, and mutual-and supports digest authentication.

103. What is authorization?

Answer: The process by which access to a method or resource is determined. Authorization depends on the determination of whether the principal associated with a request through authentication is in a given security role. A security role is a logical grouping of users defined by the person who assembles the application. A deployer maps security roles to security identities. Security identities may be principals or groups in the operational environment.

104. What is authorization constraint?

Answer: An authorization rule that determines who is permitted to access a Web resource collection.

105. What is B2B?

B2B stands for Business-to-business.

106. What is backing bean?

Answer: A JavaBeans component that corresponds to a JSP page that includes JavaServer Faces components. The backing bean defines properties for the components on the page and methods that perform processing for the component. This processing includes event handling, validation, and processing associated with navigation.

107. What is basic authentication?

Answer: An authentication mechanism in which a Web server authenticates an entity via a user name and password obtained using the Web application's built-in authentication mechanism.

108. What is bean-managed persistence?

Answer: The mechanism whereby data transfer between an entity bean's variables and a resource manager is managed by the entity bean.

109. What is bean-managed transaction?

Answer: A transaction whose boundaries are defined by an enterprise bean.

110. What is binding (XML)?

Answer: Generating the code needed to process a well-defined portion of XML data.

111. What is binding (JavaServer Faces technology)?

Answer: Wiring UI components to back-end data sources such as backing bean properties.

112. What is build file?

Answer: The XML file that contains one or more asant targets. A target is a set of tasks you want to be executed. When starting asant, you can select which targets you want to have executed. When no target is given, the project's default target is executed.

113. What is business logic?

Answer: The code that implements the functionality of an application. In the Enterprise JavaBeans architecture, this logic is implemented by the methods of an enterprise bean.

114. What is business method?

Answer: A method of an enterprise bean that implements the business logic or rules of an application.

115. What is callback methods?

Answer: Component methods called by the container to notify the component of important events in its life cycle.

116. What is caller?

Answer: Same as caller principal.

117. What is caller principal?

Answer: The principal that identifies the invoker of the enterprise bean method.

118. What is cascade delete?

Answer: A deletion that triggers another deletion. A cascade delete can be specified for an entity bean that has container-managed persistence.

119. What is CDATA?

Answer: A predefined XML tag for character data that means "don't interpret these characters," as opposed to parsed character data (PCDATA), in which the normal rules of XML syntax apply. CDATA sections are typically used to show examples of XML syntax.

120. What is certificate authority?

Answer: A trusted organization that issues public key certificates and provides identification to the bearer.

121. What is client-certificate authentication?

Answer: An authentication mechanism that uses HTTP over SSL, in which the server and, optionally, the client authenticate each other with a public key certificate that conforms to a standard that is defined by X.509 Public Key Infrastructure.

122. What is comment?

Answer: In an XML document, text that is ignored unless the parser is specifically told to recognize it.

123. What is commit?

Answer: The point in a transaction when all updates to any resources involved in the transaction are made permanent.

124. What is component contract?

Answer: The contract between a J2EE component and its container. The contract includes life-cycle management of the component, a context interface that the instance uses to obtain various information and services from its container, and a list of services that every container must provide for its components.

125. What is component-managed sign-on?

Answer: A mechanism whereby security information needed for signing on to a resource is provided by an application component.

126. What is connector?

Answer: A standard extension mechanism for containers that provides connectivity to enterprise information systems. A connector is specific to an enterprise information system and consists of a resource adapter and application development tools for enterprise information system connectivity. The resource adapter is plugged in to a container through its support for system-level contracts defined in the Connector architecture.

127. What is container-managed persistence?

Answer: The mechanism whereby data transfer between an entity bean's variables and a resource manager is managed by the entity bean's container.

128. What is container-managed sign-on?

Answer: The mechanism whereby security information needed for signing on to a resource is supplied by the container.

129. What is container-managed transaction?

Answer: A transaction whose boundaries are defined by an EJB container. An entity bean must use container-managed transactions.

130. What is content?

Answer: In an XML document, the part that occurs after the prolog, including the root element and everything it contains.

131. What is context attribute?

Answer: An object bound into the context associated with a servlet.

132. What is context root?

Answer: A name that gets mapped to the document root of a Web application.

133. What is conversational state?

Answer: The field values of a session bean plus the transitive closure of the objects reachable from the bean's fields. The transitive closure of a bean is defined in terms of the serialization protocol for the Java programming language, that is, the fields that would be stored by serializing the bean instance.

134. What is CORBA?

Answer: Common Object Request Broker Architecture. A language-independent distributed object model specified by the OMG.

135. What is create method?

Answer: A method defined in the Interview Questions - Home interface and invoked by a client to create an enterprise bean.

136. What are credentials?

Answer: The information describing the security attributes of a principal.

137. What is CSS?

Answer: Cascading style sheet. A style sheet used with HTML and XML documents to add a style to all elements marked with a particular tag, for the direction of browsers or other presentation mechanisms.

138. What is CTS?

Answer: Compatibility test suite. A suite of compatibility tests for verifying that a J2EE product complies with the J2EE platform specification.

139. What is data?

Answer: The contents of an element in an XML stream, generally used when the element does not contain any subelements. When it does, the term content is generally used. When the only text in an XML structure is contained in simple elements and when elements that have subelements have little or no data mixed in, then that structure is often thought of as XML data, as opposed to an XML document.

140. What is DDP?

Answer: Document-driven programming. The use of XML to define applications.

141. What is declaration?

Answer: The very first thing in an XML document, which declares it as XML. The minimal declaration is . The declaration is part of the document prolog.

142. What is declarative security?

Answer: Mechanisms used in an application that are expressed in a declarative syntax in a deployment descriptor.

143. What is delegation?

Answer: An act whereby one principal authorizes another principal to use its identity or privileges with some restrictions.

144. What is deployer ?

Answer: A person who installs J2EE modules and applications into an operational environment.

145. What is deployment?

Answer: The process whereby software is installed into an operational environment.

146. What is deployment descriptor?

Answer: An XML file provided with each module and J2EE application that describes how they should be deployed. The deployment descriptor directs a deployment tool to deploy a module or application with specific container options and describes specific configuration requirements that a deployer must resolve.

147. What is destination?

Answer: A JMS administered object that encapsulates the identity of a JMS queue or topic. See point-to-point messaging system, publish/subscribe messaging system.

148. What is digest authentication?

Answer: An authentication mechanism in which a Web application authenticates itself to a Web server by sending the server a message digest along with its HTTP request message. The digest is computed by employing a one-way hash algorithm to a concatenation of the HTTP request message and the client's password. The digest is typically much smaller than the HTTP request and doesn't contain the password.

149. What is distributed application?

Answer: An application made up of distinct components running in separate runtime environments, usually on different platforms connected via a network. Typical distributed applications are two-tier (client-server), three-tier (client-middleware-server), and multitier (client-multiple middleware-multiple servers).

150. What is document?

Answer: In general, an XML structure in which one or more elements contains text intermixed with subelements.

151. What is Document Object Model?

Answer: An API for accessing and manipulating XML documents as tree structures. DOM provides platform-neutral, language-neutral interfaces that enables programs and scripts to dynamically access and modify content and structure in XML documents.

152. What is document root?

Answer: The top-level directory of a WAR. The document root is where JSP pages, client-side classes and archives, and static Web resources are stored.

153. What is DTD?

Answer: Document type definition. An optional part of the XML document prolog, as specified by the XML standard. The DTD specifies constraints on the valid tags and tag sequences that can be in the document. The DTD has a number of shortcomings, however, and this has led to various schema proposals. For example, the DTD entry says that the XML element called username contains parsed character data-that is, text alone, with no other structural elements under it. The DTD includes both the local subset, defined in the current file, and the external subset, which consists of the definitions contained in external DTD files that are referenced in the local subset using a parameter entity.

154. What is durable subscription?

Answer: In a JMS publish/subscribe messaging system, a subscription that continues to exist whether or not there is a current active subscriber object. If there is no active subscriber, the JMS provider retains the subscription's messages until they are received by the subscription or until they expire.

155. What is EAR file?

Answer: Enterprise Archive file. A JAR archive that contains a J2EE application.

156. What is ebXML?

Answer: Electronic Business XML. A group of specifications designed to enable enterprises to conduct business through the exchange of XML-based messages. It is sponsored by OASIS and the United Nations Centre for the Facilitation of Procedures and Practices in Administration, Commerce and Transport (U.N./CEFACT).

157. What is Java API for XML Processing (JAXP)?

Answer: An API for processing XML documents. JAXP leverages the parser standards SAX and DOM so that you can choose to parse your data as a stream of events or to build a tree-structured representation of it. JAXP supports the XSLT standard, giving you control over the presentation of the data and enabling you to convert the data to other XML documents or to other formats, such as HTML. JAXP provides namespace support, allowing you to work with schema that might otherwise have naming conflicts.

158. What is Java API for XML Registries (JAXR)?

Answer: An API for accessing various kinds of XML registries.

159. What is Java API for XML-based RPC (JAX-RPC)?

Answer: An API for building Web services and clients that use remote procedure calls and XML.

160. What is Java IDL?

Answer: A technology that provides CORBA interoperability and connectivity capabilities for the J2EE platform. These capabilities enable J2EE applications to invoke operations on remote network services using the Object Management Group IDL and IIOP.

161. What is Java Secure Socket Extension (JSSE)?

Answer: A set of packages that enable secure Internet communications.

162. What is Java Transaction API (JTA)?

Answer: An API that allows applications and J2EE servers to access transactions.

163. What is Java Transaction Service (JTS)?

Answer: Specifies the implementation of a transaction manager that supports JTA and implements the Java mapping of the Object Management Group Object Transaction Service 1.1 specification at the level below the API.

164. What is JavaBeans component?

Answer: A Java class that can be manipulated by tools and composed into applications. A JavaBeans component must adhere to certain property and event interface conventions.

165. What is JavaMail?

Answer: An API for sending and receiving email.

166. What is local subset?

Answer: That part of the DTD that is defined within the current XML file.

167. What is tag?

Answer: In XML documents, a piece of text that describes a unit of data or an element. The tag is distinguishable as markup, as opposed to data, because it is surrounded by angle brackets (< and >). To treat such markup syntax as data, you use an entity reference or a CDATA section.

168. What is template?

Answer: A set of formatting instructions that apply to the nodes selected by an XPath expression.

169. What is tool provider?

Answer: An organization or software vendor that provides tools used for the development, packaging, and deployment of J2EE applications.

170. What is transaction attribute?

Answer: A value specified in an enterprise bean's deployment descriptor that is used by the EJB container to control the transaction scope when the enterprise bean's methods are invoked. A transaction attribute can have the following values: Required, RequiresNew, Supports, NotSupported, Mandatory, or Never.

171. What is transaction?

Answer: An atomic unit of work that modifies data. A transaction encloses one or more program statements, all of which either complete or roll back. Transactions enable multiple users to access the same data concurrently.

172. What is transaction isolation level?

Answer: What is transaction isolation level The degree to which the intermediate state of the data being modified by a transaction is visible to other concurrent transactions and data being modified by other transactions is visible to it.

173. What is transaction manager?

Answer: Provides the services and management functions required to support transaction demarcation, transactional resource management, synchronization, and transaction context propagation.

174. What is Unicode?

Answer: A standard defined by the Unicode Consortium that uses a 16-bit code page that maps digits to characters in languages around the world. Because 16 bits covers 32,768 codes, Unicode is large enough to include all the world's languages, with the exception of ideographic languages that have a different character for every concept, such as Chinese.

175. What is Universal Description, Discovery and Integration (UDDI) project?

Answer: An industry initiative to create a platform-independent, open framework for describing services, discovering businesses, and integrating business services using the Internet, as well as a registry. It is being developed by a vendor consortium.

176. What is Universal Standard Products and Services Classification (UNSPSC)?

Answer: A schema that classifies and identifies commodities. It is used in sell-side and buy-side catalogs and as a standardized account code in analyzing expenditure.

177. What is unparsed entity?

Answer: A general entity that contains something other than XML. By its nature, an unparsed entity contains binary data.

178. What is user data constraint?

Answer: Indicates how data between a client and a Web container should be protected. The protection can be the prevention of tampering with the data or prevention of eavesdropping on the data.

179. What is user (security)?

Answer: An individual (or application program) identity that has been authenticated. A user can have a set of roles associated with that identity, which entitles the user to access all resources protected by those roles.

180. What is validating parser?

Answer: A parser that ensures that an XML document is valid in addition to being well formed. See also parser.

181. What is value-binding expression?

Answer: A JavaServer Faces EL expression that refers to a property of a backing bean. A component tag uses this expression to bind the associated component's value or the component instance to the bean property. If the component tag refers to the property via its value attribute, then the component's value is bound to the property. If the component tag refers to the property via its binding attribute then the component itself is bound to the property.

182. What is virtual host?

Answer: Multiple hosts plus domain names mapped to a single IP address.

183. What is W3C?

Answer: World Wide Web Consortium. The international body that governs Internet standards. Its Web site is http://www.w3.org/.

184. What is WAR file?

Answer: Web application archive file. A JAR archive that contains a Web module.

185. What is warning?

Answer: A SAX parser warning is generated when the document's DTD contains duplicate definitions and in similar situations that are not necessarily an error but which the document author might like to know about, because they could be. See also fatal error, error.

186. What is Web service?

Answer: An application that exists in a distributed environment, such as the Internet. A Web service accepts a request, performs its function based on the request, and returns a response. The request and the response can be part of the same operation, or they can occur separately, in which case the consumer does not need to wait for a response. Both the request and the response usually take the form of XML, a portable data-interchange format, and are delivered over a wire protocol, such as HTTP.

187. What is well-formed?

Answer: An XML document that is syntactically correct. It does not have any angle brackets that are not part of tags, all tags have an ending tag or are themselves self-ending, and all tags are fully nested. Knowing that a document is well formed makes it possible to process it. However, a well-formed document may not be valid. To determine that, you need a validating parser and a DTD.

188. What is Xalan?

Answer: An interpreting version of XSLT.

189. What is XHTML?

Answer: An XML look-alike for HTML defined by one of several XHTML DTDs. To use XHTML for everything would of course defeat the purpose of XML, because the idea of XML is to identify information content, and not just to tell how to display it. You can reference it in a DTD, which allows you to say, for example, that the text in an element can contain < em > and < b > tags rather than being limited to plain text.

190. What is XLink?

Answer: The part of the XLL specification that is concerned with specifying links between documents.

191. What is XLL?

Answer: The XML Link Language specification, consisting of XLink and XPointer.

192. What is XML?

Answer: Extensible Markup Language. A markup language that allows you to define the tags (markup) needed to identify the content, data, and text in XML documents. It differs from HTML, the markup language most often used to present information on the Internet. HTML has fixed tags that deal mainly with style or presentation. An XML document must undergo a transformation into a language with style tags under the control of a style sheet before it can be presented by a browser or other presentation mechanism. Two types of style sheets used with XML are CSS and XSL. Typically, XML is transformed into HTML for presentation. Although tags can be defined as needed in the generation of an XML document, a document type definition (DTD) can be used to define the elements allowed in a particular type of document. A document can be compared by using the rules in the DTD to determine its validity and to locate particular elements in the document. A Web services application's J2EE deployment descriptors are expressed in XML with schemas defining allowed elements. Programs for processing XML documents use SAX or DOM APIs.

193. What is XML registry?

Answer: An infrastructure that enables the building, deployment, and discovery of Web services. It is a neutral third party that facilitates dynamic and loosely coupled business-to-business (B2B) interactions.

194. What is XML Schema?

Answer: The W3C specification for defining the structure, content, and semantics of XML documents.

195. What is XPath?

Answer: An addressing mechanism for identifying the parts of an XML document.

196. What is XPointer?

Answer: The part of the XLL specification that is concerned with identifying sections of documents so that they can be referenced in links or included in other documents.

197. What is XSL-FO?

Answer: A subcomponent of XSL used for describing font sizes, page layouts, and how information flows from one page to another.

198. What is keystore?

Answer: A file containing the keys and certificates used for authentication.

199. What is local subset?

Answer: That part of the DTD that is defined within the current XML file.

200. What is managed bean creation facility?

Answer: A mechanism for defining the characteristics of JavaBeans components used in a JavaServer Faces application.

201. What is message?

Answer: In the Java Message Service, an asynchronous request, report, or event that is created, sent, and consumed by an enterprise application and not by a human. It contains vital information needed to coordinate enterprise applications, in the form of precisely formatted data that describes specific business actions.

202. What is message consumer?

Answer: An object created by a JMS session that is used for receiving messages sent to a destination.

203. What is message-driven bean?

Answer: An enterprise bean that is an asynchronous message consumer. A message-driven bean has no state for a specific client, but its instance variables can contain state across the handling of client messages, including an open database connection and an object reference to an EJB object. A client accesses a message-driven bean by sending messages to the destination for which the bean is a message listener.

204. What is message producer?

Answer: An object created by a JMS session that is used for sending messages to a destination.

205. What is mixed-content model?

Answer: A DTD specification that defines an element as containing a mixture of text and one more other elements. The specification must start with #PCDATA, followed by diverse elements, and must end with the "zero-or-more" asterisk symbol (*).

206. What is method-binding expression?

Answer: A JavaServer Faces EL expression that refers to a method of a backing bean. This method performs either event handling, validation, or navigation processing for the UI component whose tag uses the method-binding expression.

207. What is method permission?

Answer: An authorization rule that determines who is permitted to execute one or more enterprise bean methods.

208. What is mutual authentication?

Answer: An authentication mechanism employed by two parties for the purpose of proving each other's identity to one another.

209. What is namespace?

Answer: A standard that lets you specify a unique label for the set of element names defined by a DTD. A document using that DTD can be included in any other document without having a conflict between element names. The elements defined in your DTD are then uniquely identified so that, for example, the parser can tell when an element <name> should be interpreted according to your DTD rather than using the definition for an element <name> in a different DTD.

210. What is naming context?

Answer: A set of associations between unique, atomic, people-friendly identifiers and objects.

211. What is naming environment?

Answer: A mechanism that allows a component to be customized without the need to access or change the component's source code. A container implements the component's naming environment and provides it to the component as a JNDI naming context. Each component names and accesses its environment entries using the java:comp/env JNDI context. The environment entries are declaratively specified in the component's deployment descriptor.

212. What is normalization?

Answer: The process of removing redundancy by modularizing, as with subroutines, and of removing superfluous differences by reducing them to a common denominator. For example, line endings from different systems are normalized by reducing them to a single new line, and multiple whitespace characters are normalized to one space.

213. What is North American Industry Classification System (NAICS)?

Answer: A system for classifying business establishments based on the processes they use to produce goods or services.

214. What is notation?

Answer: A mechanism for defining a data format for a non-XML document referenced as an unparsed entity. This is a holdover from SGML. A newer standard is to use MIME data types and namespaces to prevent naming conflicts.

215. What is OASIS?

Answer: Organization for the Advancement of Structured Information Standards. A consortium that drives the development, convergence, and adoption of e-business standards.

216. What is OMG?

Answer: Object Management Group. A consortium that produces and maintains computer industry specifications for interoperable enterprise applications. Its Web site ishttp://www.omg.org/.

217. What is one-way messaging?

Answer: A method of transmitting messages without having to block until a response is received.

218. What is ORB?

Answer: Object request broker. A library that enables CORBA objects to locate and communicate with one another.

219. What is OS principal?

Answer: A principal native to the operating system on which the J2EE platform is executing.

220. What is OTS?

Answer: Object Transaction Service. A definition of the interfaces that permit CORBA objects to participate in transactions.

221. What is parameter entity?

Answer: An entity that consists of DTD specifications, as distinct from a general entity. A parameter entity defined in the DTD can then be referenced at other points, thereby eliminating the need to recode the definition at each location it is used.

222. What is parsed entity?

Answer: A general entity that contains XML and therefore is parsed when inserted into the XML document, as opposed to an unparsed entity.

223. What is parser?

Answer: A module that reads in XML data from an input source and breaks it into chunks so that your program knows when it is working with a tag, an attribute, or element data. A nonvalidating parser ensures that the XML data is well formed but does not verify that it is valid. See also validating parser.

224. What is passivation?

Answer: The process of transferring an enterprise bean from memory to secondary storage.

225. What is persistence?

Answer: The protocol for transferring the state of an entity bean between its instance variables and an underlying database.

226. What is persistent field?

Answer: A virtual field of an entity bean that has container-managed persistence; it is stored in a database.

227. What is POA?

Answer: Portable Object Adapter. A CORBA standard for building server-side applications that are portable across heterogeneous ORBs.

228. What is point-to-point messaging system?

Answer: A messaging system built on the concept of message queues. Each message is addressed to a specific queue; clients extract messages from the queues established to hold their messages.

229. What is primary key?

Answer: An object that uniquely identifies an entity bean within a home.

230. What is principal?

Answer: The identity assigned to a user as a result of authentication.

231. What is privilege?

Answer: A security attribute that does not have the property of uniqueness and that can be shared by many principals.

232. What is processing instruction?

Answer: Information contained in an XML structure that is intended to be interpreted by a specific application.

233. What is programmatic security?

Answer: Security decisions that are made by security-aware applications. Programmatic security is useful when declarative security alone is not sufficient to express the security model of an application.

234. What is prolog?

Answer: The part of an XML document that precedes the XML data. The prolog includes the declaration and an optional DTD.

235. What is public key certificate?

Answer: Used in client-certificate authentication to enable the server, and optionally the client, to authenticate each other. The public key certificate is the digital equivalent of a passport. It is issued by a trusted organization, called a certificate authority, and provides identification for the bearer.

236. What is publish/subscribe messaging system?

Answer: A messaging system in which clients address messages to a specific node in a content hierarchy, called a topic. Publishers and subscribers are generally anonymous and can dynamically publish or subscribe to the content hierarchy. The system takes care of distributing the messages arriving from a node's multiple publishers to its multiple subscribers.

237. What is query string?

Answer: A component of an HTTP request URL that contains a set of parameters and values that affect the handling of the request.

238. What is queue?

Answer: See point-to-point messaging system.

239. What is RAR?

Answer: Resource Adapter Archive. A JAR archive that contains a resource adapter module.

240. What is RDF?

Answer: Resource Description Framework. A standard for defining the kind of data that an XML file contains. Such information can help ensure semantic integrity-for example-by helping to make sure that a date is treated as a date rather than simply as text.

241. What is RDF schema?

Answer: A standard for specifying consistency rules that apply to the specifications contained in an RDF.

242. What is realm?

Answer: See security policy domain. Also, a string, passed as part of an HTTP request during basic authentication, that defines a protection space. The protected resources on a server can be partitioned into a set of protection spaces, each with its own authentication scheme or authorization database or both.

In the J2EE server authentication service, a realm is a complete database of roles, users, and groups that identify valid users of a Web application or a set of Web applications.

243. What is reentrant entity bean?

Answer: An entity bean that can handle multiple simultaneous, interleaved, or nested invocations that will not interfere with each other.

244. What is reference?

Answer: See entity reference.

245. What is registry?

Answer: An infrastructure that enables the building, deployment, and discovery of Web services. It is a neutral third party that facilitates dynamic and loosely coupled business-to-business (B2B) interactions.

246. What is registry provider?

Answer: An implementation of a business registry that conforms to a specification for XML registries (for example, ebXML or UDDI).

247. What is relationship field?

Answer: A virtual field of an entity bean having container-managed persistence; it identifies a related entity bean.

248. What is remote interface?

Answer: One of two interfaces for an enterprise bean. The remote interface defines the business methods callable by a client.

249. What is remove method?

Answer: Method defined in the home interface and invoked by a client to destroy an enterprise bean.

250. What is render kit?

Answer: A set of renderers that render output to a particular client. The JavaServer Faces implementation provides a standard HTML render kit, which is composed of renderers that can render HMTL markup.

251. What is renderer?

Answer: A Java class that can render the output for a set of JavaServer Faces UI components.

252. What is request-response messaging?

Answer: A method of messaging that includes blocking until a response is received. What is resource adapter. A system-level software driver that is used by an EJB container or an application client to connect to an enterprise information system. A resource adapter typically is specific to an enterprise information system. It is available as a library and is used within the address space of the server or client using it. A resource adapter plugs in to a container. The application components deployed on the container then use the client API (exposed by the adapter) or tool-generated high-level abstractions to access the underlying enterprise information system. The resource adapter and EJB container collaborate to provide the underlying mechanisms-transactions, security, and connection pooling-for connectivity to the enterprise information system.

253. What is resource adapter module?

Answer: A deployable unit that contains all Java interfaces, classes, and native libraries, implementing a resource adapter along with the resource adapter deployment descriptor.

254. What is resource manager?

Answer: Provides access to a set of shared resources. A resource manager participates in transactions that are externally controlled and coordinated by a transaction manager. A resource manager typically is in a different address space or on a different machine from the clients that access it. Note: An enterprise information system is referred to as a resource manager when it is mentioned in the context of resource and transaction management.

255. What is resource manager connection?

Answer: An object that represents a session with a resource manager.

256. What is resource manager connection factory?

Answer: An object used for creating a resource manager connection.

257. What is RMI?

Answer: Remote Method Invocation. A technology that allows an object running in one Java virtual machine to invoke methods on an object running in a different Java virtual machine.

258. What is RMI-IIOP?

Answer: A version of RMI implemented to use the CORBA IIOP protocol. RMI over IIOP provides interoperability with CORBA objects implemented in any language if all the remote interfaces are originally defined as RMI interfaces.

259. What is role (development)?

Answer: The function performed by a party in the development and deployment phases of an application developed using J2EE technology. The roles are application component provider, application assembler, deployer, J2EE product provider, EJB container provider, EJB server provider, Web container provider, Web server provider, tool provider, and system administrator.

260. What is role mapping?

Answer: The process of associating the groups or principals (or both), recognized by the container with security roles specified in the deployment descriptor. Security roles must be mapped by the deployer before a component is installed in the server.

261. What is role (security)?

Answer: An abstract logical grouping of users that is defined by the application assembler. When an application is deployed, the roles are mapped to security identities, such as principals or groups, in the operational environment.

In the J2EE server authentication service, a role is an abstract name for permission to access a particular set of resources. A role can be compared to a key that can open a lock. Many people might have a copy of the key; the lock doesn't care who you are, only that you have the right key.

262. What is rollback?

Answer: The point in a transaction when all updates to any resources involved in the transaction are reversed.

What is root?

Answer: The outermost element in an XML document. The element that contains all other elements.

263. What is SAX?

Answer: Abbreviation of Simple API for XML.

264. What is Simple API for XML?

Answer: An event-driven interface in which the parser invokes one of several methods supplied by the caller when a parsing event occurs. Events include recognizing an XML tag, finding an error, encountering a reference to an external entity, or processing a DTD specification.

265. What is schema?

Answer: A database-inspired method for specifying constraints on XML documents using an XML-based language. Schemas address deficiencies in DTDs, such as the inability to put constraints on the kinds of data that can occur in a particular field. Because schemas are founded on XML, they are hierarchical. Thus it is easier to create an unambiguous specification, and it is possible to determine the scope over which a comment is meant to apply.

266. What is Secure Socket Layer (SSL)?

Answer: A technology that allows Web browsers and Web servers to communicate over a secured connection.

What is security attributes?

Answer: A set of properties associated with a principal. Security attributes can be associated with a principal by an authentication protocol or by a J2EE product provider or both.

267. What is security constraint?

Answer: A declarative way to annotate the intended protection of Web content. A security constraint consists of a Web resource collection, an authorization constraint, and a user data constraint.

268. What is security context?

Answer: An object that encapsulates the shared state information regarding security between two entities.

269. What is security permission?

Answer: A mechanism defined by J2SE, and used by the J2EE platform to express the programming restrictions imposed on application component developers.

270. What is security permission set?

Answer: The minimum set of security permissions that a J2EE product provider must provide for the execution of each component type.

271. What is security policy domain?

Answer: A scope over which security policies are defined and enforced by a security administrator. A security policy domain has a collection of users (or principals), uses a well-defined authentication protocol or protocols for authenticating users (or principals), and may have groups to simplify setting of security policies.

272. What is security role?

Answer: See role (security).

273. What is security technology domain?

Answer: A scope over which the same security mechanism is used to enforce a security policy. Multiple security policy domains can exist within a single technology domain.

274. What is security view?

Answer: The set of security roles defined by the application assembler.

275. What is server certificate?

Answer: Used with the HTTPS protocol to authenticate Web applications. The certificate can be self-signed or approved by a certificate authority (CA). The HTTPS service of the Sun Java System Application Server Platform Edition 8 will not run unless a server certificate has been installed.

276. What is server principal?

Answer: The OS principal that the server is executing as.

277. What is service element?

Answer: A representation of the combination of one or more Connector components that share a single engine component for processing incoming requests.

278. What is service endpoint interface?

Answer: A Java interface that declares the methods that a client can invoke on a Web service.

279. What is servlet?

Answer: A Java program that extends the functionality of a Web server, generating dynamic content and interacting with Web applications using a request-response paradigm.

280. What is servlet container?

Answer: A container that provides the network services over which requests and responses are sent, decodes requests, and formats responses. All servlet containers must support HTTP as a protocol for requests and responses but can also support additional request-response protocols, such as HTTPS.

281. What is servlet container, distributed?

Answer: A servlet container that can run a Web application that is tagged as distributable and that executes across multiple Java virtual machines running on the same host or on different hosts.

282. What is servlet context?

Answer: An object that contains a servlet's view of the Web application within which the servlet is running. Using the context, a servlet can log events, obtain URL references to resources, and set and store attributes that other servlets in the context can use

283. What is servlet mapping?

Answer: Defines an association between a URL pattern and a servlet. The mapping is used to map requests to servlets.

284. What is session?

Answer: An object used by a servlet to track a user's interaction with a Web application across multiple HTTP requests. What is session bean?

An enterprise bean that is created by a client and that usually exists only for the duration of a single client-server session. A session bean performs operations, such as calculations or database access, for the client. Although a session bean can be transactional, it is not recoverable should a system crash occur. Session bean objects either can be stateless or can maintain conversational state across methods and transactions. If a session bean maintains state, then the EJB container manages this state if the object must be removed from memory. However, the session bean object itself must manage its own persistent data.

285. What is SGML?

Answer: Standard Generalized Markup Language. The parent of both HTML and XML. Although HTML shares SGML's propensity for embedding presentation information in the markup, XML is a standard that allows information content to be totally separated from the mechanisms for rendering that content.

286. What is SOAP?

Answer: Simple Object Access Protocol. A lightweight protocol intended for exchanging structured information in a decentralized, distributed environment. It defines, using XML technologies, an extensible messaging framework containing a message construct that can be exchanged over a variety of underlying protocols.

287. What is SOAP with Attachments API for Java (SAAJ)?

Answer: The basic package for SOAP messaging, SAAJ contains the API for creating and populating a SOAP message.

288. What is SQL?

Answer: Structured Query Language. The standardized relational database language for defining database objects and manipulating data.

289. What is SQL/J?

Answer: A set of standards that includes specifications for embedding SQL statements in methods in the Java programming language and specifications for calling Java static methods as SQL stored procedures and user-defined functions. An SQL checker can detect errors in static SQL statements at program development time, rather than at execution time as with a JDBC driver.

290. What is SSL?

Answer: Secure Socket Layer. A security protocol that provides privacy over the Internet. The protocol allows client-server applications to communicate in a way that cannot be eavesdropped upon or tampered with. Servers are always authenticated, and clients are optionally authenticated.

291. What is template?

Answer: A set of formatting instructions that apply to the nodes selected by an XPath expression.

292. What is tool provider?

Answer: An organization or software vendor that provides tools used for the development, packaging, and deployment of J2EE applications.

293. What is topic?

Answer: See publish-subscribe messaging system.

294. What is transaction?

Answer: An atomic unit of work that modifies data. A transaction encloses one or more program statements, all of which either complete or roll back. Transactions enable multiple users to access the same data concurrently.

295. What is transaction attribute?

Answer: A value specified in an enterprise bean's deployment descriptor that is used by the EJB container to control the transaction scope when the enterprise bean's methods are invoked. A transaction attribute can have the following values: Required, RequiresNew, Supports, NotSupported, Mandatory, or Never.

296. What is transaction isolation level?

Answer: The degree to which the intermediate state of the data being modified by a transaction is visible to other concurrent transactions and data being modified by other transactions is visible to it.

297. What is transaction manager?

Answer: Provides the services and management functions required to support transaction demarcation, transactional resource management, synchronization, and transaction context propagation.

298. What is Unicode?

Answer: A standard defined by the Unicode Consortium that uses a 16-bit code page that maps digits to characters in languages around the world. Because 16 bits covers 32,768 codes, Unicode is large enough to include all the world's languages, with the exception of ideographic languages that have a different character for every concept, such as Chinese.

299. What is Universal Description, Discovery and Integration (UDDI) project?

Answer: An industry initiative to create a platform-independent, open framework for describing services, discovering businesses, and integrating business services using the Internet, as well as a registry. It is being developed by a vendor consortium.

300. What is Universal Standard Products and Services Classification (UNSPSC)?

Answer: A schema that classifies and identifies commodities. It is used in sell-side and buy-side catalogs and as a standardized account code in analyzing expenditure.

301. What is unparsed entity?

Answer: A general entity that contains something other than XML. By its nature, an unparsed entity contains binary data.

302. What is user data constraint?

Answer: Indicates how data between a client and a Web container should be protected. The protection can be the prevention of tampering with the data or prevention of eavesdropping on the data.

303. What is user (security)?

Answer: An individual (or application program) identity that has been authenticated. A user can have a set of roles associated with that identity, which entitles the user to access all resources protected by those roles.

304. What is valid?

Answer: A valid XML document, in addition to being well formed, conforms to all the constraints imposed by a DTD. It does not contain any tags that are not permitted by the DTD, and the order of the tags conforms to the DTD's specifications.

305. What is validating parser?

Answer: A parser that ensures that an XML document is valid in addition to being well formed. See also parser.

306. What is value-binding expression?

Answer: A JavaServer Faces EL expression that refers to a property of a backing bean. A component tag uses this expression to bind the associated component's value or the component instance to the bean property. If the component tag refers to the property via its value attribute, then the component's value is bound to the property. If the component tag refers to the property via its binding attribute then the component itself is bound to the property.

307. What is virtual host?

Answer: Multiple hosts plus domain names mapped to a single IP address.

308. What is Xalan?

Answer: An interpreting version of XSLT.

309. What is XHTML?

Answer: An XML look-alike for HTML defined by one of several XHTML DTDs. To use XHTML for everything would of course defeat the purpose of XML, because the idea of XML is to identify information content, and not just to tell how to display it. You can reference it in a DTD, which allows you to say, for example, that the text in an element can contain <em> and <b> tags rather than being limited to plain text.

310. What is XLink?

Answer: The part of the XLL specification that is concerned with specifying links between documents.

311. What is XLL?

Answer: The XML Link Language specification, consisting of XLink and XPointer.

312. What is XML?

Answer: Extensible Markup Language. A markup language that allows you to define the tags (markup) needed to identify the content, data, and text in XML documents. It differs from HTML, the markup language most often used to present information on the Internet. HTML has fixed tags that deal mainly with style or presentation.

An XML document must undergo a transformation into a language with style tags under the control of a style sheet before it can be presented by a browser or other presentation mechanism. Two types of style sheets used with XML are CSS and XSL. Typically, XML is transformed into HTML for presentation. Although tags can be defined as needed in the generation of an XML document, a document type definition (DTD) can be used to define the elements allowed in a particular type of document. A document can be compared by using the rules in the DTD to determine its validity and to locate particular elements in the document. A Web services application's J2EE deployment descriptors are expressed in XML with schemas defining allowed elements. Programs for processing XML documents use SAX or DOM APIs.

313. What is XML registry?

Answer: See registry.

314. What is XML Schema?

Answer: The W3C specification for defining the structure, content, and semantics of XML documents.

315. Explain DOM and SAX Parser?

Answer: DOM parser is one which makes the entire XML passed as a tree Structure and will have it in memory. Any modification can be done to the XML.

SAX parser is one which triggers predefined events when the parser encounters the tags in XML, Event-driven parser. Entire XML will not be stored in memory. Bit faster than DOM. NO modifications can be done to the XML.

316. What types of Servlets do you know?

Answer: There are two types of Servlets - GenericServlet and HttpServlet.

317. What is the difference between HttpServlet and GenericServlet?

Answer: GenericServlet has a service() method aimed to handle requests. HttpServlet extends GenericServlet and adds support for doGet(), doPost(), doHead() methods (HTTP 1.0) plus doPut(), doOptions(), doDelete(), doTrace() methods (HTTP 1.1). Both these classes are abstract.

318. What is the difference between doGet() and doPost()?

Answer: doGet() method is limited with 2k of data to be sent, and doPost() method doesn't have this limitation. A request string for doGet() looks like the following:

http://www.server.com/servlet?param1=value1¶m2=value2&...¶mN=valu
eN

doPost() method call doesn't need a long text tail after a servlet name in a request. All parameters are stored in a request itself, not in a request string, and it's impossible to guess the data transmitted to a servlet only looking at a request string.

319. What are the methods in HttpServlet?

Answer: Methods of HttpServlet can be divided into 3 groups:

1. Initialization methods. These methods are inherited from GenericServlet interface. They include init (ServletConfig config) (allowing initializing a servlet with the prepared or existing config), ServletConfig getServletConfig() (the opposite method), destroy() (removing a servlet), ServletContext getServletContext() (to obtain the context of a servlet), log methods (logging servlet operations).
2. Request processing methods. These are the methods listed in point 2 of this document plus getLastModified(HttpServletRequest request) method.
3. Programmer-defined methods. These methods are written by a programmer and are not regulated by Sun's Servlet specification.

320. Why do you need to use session tracking?

Answer: Session tracking becomes necessary when you are exchanging any information with the visitor and don't want to lose this information. Session tracking is the most convenient and easy way of unique client identification.

321. What are the types of session tracking?

Answer: There are 4 types of session tracking: using cookies for identifying a client (reading a cookie each time a page is requested), using URL rewriting mechanism (appending the session id to each URL), using SSL built-in session tracking mechanisms and hiding the session information in hidden fields of a HTML form (e.g. login name).

322. What are cookies? Why are cookies widely used?

Answer: Cookies are little (up to 4k) pieces of text stored by the server on a client's machine. Cookies are a standard way to store persistent session information (shopping cart, client's preferences, etc.). Every Web server supports cookies, and more than 80% clients keep cookies options turned on in their Internet browsers.

323. What will happen if my servlet attempts to write a cookie to the client's machine, and his browser doesn't accept cookies?

Answer: Nothing will happen except you will be unable to read this cookie from a client.

324. Can I use JavaScript in servlets?

Answer: You can include JavaScript code to the servlet response (i.e. to the generated page), but not to the servlet code itself.

325. What are the types of protocols used in HttpServlet?

Answer: HttpServlet class was developed for usage with HTTP and HTTPS protocols.

SOME OTHER USEFUL BOOKS

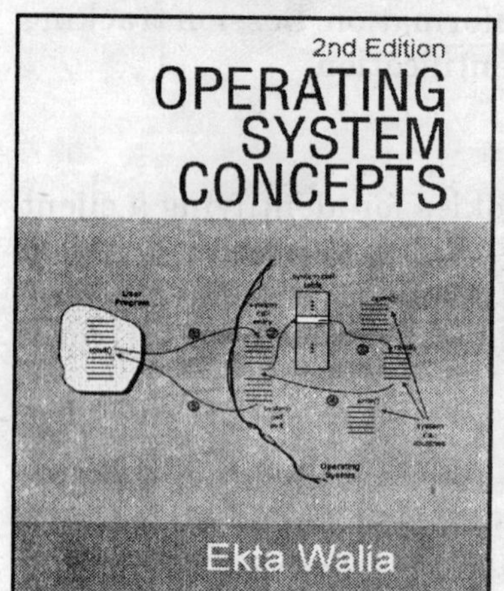